Other Titles in the Crowood AutoClassics Series

FORD CAF

Other Titles in the Crowood AutoClassics Series

FORD CAPRI

FORD CAPRI

GRAHAM ROBSON

THE CROWOOD PRESS

First published in 2007 by
The Crowood Press Ltd
Ramsbury, Marlborough
Wiltshire SN8 2HR

www.crowood.com

**British Library Cataloguing-in-Publication
Data**
A catalogue record for this book is available from
the British Library.

ISBN 978 1 86126 978 2

Typeset and designed by D & N Publishing
Lambourn Woodlands, Hungerford, Berkshire.

Printed and bound in Singapore by Craft Print
International.

Acknowledgements
This book about the Capri has been building up in
my mind for more than twenty years, and an amazing number of people have given their help,
encouragement and expertise along the way.

I want to start by acknowledging the many Ford
directors, managers, engineers and employees who
have been interviewed over the years, or have just
answered odd queries from time to time. There are
many of them, but the principal insights came from
Walter Hayes, and from those characters involved in
the Advanced Vehicle Operation (AVO) and the Special Vehicle Engineering (SVE) department, along
with Ford Motorsport at Boreham.

Accordingly, please step forward, to take a bow
– Terry Bradley, John Griffiths, Ray Horrocks, Bob
Howe, Mike Kranefuss, Rod Mansfield, Bill
Meade, Mike Moreton, Henry Taylor and Stuart
Turner, and of course I must not forget Mike
Costin, Keith Duckworth and Mike Hall at
Cosworth of Northampton.

In this book, I am extremely proud of the range
of colour images that should help to bring the story
of this car to life – in the showrooms, on the road,
and in motor sport. I owe real gratitude to Dave
Hill, who runs Ford's photographic department, to
his predecessors Fran Chamberlain and Sheila
Knapman, and in particular to my good friend and
publishing associate Charles Herridge, who plun-
dered his own stocks to help complete the story.

Without all the help I got to find images, facts,
figures and opinions, the job could never have been
finished. I know it, and I hope they all realize just
how grateful I am to them for making the impossible possible, and the difficult relatively simple.

How can I repay them? By hoping that they will
find time to delve into these pages, and to see how
we have all celebrated the life of a remarkably
successful range of cars.

Contents

Introduction

'The Car You Always Promised Yourself' – the cliché is legendary, but like all the best clichés, it is true. The Capri *was* the car that many of you promised yourselves, and over the years more than 1.9 million were sold to prove that point. For tens of thousands of drivers like me – needing wheels for business, looking for style, but wanting space for a growing family, and the lowest possible running costs – buying a Capri was an obvious choice.

In the 1970s and 1980s I bought three new Capris – a 2000GL Capri II, a 2000S Capri III and finally, oh joy, a 2.8i. In the same period, I managed to drive several 3000GTs and Ghias, and even sampled a Capri Tickford. I think I drove everything worth trying and believe I knew all about the Capri character by the time the last cars of all were built. Over the years I built up a desire to cram some of my thoughts between hard covers and see if I could tell the whole story of this remarkable car.

The Capri Lifestyle

To understand the Capri, you have to understand when it was being built – you cannot really judge the 1960s without having been there. You cannot realize just how rigidly pro-British we all were, how insular the British car market was at the time, how few imported cars we bought or foreign ideas we embraced.

Saloons had roofs, optional leather upholstery and four seats, sports cars were open-top two-seaters with optional heaters and tiny boots – and there was not much in between. People wanting exciting cars with a tin top had to look very hard for anything to amuse them.

Until, that is, the Capri came along.

The new Capri was not only a British but equally a European sensation in 1969: it changed the face of sporting motoring at miraculously low prices. At the time, it had no competition, and no other new car could match it – the sales figures proved that. Ford's marketing machine – genius-backed and fast-moving then, much more so than it is today – saw an immediate winner, and milked it for several years.

Then, after the mid-1970s, it all began to go a bit flat. Just as mini-skirts and 'flower-power' disappeared, so did Capris cover themselves up and become more staid. As Britain's inflation figures soared upwards (they were well over 20 per cent in 1974 and 1975), Capri sales slumped – and never recovered. As the 'housing estate racers' turned from their old Cortinas to Capris that were nearly as old (bringing their extrovert 'after-market' colour schemes, their dangling dollies, and their furry steering wheel covers with them) so the car's image deteriorated. Most people who had lusted after a new Capri in 1970 suddenly found that they needed an economy car five years later.

The miracle is that the Capri phenomenon had lasted for so long. However, Ford was helped by clueless opposition. With the MGB GT, British Leyland made the mistake of not developing their car, while Vauxhall did not even try until the mid-1970s. For them, it was a case of 'too timid and too late'. Ford did not mind; by the time competition blossomed, mainly in Europe from the Opel Manta, they had made their money, restyled their cars, and could coast for some years, which they did until 1986. It was a big bonus.

Influences

Again, unless you were there at the time, you will probably never know just what an impact the Capri made on the British market-place, for it was a completely new type of car. Ford had never before designed anything like it, in

---

Walter Hayes

Between 1961 and 1989, when he finally retired, Hayes was one of the most dynamic and enthusiastic supporters of all sporting and high-performance Ford programmes. Yet, by his own admission, he was really a newspaperman and not a motor industry executive, and latterly a publicist rather than a motor sport administrator.

Already famous as an editor in the world of British newspapers, he joined Ford to revolutionize their public face. Originally in charge of Ford-UK's Public Affairs department, and soon the influence behind every motor sport programme, he modernized Ford's thinking in every way, and was much involved in the birth and development of the Capri brand. It was Hayes who found the money to build the Boreham motor sport centre, who urged Ford to finance Cosworth's DFV F1 engine, and much more.

By the 1980s he had become Vice-Chairman, Ford-of-Europe, and supported the Capri for years when all around him were saying it was time to pension it off, and he did much to ensure that its long-term legend and reputation remained secure. More than anyone, some say, it was Hayes who kept Ford-Germany Motorsport in being during the financially difficult 1970s and who ushered the RS3100 project into limited production.

When he reached his 65th birthday he retired, for that was Ford's global ruling, but he was not yet ready to forget about cars. One of his later appointments was as Aston Martin's chairman, where he got the new DB7 approved, and generally revived yet another flagging organization.

Guru? Of course. Inspiration? Certainly. Influential 'top brass'? Naturally. But also a deep thinker, a visionary, a motoring enthusiast – and a very important man. Without him, in my opinion, the history of the Capri might have been much shorter than it eventually turned out to be.

---

fact it had never tried to promote motoring like this before – certainly no British car company had *ever* tried to sell a car in this way, in so many varieties.

It was a new concept. A Capri was brash, it was totally self-confident – and it succeeded. For a time it was typical of the 'swinging sixties': it was trendy, it was Carnaby Street, it was 'flower-power' – it was everything that made Britain such an exciting place to be at that time. Britain was in love with motoring – speed and sport were still acceptable, and there were few frowning faces.

Even the name Capri was inspirational. Someone, somewhere, high up in Ford's hierarchy had decided to dispense with all ideas of using a boring and long-established Ford name. Instead, came a glamorous alternative, a name that reminded everyone of enjoyment – sun, sea, summer holidays and new experiences – a combination that almost automatically brought a smile to one's face.

It was Walter Hayes who was behind the launch of the new Capri brand. As an ex-Fleet Street man, Ford's PR chief could gauge the mood of the street to perfection – that there was fun out there to be had, that there was money, and a new market ready to be captured.

What happens first in the USA, usually laps over into Europe a short time afterwards. The details may change, but the influences are the same. When developing the mighty Mustang, Ford had identified a growing youth market with money to spend, had invented the market sector to serve it and reaped the rewards. Although drivers did not know until Ford told them about it, they were being offered what their fantasies demanded.

Being part of a thriving multi-national business helped, for Ford-of-Europe was quick to learn from what Ford-USA had already discovered. Following the post-war 'baby-boom' in the USA, the boomers had grown up, there were well-paid jobs for them everywhere, they had money to spend and wanted excitement for their dollars. With the new Mustang, Ford gave it to them.

Even though it took time for the same sort of prosperous youth market to develop in Europe, Ford-of-Europe was first on the scene to massage a lot of collective egos. Ford knew they could milk the excitement and the glitz before any of its rivals were ready. Sporty motoring, they concluded, did not have to be in two-seaters, and certainly did not have to be in cars where canvas tops flapped, leaked water, and were open to vandalization.

Not only that, but they decided to bring American methods into British showrooms, probably for the very first time. In so many subtle ways, they would flatter the customer, and let him or her design their own car – the sporty car of their dreams. Produce a basic car for the customer, the theory went, then offer so many options and accessories that he or she could spend a morning, an evening or even a day tailoring it to suit them: that was a real novelty. While there might be a Capri in every street before long, it need not be at all like its neighbour's version.

No British car maker, not even Ford, had gone so far down this path before – none of them even understood what was involved. Up to then, a new model might become available in two or three guises, with two different engines, but the excitement stopped there. For the Capri, the process would go much further.

In the USA, this process – the 'mix-and-match' approach – was well-developed. In 1968, when the Capri was being finalized, the latest Mustang, for instance, already came in three different body styles, with seven different engines, three transmissions, a long list of rear axle ratios, trim and equipment options and a glossy accessory catalogue almost worth reserving for Christmas reading!

If not immediately, but within two years, Ford's marketing staff would move the same way for the Capri. Because the European market was not quite as large, neither would the list of options be as huge – but compared with the opposition, this was accessory heaven!

High Tide

For the first five years – until the Energy Crisis crippled Europe's economy – Ford and the Capri could do no wrong. For the dealers, used to selling scores of Escorts and Cortinas to uncomplaining fleets and private customers, this was marketing at the cutting edge. Because the dealers had not for six decades had a mainstream sporting car to sell, except for Escort RS types, they were proud to have such a car on the forecourt – so attractive, so appealing, in so many different versions, and especially for the way it attracted the young, and the young-at-heart, through their showroom doors.

The customers, it seems, were delighted. By comparison with the opposition, the all-important 'sticker price' of each Capri seemed amazingly cheap. Even after a brisk canter through the options list, nudging up the price by adding XL packs here, radios there, metallic colours, driving lamps and other accessories elsewhere, it was still a value package that appealed to thousands.

The Capri was also remarkably cheap to run, for by equipping it with a standard saloon-type engine, transmission and suspension, Ford had ensured saloon-type running, maintenance and repair costs. Insurance companies did not mind the Capri either – which increased its appeal even more.

It is no wonder then, that the Capri had little competition in the UK at first. British Leyland offered only the MGB GT with one engine, two transmissions and few options while Vauxhall and Chrysler had nothing at all. Chrysler dabbled with the idea of building a competitor to the Capri, but blanched when they saw the investment implications, while Vauxhall thought that a Viva coupé, called a Firenza, would do the same job: they were wrong.

Sagging Image

The original Capri – a 2+2-seater, all Detroit (and Essex!) glitz with a long bonnet but a small boot, a great deal of image but with nothing special in the chassis engineering – became Everyman's sporting car. None the less, the middle classes, the snobs and the traditionalists all stayed faithful to their MGs and their Triumphs, and were initially reluctant to embrace the Capri when they needed more than two seats.

Ford countered this by proving that the Capri was a *real* sports car – at top level with Capris that won major touring car races, and lower down with one-make events in front of large crowds. Somehow, though, there was always the reservation that the Capri looked more American than British, and that it was still a bit too brash for gentlemen to buy.

The Capri II – smooth and rounded where the original had been craggy, more spacious and versatile than before, went a long way to counter that. A better all-round car, the ride and handling was softer, better behaved, and more GT than sports car this time around, but the market was changing fast.

In 1973–74 the problem was that motoring, and motor cars, were shocked to the core by the sudden eruption of the Energy Crisis, by the very real threat of petrol rationing that followed, by the imposition of speed limits where none were justified, and by the rapid rise of noisy and well-connected environmental 'do-gooders' who suggested that motor cars should be for transportation, not for enjoyment – that trains, buses and even bicycles were altogether more sensible.

First in the USA, and soon afterwards in Europe, the market for extrovert sporting cars collapsed. The USA, which had been the Capri's largest export market in the early 1970s, stopped buying the German-built types in favour of its own smaller Mustangs.

Inflation soared, costs rocketed, in Britain the miners went on strike for more money, managing to reduce the country to a three-day week and a lights-out winter, and suddenly the urge to enjoy ourselves in a car ebbed away. Over in Detroit, Ford-USA found that the 'ponycar' market (*see* panel on page 16) was dissolving rapidly around it, and Europe soon followed suit.

Even the Capri II struggled. It did not help that highly-publicized examples turned up in all the wrong places: on TV (*Minder*, *The Professionals* and *The Sweeney*, for instance) where their owners were small-time villains or uncouth cops; at kerb-sides, where the older types were well down in the 'banger' league; and in scrapyards where the early, poorly protected Capris were turning up.

Out in the market-place, in any case, Ford was now running to stand still. Like its big rivals, it faced huge competition from Japanese imports, and it spent billions on new, small front-wheel-drive cars that left nothing over for frivolities. The fact that a second Energy Crisis, less fierce than the first, but equally depressing, struck Europe in 1979–80, did little to help. Sporty cars? Well, not any more, it seemed, for the USA had turned against them. Not only models, but complete sports car ranges – MG, Triumph and Fiat among them – all disappeared at the end of the 1970s.

Survival

Money-men will tell you that after this Ford only kept making Capris – fewer and fewer of them, every year – because they could afford to do so, and that they treated it as an indulgence. In a way, this was the MGB syndrome all over again. As a business proposition, where investment capital had to be repaid, the Capri had probably paid for itself long before the end of the 1970s, the accountants were delighted, and every car sold after that was a bonus.

With space to spare at Cologne, Ford carried on making Capris in the 1980s, spending no more than necessary on updating them and spending nothing on improving their image. That image, in any case, was now set in stone, for the style had not really changed since 1974. Capri fans that changed their cars every two years or so were now reluctant to buy yet again – after three or four models, they thought, what was new? How do I know? Because it happened to me, and I was a typical Capri customer.

The final fling came with the fastest Capris of all. Although there were no exciting new Ford engines still to be fitted, the Cologne V6 was still versatile. Not only did the Special Vehicle Engineering (SVE) department develop the 160bhp 2.8i – which was the best-handling Capri of all time – but Ford also backed Tickford's extrovert turbocharged Tickford model. Amazingly, far more development went into the 2.8i in the last three years than the Capri ever had in the late 1970s – but not many of us experienced it. Think, if you will, what a Capri Ghia of the 1970s could have been like, if the Brooklands leather trim and the five-speed transmission had been available.

The fact is that we were all getting bored with looking at the Capri by the 1980s. In 1980 just 31,187 Capris were sold in the UK,

but only 11,075 in 1985, a statistic that speaks for itself.

Afterlife

Today, as every Ford enthusiast surely knows, Capri 3000s and 2.8is (particularly the Brooklands type) are extremely popular. Other models, 1300s, 1600s and V4-engined 2000s, on the other hand, are usually ignored.

Where did it all go wrong? Nowhere, in my opinion – except that Ford kept on selling the same old style for far too long. The moral of the story? Only that the Capri was a car of its time, and no matter how hard Ford tried they could not make it all happen again. None the less, the legend continues and we should all be delighted because of that.

Timeline

September 1961	First use of the Capri name on a British Ford, a two-door coupé version of the Classic saloon. No relation to future Capris.
April 1964	Launch of the Mustang in the USA. Thoughts then turned to doing a Mustang on a smaller platform in Europe. The birth of the Colt project that became the Capri.
January 1969	Ford introduced the Capri, as the 'Car You Always Promised Yourself', originally to be built at Halewood in the UK and at Cologne in Germany. Ford showed prototype Capris with brand-new 120bhp/double overhead-camshaft/1.6-litre/16-valve Cosworth BDA-type engines, but that project was soon cancelled.
October 1969	Introduction of the V6-engined Capri 3000GT, prices starting at £1,291.
1970	The German-assembled Capri went on sale in the USA through Lincoln-Mercury division dealerships.
March 1970	Introduction of the up-market, better-trimmed, Capri 3000E.
September 1970	General uprating of 4-cylinder Kent engines, 1971 model Capris to have more power than before, starting at 57bhp, with 86bhp for the 1600GT type.
January 1971	Rationalization of option packs – only base, L, XL, XLR and E were still available.
October 1971	Ford-UK made further changes to the Capri range. The 72bhp/1300GT version was dropped. In a general Ford uprating of V-engines, the 3000GT/3000E types got 138bhp and more torque than before. 'Works' Capris, with 2.9-litre Cologne V6 engines, won the European Touring Car Championship.
June 1972	The first of the limited-edition special-run Capris appeared – 1600GTs, 2000GTs and 3000GTs – called 'Specials', with enhanced trim, furnishing and equipment; all with the bonnet 'power bulge' previously confined to V6-types.
September 1972	Ford announced a mid-life facelift for the Capri I. All cars got big headlamps, bonnet bulges, new-style wheels and a new-style facia (to be carried forward to the Capri II hatchback in 1974). The old-style 86bhp/1600GT Kent was dropped in favour of an 88bhp/1600 Pinto engine. Capri 3000Es gave way to a new four-headlamp 3000GXL. 'Works' Capris, with 2.9-litre Cologne V6 engines, won the European Touring Car Championship.
November 1973	Introduction of the very limited production Capri RS3100 – like the 3000GT, but with a 3.1-litre/148bhp engine, and large rear 'duck-tail' spoiler. This was an 'homologation special' for racing with the 3.4-litre Cosworth GA-type V6 engine.
1974	'Works' Capri RS3100s, with 3.4-litre/455bhp engines, won four major long-distance European Touring Car races.
February 1974	The Capri II took over, with a completely new style and engine line-up. Same basic platform and suspension as before, but a rounder, smoother and more spacious cabin, with a hatchback feature.
May 1974	Introduction of the Ghia badge for top of the range trim/equipment packages on many of its models.
March 1975	Announcement of the Midnight special-edition models at the Geneva Motor Show, the first of the Capri S types. Kitted out in black, with gold pinstriping and ultra-special wheels, plus firmed-up suspension and damping, in 1.6-, 2- and 3-litre forms.

Timeline *continued*

October 1975	Many equipment changes and improvements initiated for 1976. Capri II range re-aligned as base, L, GL, S (once the Midnight, now to be the mainstream version) and Ghia types. No engine changes, but all types got trim/equipment upgrades and 3-litre types got power-assisted steering as standard.
February 1976	Reacting to post-Energy Crisis fuel price panics, Ford introduced a super-economy version of the Capri 1300, with a 50bhp Kent engine: it was a complete failure!
Summer 1976	Halewood assembly gradually ran down, ending completely in October 1976: all future Capri assembly was concentrated at Cologne. Total Halewood assembly was 398,440 in seven years.
March 1978	Capri III (four headlamps, better trim and general upgrade of equipment) took over from the Capri II, as a facelift on an existing style. No changes to the platform, the suspension or the engine range.
March 1980	Introduction of the GT4 limited-edition models, a trim and decoration job. The culling of unpopular models began with the slow-selling 88bhp/1.6-litre 1600S being dropped.
March 1981	Introduction of the Capri 2.8i – the first UK-market version to use the Cologne V6 engine and the first to have fuel-injection (160bhp), with its chassis re-developed by Rod Mansfield's Special Vehicle Engineering (SVE) department. The old 3000 was dropped at this time, and the Ghia badge disappeared.
January 1982	More range rationalization, with the Capri 1300 finally being dropped.
May 1982	Announcement of a further limited-edition Capri, the Cabaret.
1983	After prototypes were shown in 1981, Ford backed limited production of the Capri Tickford, a sophisticated conversion based on the 2.8 Injection (2.8i) with a 205bhp turbocharged engine. Recognized by an extrovert body kit, including spoilers and side skirts. Only 100 new Tickfords would be sold, the last in 1987.
Autumn 1983	Further improvements to the Capri 2.8i included the fitting of the Sierra-type 5-speed overdrive gearbox instead of the old Granada-type box, offering long-legged cruising.
January 1984	Introduction of the Laser limited-edition models – 1600s and 2000s – eventually turning this into the 'run-out' standard version of the 4-cylinder cars.
September 1984	The 2.8i was re-designated a 'Special' for 1985, complete with limited-slip differential, and new-style seven-spoke dished-alloy road wheels.
Late 1986	Ford previewed the imminent end of the Capri, announcing that production would close down in December.
December 1986	The last-ever Capri, a 280 Brooklands, was built in Cologne. Total Capri production – 1968–86 – was more than 1.9 million.
February 1987	Although already built, a final run of 2.8i models, to be called 280 Brooklands, was announced. Painted in Brooklands (British Racing) Green, with leather upholstery, these cost £11,999 each and 1,038 such cars were built.
Spring 1987	The last Capris were finally sold from showrooms, the 280 Brooklands instantly becoming a collector's piece. Security provision was primitive, so many were stolen in the next few years!

1 'Total Performance' – The Prelude to the Capri

Origins? For the Capri, there was probably one seminal moment. Everything that followed – the concept, the styling, the advertising and the marketing thrust – stemmed from 17 April 1964. You may not be old enough to know much about that time, but it was the month in which Ford-USA introduced the Mustang.

Along with the Consul Classic saloon on which it was based, the Capri of 1961 had a heavily sculptured front-end style, complete with four headlamps. Neither the style, nor the four-lamp motif, would appear on the entirely different sporting Capri that would follow in 1969.

The first time that the model name of Capri appeared on a European Ford was in 1961, when it was used on the Classic Capri coupé. This car was based on the Consul Classic saloon, and initially only had a 54bhp/1340cc engine.

For a moment then, please indulge me. Take a journey back in time, well over forty years, to see just how Ford-USA was changed by the arrival of the sporty Mustang. Before then, it was selling Falcons, Fairlanes and Galaxies – shed-loads of fast-selling family cars without an ounce of character or performance attraction. Then came the Mustang, leaning towards the young driver market, stylish to a fault, stuffed full of testosterone, and available in six different engines and two body styles.

The point of the Mustang was that Lee Iacocca's team from Ford Division, Ford-USA, made sure it would appeal to many different people: there would be derivatives not only for the performance-crazed youngster in Main

---

Capri – What's in a Name?

Although it is *this* Capri ('our' Capri) that made the model name famous for all time, it was not the first (nor, indeed, the last) time that the name of this Mediterranean island was used on a Ford product.

As far as I can see, the original Capri-badged car was the Lincoln Cosmopolitan Capri Coupé of 1950 (Lincoln being a Ford Motor Company brand), which then became a pure Lincoln Capri for the 1952 model year. This large V8-engined range of cars (coupés, saloons and convertibles) then carried on throughout the 1950s.

By 1961 Lincoln had begun to concentrate on Continentals (without the Capri name), which meant that the name could then be taken up for the Ford-UK Classic Capri coupé (this was the first UK Ford, incidentally, to use the Cortina GT-type engine, as developed by Cosworth), while a little later, over in the USA, a (Ford-owned) Mercury Comet Capri appeared in late 1965, and was built for two years.

The *real* European Capri took over in 1969, and made the model name famous across the world. Then it all got complicated. Over in the USA, the European-built Capri (that had sold in large quantities from 1970–77) was finally dropped, and from late 1978 a new (Ford-USA) Mercury Capri Coupé appeared, this being no more than a new-generation Ford-USA Mustang 'in a party frock'.

In the USA, the Mercury Capri ran until 1986, after which, and quite coincidentally, both American and European types died at the same time.

On the other hand, it seemed that Ford could not quite bring itself to kill off the model name. In late 1991 Ford-Australia launched a transverse-engined front-wheel-drive 2+2-seater sports car based on the Mazda 323 model (Ford already had strong links with the Japanese concern), calling it a Capri and, just to complicate matters, when examples of that car were sold in the USA, they were re-badged as the Mercury Capri.

By the end of the 1990s, the Capri name had gone back into the trade mark 'stock cupboard', but I have no doubt that Ford will re-launch it one day.

Although the original Capri was not astonishingly beautiful, nor a high-performance machine, it did, at least, have a very large luggage boot. On the next Capri those attributes would be reversed.

This was the Classic Capri of 1961, the first European Ford model to pick up that later famous name. Structurally, and in their styling, the two cars had nothing at all in common.

Street, Detroit; the racing car fan; the trendy types on Rodeo Drive in Los Angeles; but also the pensioner in Florida.

It was a sensation. Between April and September 1964, Ford built more than 120,000 Mustangs, the millionth car followed within two years, and at a stroke, a new category of all-American car – soon known as the 'ponycar' – was born. No wonder, therefore, that Ford's corporate thoughts soon turned to repeating

One of the main marketing attractions of the original USA-built Mustang was that it was available with an extensive range of engines, transmissions, dress-up kits, and a choice of coupé or convertible styles. Although this car certainly inspired the birth of the Capri of 1969, Ford never offered a convertible version of their new machine.

By 1967, the Mustang had already built a reputation as Ford's icon of 'Total Performance'. The style of this 1967 model (which was a lightly face-lifted version of the original) shows how the original long bonnet/fast-back/short-tail proportions would be taken up by the European Capri.

'Ponycars' – Starting A European Trend

It was the American media that came up with the evocative word 'ponycar' – *Motor Trend* apparently taking credit for its invention – and applied it to the original Mustang of 1964. It is important to realize that the North Americans had already invented the 'muscle car' category – but this applied to machines with vast V8 engines, and more performance than the old-style chassis, suspension and brakes could cope with. The Mustang, clearly, was not in that grouping so the new descriptive name 'ponycar' came in to suit.

Just as soon as the compact four-seater Mustang was established in the USA, its rivals in Detroit started to develop competitors for what was clearly a new and booming market. The Plymouth Barracuda arrived at about the same time, but the original Chevrolet Camaro/Pontiac Firebird twins were much more significant, another worthy rival being the AMC (Rambler) Javelin.

Over on this side of the Atlantic, the Capri was the original type of European 'ponycar' (though Fiat might claim that their 124 Sport Coupé got there first) and was soon rivalled by the Opel Manta Coupé. Toyota's Celica soon joined in.

the trick in Europe. It was in this way, in the mid-1960s, that the Capri was conceived.

At this juncture, in any case, the time was ripe for European Ford companies to make a dash towards making more sporty cars. As recently as 1962 Ford had embraced a new and more high-profile marketing posture that revolved around the aggressive, muscle-flexing, headline: 'Total Performance'. Not only would new Ford cars take on more and more sporting and higher-performance attitudes, but there would be aggressively-mounted motor sport programmes to go with them. First in rallies, then in saloon car racing, followed up by the GT40 racing sports car programme and, from 1967, involvement in F1, via the Ford-financed and badged Cosworth DFV engine project.

This marketing thrust, therefore, needed to be backed up by the launch of new models to reinforce it. If BMC could sell tens of thousands of MGs and Austin-Healeys, and similarly Triumph with its Spitfires and TRs, surely Ford, with its unrivalled distribution and marketing strengths, could beat them at their own game?

The 'Colt' – American Concept, European Engineering

'If we can do it here, we can do it in Europe' – that was the theme behind the start-up of a sporty new 2+2-seater coupé concept that was inspired by the Mustang. Ford's European car-making subsidiaries − British and German, respectively − were profitably producing essentially mundane cars in big numbers, but neither of them had anything seriously sporty to sell. Perhaps the shapes and the concepts that started life in Dearborn, Michigan might eventually do it for them.

Not only that, but 'Uncle Henry' (most Ford enthusiasts called him by that name at the time!) was pragmatic and resourceful. Rather than develop a sporty car that was new from the ground up, he would do it 'the Mustang way' – by utilizing an existing chassis/platform, with suspensions, engines and transmissions that were already in existence. That was the way in which a car, soon coded the Colt, could be brought in with a minimum of capital investment, where most of the money would be spent on a new body shell and on marketing.

However, Ford did not believe there was sufficient demand for a convertible in Europe (in nineteen years and almost two million examples what became the Capri would only ever be a closed coupé, or coupé/hatchback) and the thinking behind the layout of the Colt was modelled on that of the then-new Mustang.

The decision to provide 2+2 seating (Ford tried to convince the world that the Capri was really a full four-seater, but any normal-sized adult who has tried to travel for a long distance in the rear seat would tell them otherwise!) was important. At a stroke, it would provide Ford with a Unique Selling Proposition (USP) over most of its theoretical rivals, and it would be a seductive offering to tens of thousands of family men who wanted something a bit more special than a four-door saloon car.

There would be one basic body style with many different trim and dress-up packs, and a whole range of engines. As far as the style and packaging were concerned, the same engine bay had to be big enough to accept anything from a 1.3-litre 'four' to a 3-litre V6 (the fact that Ford-South Africa eventually managed to squeeze a Mustang-sized V8 into place was a lucky bonus that Ford-Europe did not envisage at the time), and the transmission tunnel had to make space for light, medium-duty and heavy-duty manual gearboxes, or European-sized three-speed automatic transmissions.

At this point, incidentally, it is worth analysing why it took so long to turn the Colt into the Capri production car. It was not because too many people dragged their feet, but that this was a period in which Ford had a mountain of other projects, all of them demanding many millions of dollars to make them viable. The Colt/Capri, accordingly, had to take its turn for attention, following this long line-up:

1965   Launch of the all-new Transit.
          Introduction of the all-new Essex V4/V6 engines.
1966   Launch of the Zephyr/Zodiac Mk IV family car.
          Launch of the second-generation Cortina.
1967   Formation of Ford-of-Europe.
          Completion of the new Ford-UK technical centre at Dunton, in Essex.
1968   Launch of the new Escort saloons, estate cars and vans.

Although it was important, clearly the Colt project could hardly take precedence over any of the other new model programmes, so it went ahead on a measured basis. Because the Colt was to take shape like the Mustang had done, by using the basis of an existing family car, but disguising this under a more sporty style, with a wide range of engines, the absolutely crucial decisions that had to be taken were which existing Ford should form that basis, and which existing platform should form the basis of the new coupé?

Although, in theory, there were several possibilities in the modern range, most were eliminated after technical and manufacturing study:

This was the original Corsair saloon, as launched in 1973. Although the style of this saloon bore no relation to the Capri that would follow, the original Capri used a lightly modified version of its under-frame, platform and running gear, though Ford would not admit it at the time.

Escort	The platform was thought to be too small and too narrow, with a small engine bay. The chassis was basically not sporty enough.
Zephyr/ Zodiac	Too large, too heavy, with very soft, underdeveloped independent rear suspension.
Taunus 12M	Old-fashioned platform, front-wheel-drive, only V4 engines (Germany) compatible with the chassis and transmission.

Taunus 17M/20M	Too long, only engineered for V-layout engines, with little sporting heritage. This was discouraging but there were also the:
Cortina	Platform basically acceptable, but extra length and width would be desirable. Good motor sport heritage on races and rallies, and the
Corsair	Platform wheelbase stretched from Cortina by 3in (76mm) so even more suitable.

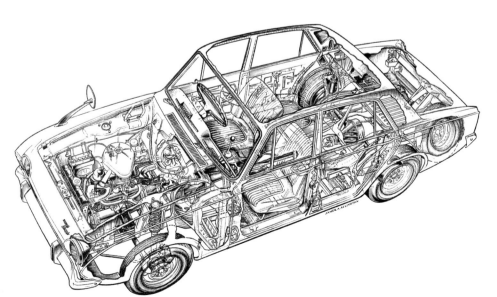

This was Ford's original cutaway drawing of the Corsair of 1963–64. Seasoned engineers will look at the details, and see where the Capri gained much of its underpinnings.

Accordingly, it was not long before what we might now call the 'packaging engineers' began to home in on the Cortina/Corsair platform. It did not take long, either, for them to decide that this might just be, as they say, 'a marriage made in heaven', as the longer of the two Cortina/Corsair platforms proved to be ideal for the purpose. The fact that the styling themes all followed the Mustang approach – long nose, short tail – meant that the engine bay proved capable of accepting every engine that might be considered, while a great deal of work had already gone into turning the Cortina into a successful competition car. If the engineers could not repeat the same trick and turn this into a viable and attractive sports coupé, then they would have a lot of questions to answer.

In the beginning, therefore, the Colt began to evolve around a little-modified Cortina/Corsair platform though, as development and detail design progressed, the new car's platform became more and more specialized. By the time the team was ready to freeze the design for production tooling to be commissioned, the Colt platform had become almost entirely unique. Although it was easy for pundits to glibly talk about 'two-door Cortinas', this was simply not true.

Glamour in more ways then one – the original Corsair in a sylvan setting with F1 Champion Jim Clark and supermodel Jean Shrimpton. It was Corsairs like this that formed the original mechanical basis of the Capris that were to follow.

Capri Platform – Origins?

As explained in the main text, the Capri had its own unique platform, but over time this evolved from the basis of one of Ford's mass-production saloons.

   Here is a simple comparison of 'platform architecture', showing how all three cars were related. Figures quoted are for original versions of those models:

Model	Year introduced	Wheelbase (in)	Front track (in)	Rear track (in)
Cortina I	1962	98	49.5	49.5
Corsair	1963	101	50	49.5
Cortina II	1966	98	52.5	51
– and –				
Capri I	1969	100.8	53	52

This really confirms the way that in the project stage the Capri platform grew out of the Corsair platform (disregarding the 0.2in (5mm) difference in wheelbase dimensions, which Ford presumably 'forgot' to mention when the Corsair was launched …), though the front and rear tracks were significantly wider. We must not forget either, that the Capri had rack-and-pinion steering, whereas the Cortina and Corsair did not.

   Even so, by the time it went into production, there had been so many development changes that the Capri platform was unique, though a few bits and pieces seem to have been in common with the Cortina II/Corsair of the period. Incidentally, the Corsair itself would be withdrawn in June 1970, just as the Capri was hitting full output.

   Did this basic platform-sharing make financial/capital investment sense? Certainly, and it would still do so today – for 1.9-million sales must have been profitable by any accounting standards.

In the meantime, the biggest pressure of all had been on the design and styling engineers, who needed to produce a smart new 2+2-seater layout that Ford management would sign off. At this stage, please note, this was to be a Ford-UK product, for Ford-of-Europe did not yet exist – and when it did, the first priorities for joint projects would be the Transit van and the Escort family car.

So who, exactly, styled the original Capri? As ever, what was publicized when the car was new, and what was really true, did not become clear until years after the cars had been retired. In 1969, as far as Ford's image-builders were concerned, the Capri had evolved as a result of smooth, cordial and altogether selfless co-operation between the USA, the UK and Germany. The real truth, it seems, is that it was Ford-USA that inspired the original packaging, and Ford-UK that produced the final shape.

In the beginning, so legend went, the car evolved under the guidance of Uwe Bahnsen, a noted Ford designer and stylist, but this assertion clearly raised the hackles of Susan Spear-Bates. In a letter published in the American magazine *Collectible Automobile* in 2003, she told quite a different story:

> My father, Gil Spear, then running the Ford Advanced Vehicle Design Studio, in Dearborn, Michigan, was totally responsible for its [the Capri's] origination. Mr Bahnsen, if he was hired at that time, was an employee of the German Ford company, then still a separate entity from the American and British Ford companies. He would have had no knowledge or input into the design of the Capri. There was very strict secrecy regarding all the designs originating out of the American advanced styling studio.
>
> Design Vice-President Gene Bordinat and his assistant Bob Maguire, decided to send some of the models to affiliated companies in the hope that the designs might stimulate new ideas for the Ford companies in England and Germany. It was determined that the Colt had the most to offer, and was sent to England with no ceremony.

Ford persisted for more than a year with its original styling proposal. Here a prototype is depicted, full side-view.

This full side-view dated 1965–66 was of an early clay model, with much change still to be made.

This was an alternative style proposal for a rather more rounded shape than that which was eventually chosen. It never got beyond this offering.

It was a surprise when the English product planners, headed by Alex Trotman, were excited about the design and began working on a running prototype. That was when they requested that my Dad move to England and work on it with them. I was beginning my second year of college when we moved to England and was well aware of his work on the Capri. The combined prototype turned out to have almost the exact dimensions and appearance as my father's original design.

No one, however, seems to argue with the fact that the first full-size style models were completed (though not inspired) in Europe, and that all feasibility and development went ahead on the basis of a Corsair-length wheelbase/platform and rolling chassis. We now know that the full-size clay model eventually chosen for refinement (and, more importantly) for production, was American.

Perhaps the American style was less aerodynamically-efficient than it might have been, but according to various Ford sources it had more 'snap' and pizzazz than the European offerings: Ford-USA, after all, had produced the Mustang, and knew (or was convinced that it knew) what was needed. As with almost all styling themes, however, it had to be shown to management teams, and then to customers at

a secret 'clinic', before it could be signed off. The fact is – and maybe this is something of a blessing – that the full-size clay model offered was not that which finally got approval.

Even before any serious mechanical engineering had gone ahead, by 1966 Ford had built up two startlingly realistic full-size, non-function, glass-fibre models of the Colt, both of them 2+2-seater coupés and visually similar in many ways, dubbing them 'Flowline' and 'GBX'. Like all subsequent related projects, these effectively put Escort-size two-door cabins on Corsair platforms, though the seats were lowered considerably, and legs had to be stretched out, for the roof was much lower. Even at that stage there were paired false air intake louvres ahead of each rear wheel arch cut-out, with small depressions in the wing pressings to suit.

At that moment these did not carry Ford or any related badging to point out their identity – a detail that was relevant for what was to follow. At this time, it is important to realize that they carried a side-window profile that Ford eventually denoted as the 'hockey-stick' line.

The company then embarked on an ambitious tour of Europe, holding what was a really innovative series of customer 'clinics', where the cars were shown to selected individuals in showroom conditions, with rival

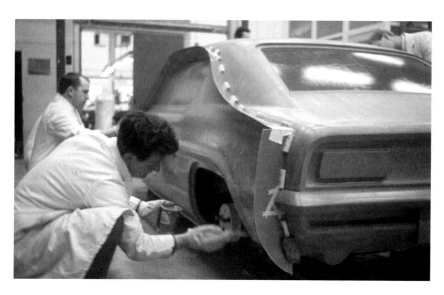

Looks very life-like, doesn't it? But this Capri was only a full-size mock-up, not a real steel car, ready for viewing by management.

Assessing public reaction at a private viewing 'clinic' in London, in 1966. This was a full-size GRP model, showing off the small rear side window that would eventually be rejected before the final shape was agreed.

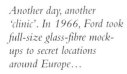

Another day, another 'clinic'. In 1966, Ford took full-size glass-fibre mock-ups to secret locations around Europe…

…where they asked, and got, brutally honest opinions on the proposed shape from private individuals, who were never told what make of car was being considered. One negative feature thrown up at these clinics was the lack of visibility to the outside world through the tiny rear side windows.

cars also displayed alongside. Those observers did not know what company was involved, but they were asked to comment on their merits.

This road show travelled far and wide – starting in London, then Cologne, Brussels, Amsterdam, Milan, Hamburg and Geneva – before the marketing team then returned to Essex to collate, sift and analyse the public's opinions. These, in the main, were encouraging, though even at that stage it was clear that there was unease about the shape of the cabin side windows, especially regarding the lack of light it gave to the rear seat passengers.

The next critical date came in July 1966, when a Ford-UK board meeting, headed by chairman Stan Gillen, elected to go ahead with the Colt. No less a personality than Henry Ford II (who had recently journeyed to Europe to see his company's race cars win the Le Mans 24-hour sports car race) was also involved at this time. The intention then was only to build the Colt on one site – the forecast capital investment of £20 million seemed to be high (in the end it cost £22 million, which most people would now rate as a real bargain), but approval was secured.

The intention was to get the car ready within two years – this was an ambitious but not impossible target (especially as existing running gear was to be used) – and according to the initial planning it was to be launched in the autumn of 1968, at the London Motor Show.

Unlike many of its rivals (and this might explain why Ford still exists, and why some of those rivals have since gone to the wall!), much planning, analysis and preparation was to be carried out before the car was introduced. Although the very first lash-up prototypes (which used carved-about Corsair platforms) were built in the autumn of 1966, product planning was still working on almost every detail.

It is worth recalling that Ford's product planning office had first become famous for its work on the original Cortina of 1962 (the much-fabled Archbishop project, which was master-minded by Terry Beckett): since that time, the department, its function and its importance, had grown and grown.

Along with the sales and marketing staffs, they concluded that the North American Mustang approach would also work well in the UK, which is to say that although there would only be one basic style – the 2+2-seater coupé – this should be made available with a number of different engines and a positive flurry of dress-up or tune-up packs. This explains – and

Wind-tunnel testing of an early prototype. Those were the days before computers, so results were gained after much laborious work, and modification by hand.

I will return to this in the next chapter – the appearance of X, L and R packs, and several combinations of them.

Looking back, the truly important decision was that the new car would be made available with engines spanning 1.3-litre/52bhp, all the way up to 3-litre/128bhp. This, at a stroke, embarrassed all of Ford's rivals, who could not match, or had not thought to match, such variety. As an example, at this time the MGB GT was only available with a single type of 1.8-litre/95bhp engine, and no dress-up packs, or even an automatic transmission option.

The practice of making one model range available with a whole variety of engines had originated in the USA, and was only just being introduced to British cars with Ford very much in the vanguard of progress. In 1966–67, for instance, the Cortina Mk II was announced with a choice of three body styles and four engines, whereas its most important rival, the BMC Austin/Morris B-Series range, had only two bodies and two engines. Accordingly, by using its marketing strengths, and its growing ability to play the 'mix-and-match' game, Ford intended to make the Colt accessible to everyone.

By the mid-1960s Ford-UK was assembling cars on two sites – Dagenham in Essex and Halewood on Merseyside. Dagenham was already bursting at the seams, but there was still space at Halewood (which was a brand-new plant) for a new model to be added. Not only that, but the Corsair, on whose platform and basic running gear the Colt was based, was also being assembled at Halewood. It did not take long, therefore, to conclude that the Colt should be assembled at Halewood too.

This is the moment when the formation of Ford-of-Europe, and its effect on the Colt programme, should be mentioned. Up until that point Ford-UK and Ford-Germany had operated strictly separately from one another. Although both theoretically sold their own cars to the other subsidiary's market, this was no more than a minor irritant. It was in other European countries – France, Italy, Belgium and Holland were perfect examples – where

what was cynically described as the 'two fishing lines' approach (for the same customer) was always present. It was quite normal, for instance, to visit a Ford dealer showroom in one of those countries to find a Cortina alongside a Taunus 12M.

This, though, was a situation that could not persist. Because Henry Ford II controlled all the purse-strings in Dearborn, he had to approve of every major investment in 'his' company. Although he was well-travelled, and certainly knew much more about Europe than his underlings (Lee Iacocca, for example, who had become known as the 'father of the Mustang' was particularly scathing about the European operations, but never stayed over on this side of the Atlantic long enough to learn more), he was not about to throw money at new factories without a lot of analysis.

Inexplicably, in fact, it would take him several more years to acknowledge that there was little economic sense in making similar, though not identical, products in two different factories, and not to take advantage of the obvious economies of scale. From 1965 John Andrews became Vice-President in charge of a rather loosely-linked European Group Operation, but it was not until mid-1967 that Mr Ford finally made the big decision.

On a visit to Paris, immediately before Ford dominated the Le Mans race of 1967, he called Andrews from his suite at the Plaza d'Athénée hotel, to tell him: 'What we need is a Ford-of-Europe, to knock a few heads together and make things happen faster. And it's no good looking to Dearborn, they have enough on their plate. You have got to do it yourself. Make Ford-of-Europe'.

This, then, was Andrews' big project for the next few years and, to his and his immediate colleagues' credit, the move towards amalgamation came very quickly indeed. By this stage, in any case, the UK and Germany were building 'the common van' (as the Ford Transit was known, internally, for some time), and the next obvious step was to insert the still-secret Escort project into a German plant too. In both cases, each of these products was to be built on two sites, one in the UK and one in Europe.

After that – and it is just as obvious today as it became clear in 1967 – the Colt project should follow suit, and before the entire project was finally signed off – effectively when the Colt became the Capri – it had been decided to commission two sets of body shell tooling so that cars could be built at Halewood and at Cologne in Germany. At this time Ford could not have known that demand would eventually be so high that a third assembly line, at the new Ford Escort factory at Saarlouis in Germany, near the French border, would also be needed.

This was the moment at which the problems, and the benefits, of building cars on two sites, separated by several hundred miles, became obvious. While it was clearly feasible to commission two sets of body shell tooling, it made no sense for tens of thousands of heavy, bulky and expensive pieces of kit, such as engines and transmissions, to be shuffled from country to country. Why send engines and gearboxes from Dagenham to Cologne (or vice versa) when suitable alternatives were already being built there?

This was when the product planning staffs in the UK and Germany got together, and it was soon agreed that cars made in the UK would use British engines and transmissions, while cars made in Germany would use German engines and transmissions. This policy, in fact, would only hold firm for three years, after which Ford-Germany began to build a 3000GT/3000GXL model with a Dagenham-produced V6 engine and related transmissions. Fortunately, because the engine bay was relatively roomy, there never seemed to be any real trouble in packaging the different engines, even when air-conditioning and other add-on gizmos had to be added.

Naturally, too, a great deal of management liaison, planning, engineering design and development work was carried out on both sides of the English Channel, and important personalities seemed to spend a great deal of their time on Ford Air – Ford's own small

dedicated airline – which provided regular daily shuttle flights between London Stansted and Cologne-Bonn airports.

Even so, because the Colt had originally been meant to progress as a Ford-UK project, the bulk of the original design, engineering and development work continued to be carried out at the newly-opened technical centre at Dunton in Essex (then, and today, a dominant building complex just south of the A127 near Basildon), where John Hitchman ran the engineering side of the project. At first the Germans needed to do little more than to concentrate on making sure that their engines and transmissions would fit comfortably into the shell.

Such was the way that Ford-of-Europe evolved, progressing rapidly towards complete cross-border integration, each team began to take over some functions from the other. Once the modern proving ground facilities at Lommel in Belgium came on stream, the majority of the road testing took place over there.

Even so, as 1967 progressed, two important problems had to be resolved. One was that a model name had to be chosen for the new car, and the other was that the style and design had to be signed off (which meant that management had to give it formal approval).

Although most Ford top managers seemed to have broadly approved of the style as presented to them in 1966, there was the niggling feeling that the public's resistance to the 'hockey-stick' side-window profile was justified. It was not merely that 'clinic' visitors did not like the looks of the car, but that they did not like the rather claustrophobic atmosphere bestowed on the rear seats by the large expanse of metal (and restricted glass area) to each side of them.

Although approval had already been given for much of the body press tooling to be manufactured by this time (and there seemed to be no justification for altering the main proportions of the cabin itself), there was still time to do something about the window profiles, so the shape was altered in the Dunton Design

In 1967 and 1968, much prototype testing took place on snow in Scandinavia, with square-window-style cars.

studios to what we now know as the C-bend rear side window shape. That, in modified form, would persist throughout the life of the car, and was extremely popular. Final approval of the modified style came in October 1967 – and the first off-tools cars were produced at Halewood in November 1968.

Naming the car itself took longer. For a time Ford hoped that they might call the car the Colt, after a smaller derivative of the Mustang theme, but it was not long before company lawyers and trade mark experts discovered that Mitsubishi of Japan had already registered the Colt name for themselves.

There was no way around this but, fortunately for everyone, someone remembered that the Capri model name had recently been used on a Ford-UK coupé – the Classic Capri of 1961–64 – and was once again available. Since the Capri was already trade-mark protected all round the world, it was adopted for the new car and would of course stay with it for the next two decades. That name, I understand, was finally and formally adopted in November 1967, a full year ahead of series production beginning.

Not that naming new Fords was always as trouble-free as that. Many years later, according to the official story put out by Ford at the time, when the new Focus was previewed at the Geneva Motor Show in 1998, discussions about its name, and an alternative that was never revealed, were not concluded until twenty-four hours before the show's doors actually opened to the world's media.

Engineering – The Bare Bones

Once the paper studies had been made (and, believe me, there was much of that at Ford at this time), engineering work got going at encouraging speed. In the UK, initial work concentrated on installing existing engines – in-line 4-cylinder 1298cc and 1599cc units and the 1996cc V4 – and their related four-speed all-synchromesh gearboxes, while in Germany the same tasks revolved around the entire existing family of German-made Cologne V4 and V6 power units.

Even so, it would be quite wrong to assume that this was little more than a re-packaging job inside a new body style and on an existing platform. While the idea of using the same basic pressed-steel platform as the Corsair family car had merit, that platform could not easily be used without significant modification. In the end, as we now know, panel after panel was altered as time passed and it effectively became unique.

Although the engine/transmission/drive line/rear axle installations were conventional by Ford standards, there was still the challenge of fitting rack-and-pinion steering up front and finding sufficient rear axle 'bump' movement at the rear. Rear axle movement was never really sufficient on this car, nor indeed on its successors, so all Capris had a rather hard rear-end ride. The facts were that rear wheel movement was 6.65in (169mm), compared with 8.31in (211mm) on a Cortina.

For those wanting a sports coupé, that was fine, but those moving over from a Cortina or a Corsair could find it hard going. Not only to take account of the limited wheel/axle movements, but to provide sporting character, the entire suspension package was stiffened up – 90lb/in wheel rate compared with 74lb/in on the Cortina at the front, 100lb/in compared with 90lb/in at the rear.

Rack-and-pinion steering, its merits and its installation quirks, was still relatively new to Ford. When work began on the Capri there was no Ford road car with rack-and-pinion steering (the GT40 doesn't count!), though such a fitting featured on the new Escort family that was close to being launched.

Cortinas, Lotus-Cortinas and Corsairs all relied on a less accurate re-circulating ball layout. Some years ago, in a related book, another author suggested that the Lotus-Cortina was given rack-and-pinion steering, but this is quite wrong. It was the Cortina Mk III, which was due for launch at the end of 1970, that would get a rack-and-pinion installation.

Except in detail, the new car's independent front suspension followed the party line, by having the very successful MacPherson strut layout, which Ford had originally pioneered way back in 1950 with the Consul/Zephyr family car range. The Capri, of course, had wider front and rear track measurements than the Cortina Mk II/Corsair 2000E on which it

was based, but the actual basic hardware – track control arms at the front, axle tubes at the rear – was the same.

Spring rates and damper settings, of course, were specifically developed for the Capri, but the hardware, the general layout and, in many cases, the detail, was often like that of the Cortina/Corsair family.

Twin radius arms were used to control the articulation of the rear axle on all models, just as it had originally been on the Cortina GT/Lotus-Cortina and the hottest Corsairs. Unhappily, such radius arms might have performed a function job but they were also very efficient at transmitting road noises, thumps and bangs from the rear axle and suspension. Ford, whose sales force was obsessed with the reduction of Noise, Vibration and Harshness (NVH) at this time cast a beady eye on this, and resolved to make changes in mid-run. This was done in 1972 when the radius arms disappeared, a slim rear anti-roll-bar took over, and no one apparently complained.

Prototype testing occupied much of 1967–68, with a great deal of high-speed endurance mileage building up in Europe, especially at the Lommel proving ground. Only ten prototypes (and five cars that had to be destroyed in compulsory head-on 30mph (48km/h) barrier crash tests) were used – this being the sort of tiny figure that makes latter-day engineers and managers wince, then sigh with envy. If a

Irresistible really, the chance to show a full rear view, with spinning driving wheels, on snow in Scandinavia.

This was prototype testing in January 1968, the car having its instrumentation checked prior to another cold weather trial.

new-type Capri was ever produced in the late 2000s, you could reckon on hundreds of pro-totypes/pilot-run cars and many crash-test cars, which would have to be shunted from all angles, being needed instead.

Because Ford was obsessed with not letting the opposition know everything at too early a stage, when it sent cars overseas from Essex it often chartered four-engined Carvair (car ferry) aircraft from British Air Ferries, that oper-ated from Southend – which was conveniently close to Dunton – and made sure that its cars carried box-section disguises at front and rear.

It is worth emphasizing that at this stage there was no question of developing super-powerful cars, for the Colt was not immedi-ately meant to be a tyre-stripping monster. Development testing was concentrated on 1.3-litre and 1.6-litre engines at first, with 2-litre V4-engined cars following later. We now know that the first 3-litre-engined prototype was not built until the beginning of 1969, when the basic range was about to break cover. When the Capri *was* launched, Ford admitted

Two heavily disguised prototypes ready to go off to Europe, on test, in one of the British Air Ferries car ferry planes, which were most conveniently based at Southend.

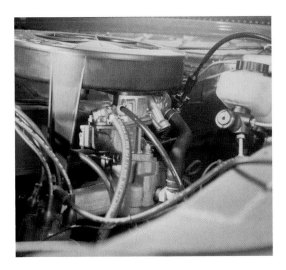

Even at this stage, the engine bay layout was almost settled.

The layout of the Capri facia was only settled at a late stage in 1968, this being what Ford called the 'hi-line' layout, complete with six dials and a full range of switches, controls and a position for the radio.

that a 3-litre type would follow, but would not appear until October 1969. A specification was released, but it was incomplete.

By mid-1968, the stylists and the engineers had done everything (often more) than was asked of them, and were ready to hand over the job to two widely-separated sites – Halewood and Cologne. At Halewood, which was already churning out thousands of Escort saloons, estate cars and vans every week, we now know that the very first pilot-built Capris were manufactured in November 1968. Because the engines, transmissions and most of the chassis hardware were already familiar to the production engineers, the rate of production ramped up just as fast as components were available.

Now, as 1969 blossomed, it was up to the customer.

2 Capri I – 'The Car You Always Promised Yourself'

Most Capri owners remember one very important date – Friday, 24 January 1969 – for that was when the original car was unveiled, at the Brussels Show. It was a typical Walter Hayes operation. Instead of showing off the car on opening day, when the limelight would have to be shared with other car-makers, he chose to launch it a week later.

Until then, visitors to the show saw the Ford stand dominated by a large, glittering, silver-foil-covered packing case, all tied up with 2-foot wide blue ribbon, and revolving on a turntable. In front of it were notices in French and in Flemish (this was in Brussels, don't forget) that stated that the 'Car of Your Wildest Dreams' would be unveiled on 24 January.

I was actually a staff member of *Autocar* at this time, and had already been to Capri previews, but there was no doubt that Ford had done a great job in hyping-up this launch. As

Finished at last. The pre-launch photo-shoot was apparently exhausting for all concerned!

Can she really have been expecting this photograph to be taken? A blonde model caught in the driving seat of a press car before the launch in 1969.

my colleague Michael Scarlett wrote in his show report:

> Five goggle-box-sized screens round the box flash half-second pictures every second of a car which looks like a small Ford Mustang. If you take the trouble, as many do, to get down on your knees to see under the box – it's got no bottom – you see that the panels hide a normal Ford live axle back

There may be a Freudian message here, but what is it?

end, MacPherson strut front suspension, rack-and-pinion steering and no engine, gearbox or propeller shaft. If you are as intrigued as Ford obviously want you to be, you had to wait until today [24 January] and either buy an airline ticket to Brussels, a bus ticket to your Ford dealers, or a copy of Autocar.

Autocar, in fact, had fallen for the hype in a big way, and for very good commercial reasons. Normally published on a Thursday, the magazine went ahead with that pretence, wrote a seven page description of the new car – and published a day late, on 24 January!

Under the headline 'What a Difference A Day Makes' (a popular song title of the period), the magazine's editorial (which I wrote) stated that:

> For us, this week, Thursday is Friday or, in other words, we are a day later than usual. Deliberately.
>
> The very good reason becomes clear in the following pages: the announcement of Ford's outstanding and additional new range – the Capris. By waiting 24 hours to fit in with the maker's plans for their release, we are able to give you the full story on the day.

(*Motor*, the big rival, which published on a Wednesday, was furious!)

New Style, Familiar Engineering

Even before the Capri was announced and went on sale, Ford dealers were taken to Malta to try out the pilot-built examples in winter sunshine, after which the same machines were shipped to Cyprus and refurbished so that the world's press could also enjoy the experience.

Even before then, Ford's marketing people had to make many decisions about pricing, equipment and options. The strategy was to emulate what their North American colleagues were already doing with the Mustang (and with other, less sporty, Fords too). One basic style would be provided (there never were any serious plans to provide convertibles, or more spacious saloon car types), but

the customer would then almost be able to design his or her car around a brochure, which not only included engine and transmission choices, but a number of dress-up packs too.

Dress-up packs, described later in this chapter, sometimes concentrated on the exterior styling, sometimes on the interior, and would sometimes be doubled- or even trebled-up to combine every attribute. For the production engineers, and their staff who had to schedule the cars, this showed every sign of being an on-going headache. It was.

Cleverly – in fact very cleverly – in all its launch publicity Ford suggested that Capri prices started from only £890, which was true enough, but it did not tell the complete story. £890 might seem to under-cut, for example,

Terry Collins' masterly cutaway drawing shows off the proportions of the original Capri. When studied from three-quarter rear, this does not emphasize the small size of the boot and the long nose of all original Capris …

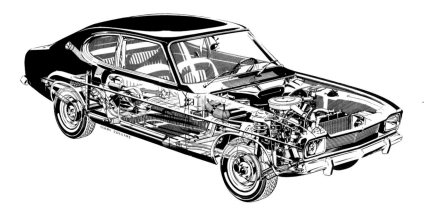

… the alternative three-quarter front view showing all the details of the front suspension and engine bay.

Original-type Capris, built from 1969 to the end of the 1972 model year run, were all fitted with this rather modest tail-lamp cluster.

A head-on view of an original-style Capri (this was one of the batch of launch models used for factory photography); this was sometimes seen with extra driving lamps, sometimes with over-riders and sometimes with a black bonnet. This is a very basic, early-specification, 1968–69 model.

Original Capri I Prices – January 1969		
Model	**Engine size /power**	**UK retail price**
1300	1298cc/52bhp	£890.39
1300GT	1298cc/64bhp	£985.70
1600	1599cc/64bhp	£936.09
1600GT	1599cc/82bhp	£1,041.83
2000GT	1996cc/93bhp	£1,087.53
Inertia-reel seat belts		£14.04
Fixed (static) seat belts		£9.49

an MGB GT's £1,217 or the £1,438 asked for a Fiat 124 Sport Coupé in the UK, but it provided a rock-bottom specification 1.3-litre engined car, with cross-ply tyres, the minimum decoration, the very minimum possible

In 1969 and 1970 they didn't come more 'entry-level' than this – no dress-up packs, mere 'soup plate' wheel trims, narrow tyres, and no visible extras. All rather cautiously registered in Sweden.

Registered in Germany, this very basic 'entry-level' specification, in plain white, shows the 'bargain-basement' level at which Capris started their career in 1969.

equipment levels, plus fixed backrest front seats and a rather unyielding slab of a rear seat (front seat safety belts, static or inertia-reel types, were compulsory fitments). Ford's build-computer at Halewood was certainly programmed to recognize such a model but I doubt if more than a handful of these base models were ever produced.

When the motoring press was introduced to the range, it saw a range of five models that were almost immediately available – 1300, 1300GT, 1600, 1600GT and 2000GT – and it was also tantalized by the promise of a Capri 'Twin-Cam' (the Cosworth BDA-equipped prototypes, which were effectively still-born, and which I describe in more detail later in this

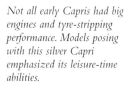

Not all early Capris had big engines and tyre-stripping performance. Models posing with this silver Capri emphasized its leisure-time abilities.

Although it was loosely based on the Cortina/Corsair under-pan, suspension and running gear, the original Capri was set up to handle in a very sporting manner.

chapter), and by the prospect of a V6-engined 3-litre derivative that would become available by the end of 1969.

The amazingly compact 2-litre V4 engine that Ford-UK announced in 1965 was one of several power units chosen for the new Capri. It had a 60-degree V-angle, and a Lanchester-type balancer shaft to make it adequately smooth.

Engines – What Choice?

In the beginning, of course (and for the next five years, as far as the factory was concerned), British versions of the Capri were available with five different engine sizes/engine tunes:

1300	1298cc	4-cylinder/52bhp
1300GT	1298cc	4-cylinder/64bhp
1600	1599cc	4-cylinder/64bhp
1600GT	1599cc	4-cylinder/82bhp
2000GT	1996cc	V4-cylinder/92.5bhp

It would be fair to say that, apart from installation details, there had been no special development in any of these engines, all of which were already in mass-production for other Ford models. All four of the in-line 4-cylinder engines were versions of the Kent engine, which powered Escorts and Cortinas, while the V4 Essex was being used, in one form or another, in Corsairs, Zephyr V4s – and Transit vans.

Sisters under the skin! The very first Ford to use the new V4 engine was the Transit van, launched in 1965, with the Corsair V4 and the Zephyr V4 soon joining in.

When the Capri was introduced to the UK in 1969, the fastest and most expensive of the original range was the V4 2-litre 2000GT.

While the Kent was known to be not only robust, neat and compact, it was also eminently tuneable – for there were also many racing and tuned-up types, including the twin-cam version that Lotus had designed for themselves and the new BDA, which is described later in this chapter.

Even though it was fitted with a contra-rotating Lanchester balancer shaft to tame the vibrations that are inherent in V4 engines, the Essex V4 was never the most refined or free-revving of power units. It is significant, surely,

that this engine was dropped in the early 1970s, to be replaced by the much more suitable (and modern!) straight-4-cylinder Pinto.

Accordingly, the most flattering thing that could be said about the Essex V4 was that it was compact and reliable. Unfortunately, it was singularly resistant to power-tuning, and because of its 60-degree v-angle, no amount of careful tuning of engine mounts could ever make it feel smooth, or sound refined. It was, however, adequately torquey, and could help the Capri 2000GT reach more than 105mph

Early-specification Capris with small or non-GT engines were fitted with this facia/steering wheel layout.

(169km/h). Indeed, until the 3000GT came along a year later, it was the fastest, and therefore the flagship, of the Capri range.

Each of the engines, of course, was matched to the same type of four-speed all-synchromesh gearbox (with what Ford called a 'single-rail' selector mechanism) that was already being used in other models such as the Cortinas and Corsairs; the low-powered types having the wide-ratio family car ratios; the 1600GT and 2000GT having the closer ratio gears as fitted to Cortina GTs, Corsair 2000Es and Lotus-Cortinas, this being colloquially known by most enthusiasts as the '2000E' gearbox.

The choice of engines to fill out this range was, to be frank, not at all logical at first. Not only was the base 1300 very puny at 52bhp, but the peak power of the 1300GT was exactly matched by that of the 1600 model. If Ford could have bothered to make an excuse it would be that all these engines were already available, and in production – and they were merely giving the customer a wide choice.

However, it was not the 1300 itself, with which a Capri could barely exceed 80mph (129km/h), that struggled to find sales, for a surprising number of these cars were bought. It was the high-revving 1300GT (an engine normally fitted to Escort GTs) that could not match up to the Capri 1600, which was more flexible, with a

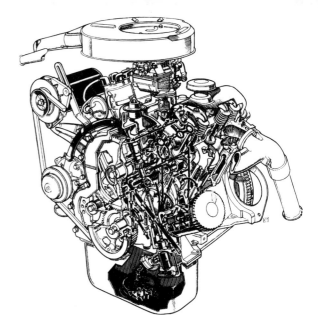

Not only was the V4 a very compact engine in width, but also in length. To ease access, the dynamo was mounted high and to the right of the cylinder block/heads assembly.

great deal more mid-range torque. Accordingly, the 1300GT was the first of the models to be abandoned – in October 1971.

Dress-Up Packages

GT-badged cars got a different facia/instrument layout than lesser varieties. Not only did they have a three-spoke steering wheel, they also had a six-instrument layout of dials, with

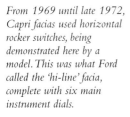

From 1969 until late 1972, Capri facias used horizontal rocker switches, being demonstrated here by a model. This was what Ford called the 'hi-line' facia, complete with six main instrument dials.

The Rostyle wheel/tyre combination was very fashionable and popular on British cars of the late 1960s and early 1970s. Such wheels were in pressed steel made by Rubery Owen in the Midlands – and at least one manufacturer (Triumph) built its cars with standard wheels, but with look-alike wheel covers replicating the Rostyle-style.

a rev-counter prominent ahead of the driver's eyes, and extra switches and controls. A Ford radio was optional on all types, as were inertia-reel safety belts (as opposed to fixed-length belts) and a Golde-type folding sunroof.

That, though, was just the beginning, for Ford then made a big play by offering not one, but five different dress-up or equipment packages, which were described (and badged) as X, L, R, XL and XLR. These, of course, were lovingly detailed in the brochures, and because so many thousands of early Capris were built that way, I now ought to summarize what went into each package.

X-Pack

'X' for Xtras? This was mainly a dress-up pack for the interior of the cars. For what now seems like a bargain price of £32.64 (roughly equivalent to about £800 today), there were reclining front seats, a shaped rear seat, a dipping rear-view mirror, a handbrake warning light on the facia, an extra interior light and – outside the cabin – twin horns and a pair of

In the early years, Capris came in one shape but many sizes, and with different dress-up packs. This studio shot shows an early car, probably a 2000GT (though details of the badge are not visible) complete with the Rostyle road wheels and the extra driving lamps that were a part of the appealing package.

reversing lights. The seats themselves certainly made that package worth buying, but they could not be separately ordered.

L-Pack

'L' for Luxury? Priced at only £15.02, this one was purely for exterior show, with identifying badges, front and rear bumper over-riders, brightwork wheel trims (not soup plates!), dummy air scoops fixed to the recesses ahead of the rear wheels, a locking filler cap, and bright metal side mouldings.

Intrinsically this added nothing to the behaviour of the car, but it provided that important bit of glitz that was attractive to some buyers. Many Capri Ls were produced in the early months.

R-Pack

'R' for Rally? Maybe, for this was perhaps the pack with the most actual (as opposed to visual) function. For £39.17, the customer got a set of the fashionable 5in rim Rostyle wheels,

This was Ford's state-of-the-art design in 1969, showing an XLR-equipped 'hi-line' facia. Which engine? We're guessing here, but with the red line on the rev-counter set at 6,000rpm, this is probably a 1600 model. The steering wheel style would be altered considerably at face-lift time in 1972 – no air-bag, of course, for these would not appear until the 1990s.

One of the original launch batch of cars, which mostly used the same TLN registration number sequence. This home market 1600 GT XLR was a perfect example of what made the car an instant bestseller when it went on sale in 1969.

There's a subliminal message from this 1969 press shot – if you bought a new Capri, you would almost inevitably have it kitted out in full XLR specification, choose the optional black bonnet, and use it to go off to enjoy all your other leisure activities.

a leather-trimmed steering wheel, fog and spot driving lamps mounted to the front bumper, a flexible map-reading lamp close to the passenger's knees, and matt black paintwork on the bonnet, the sills and the tail panel (though the paint job could be deleted if you asked for that to be noted at an early stage).

After that the mix-and-match process got even more complicated. Those awkward clients asking for combinations of the various packages were discreetly told that it could not be done, but the XL package costing £44.39 was certainly seen on many cars, while the entire XLR package (priced at £79.64 – a slight discount on individual tariffs) was in great demand, and was the specification that Ford apparently preferred to build. The X and R packs, on their own, would finally be withdrawn from the autumn of 1970, not only because of low demand, but because the production scheduling staff at Halewood wanted to put back some kind of logic into their operation.

If you wanted to impress the neighbours in 1969–70, you needed to draw their attention to the detail of the 1600GT XLR badging on the front wings.

The hidden message here was that one could use a Capri for anything, business, shopping or pleasure. This black-bonneted GT XLR was on a slipway close to pleasure boats – we mustn't forget that anti-corrosion treatment was pretty sketchy in those days!

An early XLR-equipped car at the original advertising photo-shoot in Portugal, intended to demonstrate the happy life-style approach that Ford wanted to promote.

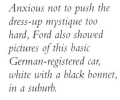

Anxious not to push the dress-up mystique too hard, Ford also showed pictures of this basic German-registered car, white with a black bonnet, in a suburb.

Transmission

Apart from the choice of engines and equipment packages, there was a choice of manual or automatic transmission. Other, rival, cars such as the MGB and the MGC had already tried this, and found that the actual demand for an automatic option was more limited than market research had suggested that it might be.

Even so, and because all the major engineering – installations, matching of characteristics, and endurance testing – had already been completed on the various saloon car programmes, the three-speed Borg Warner Type 35 automatic was made available on 1600 and 2000 models. It was not available with the 1.3-litre engine, because the power losses were thought to be too much for such under-powered power units.

How many were eventually sold? Ford never issued that sort of statistic, but anecdotal evidence suggests that no more than 5 per cent of the original Capri Is were fitted with the £89 automatic option, and even that may be a generous estimate.

BDA-Engined Capri – a Glorious Red Herring

While all this was going on, and the dealer chain was getting ready to sell cars, the showing of a new 16-valve Cosworth-designed engine, the BDA (Belt-Drive, Series A), quite over-shadowed the launch of the Capri itself. Not only did Ford bring BDA-powered Capris to the press launch, but forecast that such cars would go into production later in the year.

But it never happened. Only eight prototypes were ever built, none were ever delivered to customers and no prototypes were ever sold off. By the summer of 1969, it had all gone quiet. Much trumpeted in January 1969, the Capri-BDA died quietly within months. Whatever happened?

In a small company, one man would have made the decision. He might have looked at the Capri-BDA, looked at the alternative

Capri power which was still to come (a cheap and rugged 3-litre V6 in this case), looked at the potential cost of Cosworth 16-valve power, and turned down his thumb. But not at Ford. Before decisions could be taken, every project had to go to committee. Submissions had to be written, meetings had to be held, sheets of finance had to be assembled – and eventually someone would take a decision.

That's the way it was in late 1968. Hayes and Competition Manager Henry Taylor had already 'invented' the BDA engine to replace the Lotus twin-cam engine, made sure that it would easily go into the Capri, then showed it off to the press. At which point the usual killjoys moved in, and made sure it was cancelled.

The BDA Engine

By 1968, the original intention was to assemble Capris in Britain and Germany, using a variety of straight-four, V4 and German V6 engines. The forecast was that almost all Capris to be ordered would have engines of 2-litres or less. As we now know, the original intention was only to make one V6-engined type – the 126bhp 2.3-litre Ford-Cologne type – there was no intention to use fancy twin-cam units.

Meanwhile, Ford's Walter Hayes was busily cementing Ford's relationship with Cosworth. Having set Keith Duckworth to design fabulously successful F2 (FVA 4-cylinder) and F1 (DFV V8) engines, he then conceived the idea of a new Cosworth-designed road car engine. In a very informal relationship, and working only with Duckworth and his chief designer Mike Hall, Hayes and Henry Taylor helped create the BDA engine. As Hall once told me:

We had just got the DFV running. It all started in May 1967, very much as a 'handshake job'. I don't think there was a written contract, but Ford gave us some money, and asked us to build about ten complete engines.

There was no specific performance target, though naturally it had to be better than the Lotus-Ford Twin-Cam. We aimed for 120bhp for the road car's engine, which it achieved quite comfortably.

I designed the whole engine, with the help of three or four detailers, and the first engine must have run in June 1968. All the work we did here, initially, was for the engine to go into a Lotus-Cortina. In fact the first road work we carried out was in two Lotus-Cortinas – I ran one of them for around 40,000 miles [64,360km].

Settling the specification – twin belt-driven overhead cams, 4-valves per cylinder, all based on the Cortina/Capri 1.6-litre cylinder block – was straightforward enough, but in 1968 it was still an engine looking for a home, because Hayes and Taylor had not yet found a use for it. Cosworth, in fact, was informally asked to make provision for it to go into several cars, as Duckworth later confirmed:

> You see, we had the problem of two sumps – one with a well at the back, one with a well at the front, and an oil pump problem. In fact the engine inclination change came as a late surprise – the engine was inclined backwards – which was a bit of a blow to us at first, as most of the oil from our cam carrier was supposed to be draining over the front.

By late 1968, prototype BDA engines were up and running on Cosworth test beds at Northampton, and were already beating their design targets. The very first BDA-engined Ford to take to the road, in fact, was a Cosworth-owned Lotus-Cortina. Even so, at that stage Ford had no car to put it in. More importantly, Cosworth was still a small company and was quite incapable of building engines in quantity.

With the introduction of the Capri looming, Hayes needed a headline-making gimmick. As historian Jeremy Walton once wrote about this derivative:

> Ford obviously felt the lack of a flagship pretty badly in Britain. Originally they didn't even have the 2-litre in production, so the announcement of the productionized Cosworth Formula 2 engine for the Capri – based on the 1600GT engine block (and bottom end reciprocating components in

production trim) – was a useful PR exercise. But there was no production future for a Capri with the 120bhp Cosworth Belt Drive A-Series (BDA).

(Perhaps it made it easy to describe, but of course the BDA was *not* a 'productionized' Cosworth Formula 2 engine (the FVA). Except that both engines had 4-valves per cylinder and twin-overhead-camshaft heads, they shared virtually no common components.)

Few Ford insiders, it seemed, ever treated this as anything but an amusing diversion. The company originally forecast that 100 of what it called the Capri Twin-Cam would eventually be sold, but as *Autocar*'s Edward Eves wrote about the engine at the time: 'Plans for its future are not final, but it is intended to build a short initial series of 100 units; some will be raced and others will be assessed by selected users, of which this journal is one'. Nothing, however, ever came of *that*.

In the winter of 1968–69, eight Capri-BDAs were hastily cobbled up from pilot-build 1600GTs, to be sent to Cyprus. Each of them had glass-fibre bonnets incorporating a bulge, eight-spoke Minilite wheels with 6in rims, and very 'prototype' exhaust systems that no one was allowed to inspect. At the time these cars retained the same 2000E gearbox as other 4-cylinder types, and had narrow (165-section) tyres.

Rare bird! This was one of eight BDA-engined Capris shown at the pre-announcement press launch. The Minilite wheels were a nice touch, and might even have been fitted if such a model had gone into production.

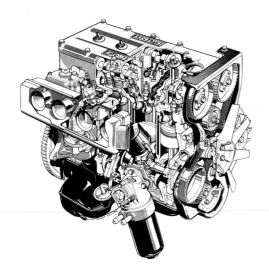

Ford showed off their brand-new 16-valve BDA engine for the first time at the Capri launch, though it was to find more fame in the Escort RS1600 and Escort RS1800 rally cars that followed in the 1970s. It fitted very comfortably into the Capri's engine bay but, strangely enough, the V6-powered versions were better performers on the road.

By January 1969 standards the Capri-BDA was the fastest of the cars offered, but within months it would of course be displaced by the heavier but far more flexible 3-litre model. Even so, journalists who tried the test cars mainly came away impressed.

Autocar's editor, Maurice Smith, thought that:

> The twin-cam, 16-valve, 4-cylinder 1600 is an altogether more responsive car, though oddly enough, the ride is slightly softer than the other versions, perhaps because of the wider, 6-inch rims. It revs freely up to 6,500rpm ... reaching 5,700rpm (an indicated 100mph [161km/h]) quickly in top.

Motor's Charles Bulmer was less complimentary, writing that:

> It is inevitable that a comparison should be made between this Cosworth-based engine and the older Lotus-Ford twin-cam unit which is optional in the Escort and Cortina. The comparison is not entirely favourable to the newcomer, which seems to have a narrower power band; there is little torque at low rpm so that bottom gear must be used for rapid acceleration out of hairpin bends.

Writing in *Autosport*, Simon Taylor was clearly delighted:

> With an engine so directly descended from the 140bhp per litre racing unit, and with so many valves and cams, I was expecting plenty of noise and harshness, but this new twin-cam is a delightful road unit ... Apparently Keith Duckworth's wife has one in her shopping Cortina and it runs happily on two-star petrol!

The general impression, in fact, was that the BDA was a fine engine and that the Capri was a promising car, but that this was probably not the best combination in which they should be sold. The engine, surely, should go into a lighter Ford, and the Capri deserved a larger engine, more in the Mustang mould?

Ford, to be honest, made it quite clear that the Capri-BDA would not be available for some months, and as those months passed it became evident that nothing more was being done. When the Capri 3-litre was introduced in October 1969, the Capri-BDA was finally forgotten.

I have never unearthed any *concrete* evidence that Ford intended to put these cars on sale. Rumours of selected Ford dealers taking delivery of cars, being told to hide them, and later to re-engine them with conventional power, are all red herrings, and the fact that a handful of private-enterprise Capri-BDAs were later built means nothing.

In 1969 Cosworth was still not equipped to produce engines in quantity – indeed, Mike Hall told me that the entire BDA assembly programme at Northampton comprised thirty-two engines, which was stretching their still-limited resources to the limit – and by their own exacting standards the design needed far more refinement and testing. In later years, of course, Cosworth expanded, and supplied thousands of castings and machined components to other engine builders for assembly, but that is another story.

For once, I actually have inside information of what happened next. In the summer of 1969 my wife and I had the pleasure of entertaining Keith Duckworth and Ford's newly-appointed Competitions Manager, Stuart Turner, to dinner. The reason was actually to introduce them to each other – they had not previously met – but one subject raised in that evening was the BDA engine. At one moment, the conversation went something like this:

Duckworth:	'What is Ford going to do with the BDA engine?'
Turner:	'I don't know. We don't yet have any plans to use it at Boreham. I've driven one of the Capris, but it would be better for us in an Escort.'
Duckworth:	'I haven't been asked to do an Escort installation yet.'
Turner:	'Can it produce more power than the Twin-Cam?'
Duckworth:	'Yes, a lot more, we've already seen 238bhp.'
Turner:	'I'll talk to Walter [Hayes] when I get back.'

The result, long-term, was that the Escort RS1600 came into existence, and we all know what happened after that. The proof that BDA production plans had not then been finalized was that it took a long time to settle on an engine builder, eventually choosing Harpers of Letchworth, which meant that RS1600 road car deliveries were delayed until May 1970. By the same token, Capri-BDA availability would also have been delayed until then.

As far as is known, none of these Capri-BDAs ever reached the public. My information is that the ex-Cyprus Capri-BDAs (which carried Greater London, as opposed to Essex, registration numbers) were eventually re-engined by being converted back to a standard 1600GT specification, and sold off.

On the Market

By modern Ford standards, the Capri was no sooner previewed than it went on sale. These days, of course, it seems to be quite normal to see a new model given the big publicity build-up, then take at least six months to become available in numbers. In all that time potential customers have no clue as to the probable price levels.

Assembly on Three Sites

For far too long, European Ford subsidiaries often competed bitterly against each other for sales in many countries: Ford-UK and Ford-Germany, in effect, were serious rivals. Not only that, but when new models were being developed, there was little co-operation between the two, and a great deal of duplication took place – the new-family of V4 and V6 engines being a perfect example of this.

Although Ford-of-Europe was set up in 1967, the Capri originally went into full production at Halewood in Britain and in Cologne in Germany, using totally duplicated sets of tooling and manufacturing facilities – but British Capri enthusiasts often forget that the majority were always assembled in Germany. European demand (and the fact that Ford-Germany also supplied Capris to the USA) meant that in 1970 a third assembly line, at the Saarlouis Escort plant very close to the French border, was also opened up though it closed down in 1974.

For the first few years, when sales and production were so high, it was easy to justify this triple-sourcing – in 1970 169,740 Capris were produced in Cologne and 84,973 at Halewood – but by 1974, when the Capri II came along, only 38,932 cars were built at Halewood compared with 146,429 in Germany. With Ford-of-Europe's strategy leaning towards a single source for cars that sold in such quantities, the decision to close down Capri assembly at Halewood was easy to take – and the last cars of all were built on Merseyside in September/October 1976.

This, incidentally, meant that Halewood became an Escort-only plant, but with this car at the height of its popularity, and Ford taking at least 30 per cent of sales in the UK market, Halewood was soon full once again.

In the early years, Ford chose to make the Capri on two sites, one in the UK and one in Germany. This aerial shot is of the Halewood complex, near Liverpool, looking east (Liverpool, therefore, is behind the camera). The large complex in the centre is the main PTA (Paint/Trim and Assembly) building where Capris and Escorts were assembled, the buildings further away being the transmissions plant where gearboxes of several types were machined and assembled.

A bodyshell going into one of the various paint preparation baths at Halewood.

Capris in the making – this is a stack of partly complete bodyshells, held in store at Halewood, before the bodyshells were then completed, went through the paint shop, and finally edged down the assembly lines before going off to their customers.

But not in 1969. By the time the Capri was launched in January 1969, thousands of cars had already been built – at Halewood in England and at Cologne in Germany. Prices were available at once, and the first deliveries were made at the beginning of February. It was a typical Walter Hayes move that, on the day the cars were finally ready to go into showrooms, an example of a Capri was parked outside busy commuter railway stations for the clientèle to see as they made their way to work.

Ford, of course, had to guess – no, I should rephrase that, for Ford's marketing staffs *never*

guessed in those days – they had to estimate how many of which models would be in the most demand in the early months. Once again, it is anecdotal evidence that tells us the well-equipped as opposed to stripped-bare, GT as opposed to ordinary, and more powerful rather than less-powerful engined types were made at first. We also know that the V4-engined 2000GT was not quite ready for sale at first, for series production of those machines did not begin until March 1969.

Even so, the new car took off like a rocket, and within months was achieving at least 3 per cent of the entire British private car market – one-seventh or one-eighth of Ford's entire domestic market share – this figure being exceeded in Germany where Cologne-built Capris also got off to a flying start.

Autocar's test report on the original 1600GT XLR summed up the initial, generous, reaction of almost everyone who saw the new car. In its opening remarks, it set the tone:

**V4 and V6 Engines –
British and German**

Years before the Colt (later Capri) range went on sale, Ford-UK laid down a compact new family of engines for use in its cars and light/medium commercial vehicles like the Transit van. Although Ford-USA controlled both companies, and laid down general strategy – which, in this case, was to insist on the evolution of new families of V-formation engines – Ford-UK and Ford-Germany were allowed to develop competing ranges. Both concerns set to, and designed new overhead-valve 60-degree V4 and V6 engines, which in each case were machined and assembled on carefully integrated transfer line equipment.

Over the years Ford-UK's new range, which was coded Essex, would span 1.7-litre (V4) to 3.1-litre (V6), while the entirely different Ford-Germany Cologne engine range would span 1.2-litre (V4) to 2.9-litre (V6). Before the commercial rationalizations made under Ford-of-Europe were established, British-built cars (which included the Capri coupé and the Corsair range) only used Ford-UK Essex V4s and V6s. The last of the Essex V6 types would be phased out in the UK in 1977, though manufacture was then transferred to Ford-South Africa, where it continued into the 1990s.

In both cases, and for dynamic balancing purposes, both types of V4 engine – British and German – used contra-rotating Lanchester balancer shafts, which were gear-driven from the nose of the crankshaft and tucked into a convenient gap in the side of the crankcase, above the oil pump and inboard of the oil filter.

This cross-section drawing of the V6 Essex engine shows how compact its 60-degree V layout actually was. Except that the V4 engines also used a crank-driven balancer shaft (in the location shown with hatchings towards the bottom left), the V4 and V6 types shared the same basic layout.

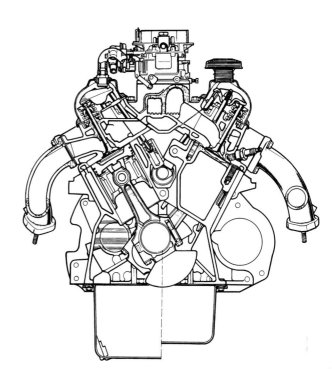

German Market: German-Built Capri Is – 1969–74

Although Capris built in Cologne and Saarlouis were structurally and functionally the same as those built at Halewood, those produced for sale in Germany and most countries in continental Europe used a different line-up of engines. Furthermore, German-built Capris with 6-cylinder engines featured a bulge in the bonnet panel: this pressing would not appear in the UK until the 3000GT was launched towards the end of 1969.

Not only were these V4 and V6 engines manufactured in Europe, but (as with British-type Capris) they were also shared with several other private cars and light commercial vehicles in the Ford-Germany range.

In the panel on page 49, I have already explained the origins and inter-linked relationship of what we call the Cologne V4 and Cologne V6 engines. In 1969, when the Capri first went into production, a wide range of these engines, from the 1.3-litre V4 to the 2.3-litre V6, were already in production, with an enlarged, 2.6-litre V6 power unit also in development.

Working on the basis that its customers did not really care what sort of engine was under the bonnet, just so long as it provided enough power and fuel economy for their needs, Ford-of-Europe provided this line-up of German-built Capris from early 1969:

1300	1305cc V4	50bhp @ 5,000rpm
1500	1498cc V4	60bhp @ 5,000rpm
1700GT	1699cc V4	75bhp @ 5,000rpm
2000GT	1998cc V6	85bhp @ 5,000rpm
		(90bhp @ 5,000 rpm on R-specification)
2300GT	2293cc V6	108bhp @ 5,000rpm

– and, from the autumn of 1969:

2300GT	2293cc V6	125bhp @ 5,500rpm

At this stage, once again, I must repeat that German-built V4 and V6 engines were totally different from the Ford-UK Essex V4s and V6s, though in product planning terms they had clearly been influenced by the same global thinking.

Trim and dress-up packs were available in the same sort of confusing variety as with British-built cars. At first every German-built car had left-hand drive, and Cologne was soon revealed as the source from which almost all US market cars would be built, though some Kent-engined US-specification Capris were originally built at Halewood.

In the next few years, change followed change, just as it did in the UK, and it is best to summarize these as follows.

March 1970 – The motor sport-intended RS2600 was previewed, and went on limited sale later in the year. This specialized Capri had a 2637cc version of the Cologne V6, was equipped with Kugelfischer fuel-injection and produced no less than 150bhp at 5,800rpm. The story of this car is described in much more detail in Chapter 3.

September 1970 – The 2600GT took over from the most powerful of the 2300GTs, having a longer-stroke version of that car's engine, with 125bhp from 2550cc. At the same juncture, the 85bhp/1998cc V6 engine option was dropped, while 1.5-litre peak power was boosted to 65bhp.

Autumn 1972 – In this mid-range face-lift/reshuffle, which involved the same style/lighting updates as on British cars, there were many changes to a car that otherwise looked basically unchanged. The most important mechanical change was that every V4-engined type was withdrawn (the engine had never been popular, nor thought smooth enough by its clientèle) in favour of versions of the still-modern overhead-camshaft Pinto in-line four, while the British 3-litre V6 Essex engine was finally made available in a German-built 3000GT/GXL.

From that point, the engine line-up was as follows:

1300	1293cc, 4–cylinder, overhead-camshaft	55bhp @ 5,500rpm
1600	1593cc, 4-cylinder, overhead-camshaft	72bhp @ 5,000rpm
1600GT	1593cc, 4-cylinder, overhead-camshaft	88bhp @ 5,700rpm
2000GT	1998cc V6	90bhp @ 5,000rpm
2300GT	2293cc V6	108bhp @ 5,000rpm
2600GT	2550cc V6	125bhp @ 5,300rpm
3000GT	2994cc V6 (Essex)	138bhp @ 5,300rpm

– and, of course the:

RS2600	2637cc V6	150bhp @ 5,600rpm

Assembly of German-built Capri Is ended in December 1973, a total of 784,000 having been made at Cologne and Saarlouis. Well over half of that total was of cars destined for sale in the USA.

Even Ford are going to be surprised at the demand for their new Capri. Forgetting the racing fastback shape for the moment, it is the best car that Ford have ever produced. With intelligent thinking behind the design and powerful marketing ahead of it, they will sell a million, and quickly at that.

The detail drawing of the car's profile and interior showed that it was a very genuine 2+2-seater, though with the front seats pushed all the way back, there was only 5in (127mm) between the front seat back-rest and the front of the rear seat cushion. For all normal purposes, though (which meant not trying to carry half a well-built rugby team inside it!), this was a compact four-seater, just as the Mustang was, on a larger scale of course, in the USA.

It tells us a lot that *Autocar*'s comment on the seats was: 'There is only enough headroom for a 5ft 8in passenger, and for adults to travel comfortably in the back the front seats need to be well forward on their runners'. (I happen to know that the technical editor, Geoffrey Howard, was 5ft 8in tall!)

Even so, Ford had clearly got the marketing approach spot on, for:

> Wherever we took the Capri there was a lot of interest in it. Not from enthusiasts as you might expect, but from ordinary family men who had always yearned for a sports car. Really it is just a saloon with very sporty lines, yet it does things without apparent effort much better than lots of so-called sports car…Like all Fords, it represents good value for money, and it is destined to be a sure-fire hit with the public and for the manufacturers.

3000GT – At Last

We all had to wait, with mounting impatience, for the launch of the brawny 3000GT that finally made its début in October 1969. Perhaps we had always been expecting too much from Ford, but the problem was that the company

Although the 3000GT and 3000E types did not outsell the 1600 types, they certainly generated all the headlines. Not only were they fast, near-120mph (193km/h) machines but they also offered exceptional value for money.

Not all Capris were equipped with the same style details – this actually being a 3000GT, complete with the XLR dress-up pack, and the black bonnet that a customer could omit from the build specification if he wanted to remain a little more anonymous. The grilles behind the doors had no function – when removed, they exposed blank metal and no fresh air access to the inside of the car.

had not taken the decision to make 3-litre engined versions of the new Capri until very late. Certainly when the styling was signed off in late 1967, no serious engineering work, or development, had taken place, and even when the rest of the range was introduced in January 1969, it is doubtful if more than one or two prototypes – and I mean that, not as an exaggeration – had been completed. None were even taken to Cyprus as a 'taster' for the media to review.

It did not help, of course, that the Capri had only been launched for two or three weeks when the original four-wheel-drive (FWD) 3-litre type was seen in TV rallycross – but that was down to Boreham's 'can-do' engineering, rather than to any long-term planning at Dunton. Neither did it help that more than one private tuning house had already completed a 3-litre engine transplant job and showed it off to the motoring press, before Ford was ready to show off the real thing.

The great day finally dawned in October 1969, just a week before the opening of the Earls Court Motor Show in London, when the 3000GT was finally launched. Even at a glance, it was clear that this had been far more seriously tackled than just as an engine transplant, for there had been engine changes, suspension modifications, and style revisions too.

Although the engine itself was basically the familiar Essex V6 of 2994cc, as found in the contemporary Zodiac, the engineers had worked away at it, not only with a newly-baffled sump and a revised oil pump pick-up, but with revised

In the early days of the Capri, the Ford Rallye Sport (RS) Club organized hilariously-contested one-model races where Capri 3000GTs were the stars, along, of course, with well-known race drivers like Graham Hill and Jack Brabham.

Not many Essex V6 engines looked so smart – for this was a pristine display power unit, which Ford had striven to keep as small as possible, even though it was a 3-litre power unit.

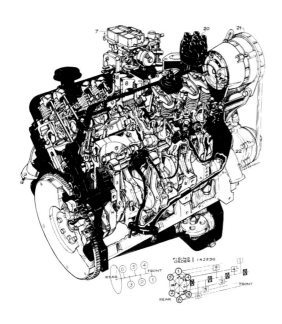

As fitted to the Capri 3000GT and 3000E types from 1969/1970, the Essex V6 engine had a high-mounted alternator positioned towards the front right of the engine bay.

bearings, and with a bit of attention to cylinder block stiffness too. Still rated at 128bhp, it was by no means a fire-breathing unit, but it was extremely torquey and (as far as Ford was concerned) it was both simple and cheap to manufacture. It was, in almost every way, the 'Big Brother' to the 2000GT's V4, which was manufactured on the same facilities at Dagenham.

The new 3000GT also got its own special four-speed gearbox, for that which was being used on other smaller-engined Capris could not cope with the torque of the V6. This basic gearbox was shared with the Zephyr/Zodiac range *and* with the Transit van. It was a compromise in more ways than one, for there was a side-opening in the casing to accept the selectors (instead of a conventional top opening); in Zodiacs there was a steering column change; and in the Transit there was a direct-acting, not remote control, central change. The rear axle ratio, of 3.22:1, was the highest yet specified for any Capri.

Some Capri jobs were more glamorous than others. Here, three race 'control' cars pose inside a dirt-track stadium, probably at races where Ford Escorts took the majority of victories.

There had been time to give the latest car a thorough make-over. To allow even more clearance for the engine (and for styling reasons too), the bonnet had a bulge in it, like the cars already being built in Cologne, the entire GT visual and equipment pack was standard, and the suspension had been revised to take account of the heavier engine and changed front/rear weight distribution.

Visually, twin exhaust pipes and 185-section radial-ply tyres gave the game away, the burble from those exhausts added to the impression, and there was an enlarged 13.5gal (61ltr) fuel tank to help feed the thirstier engine. Under the bonnet, the engine bay finally looked full, and there was a high-mounted alternator.

This, no question, was the Capri package enthusiasts had been awaiting for nearly a year. Priced on announcement at £1,291, but immediately raised to £1,386 within days of the launch – added to which the compulsory safety belts cost £14.04, and most people elected to pay £34.93 for a Ford radio – this looked like a bargain, and sales once again exceeded all expectations.

As *Autocar* testers commented, they thought it offered: 'Effortless performance and considerable refinement at a fair price. Heavier engine results in more understeer. Steering and straight-line stability improved, but ride significantly worse. Gearbox ratios not ideal'.

Although the top speed of 113mph (182km/h) and 0-60mph acceleration in 10.3 seconds came up to every expectation, in the original 3000GT there was an important shortcoming in the gear ratios provided. Apart from the quality of the change itself, which was rather clunky and quite unlike that of the smaller Ford gearboxes, the internal ratios were awkward. These, don't forget, had originally been devised for use in the heavy Zephyr/Zodiac family cars of the 1960s and as *Autocar* commented in October 1969:

One cannot really dismiss as unimportant the peculiar set of intermediate ratios in the Mk IV Zodiac gearbox, even allowing for the flexible nature of the engine. For a car with sporting pretensions, second gear is too low, which leaves an annoying gap between second and third. Observing the 5,800rpm red sector on the accurate rev counter, first, second and third give 38 [61], 55 [88.5] and 84 [135] mph [km/h] maximum respectively. This uneven spacing prevents the car accelerating as well as it could. You notice it not only during acceleration against a stop-watch, but on the road when overtaking.

For the next two years Ford seemed able to sell every Capri that they could build. No fewer

From March 1970, the 3000E became the Capri flagship model. The best-equipped, and the fastest in the range, it was very popular.

than 84,973 cars were assembled at Halewood in 1970 – which was a figure the Capri would never again reach in the UK – though twice as many cars (including the first flood of exports to the USA) were assembled in Germany. It must have come as a shock to Ford's rivals, and was certainly a pleasant and profitable surprise to Ford-of-Europe, when the millionth Capri was built in mid-1973.

In the meantime, development and improvement of the basic design, all kept the pot boiling. There wasn't a year when something important was not done to improve an already-popular car.

1970

The first glossy new arrival was that of the 3000E, which appeared in March 1970. Adding to Ford's range of 'E-for-Executive' saloons (the Cortina 1600E, the Corsair 2000E and the Zodiac Executive), this followed the same pattern. Based on the still-new 3000GT, the 3000E had all the XLR kit, to which was

added a vinyl roof covering, a push-button radio, a heated rear window, opening rear quarter windows, and special cloth-trim inserts for the seats. All this cost an extra £91, which was a bargain, and once again Ford had a marketing success on their hands.

Along with other Ford passenger cars, from September 1970 the Capri received more powerful Kent engines, the 1600GT now produced 86bhp, for instance, instead of 82bhp – this being achieved by the usual tuner's expertise of modified cylinder heads shaping – a different camshaft profile and altered carburation.

At the same time, the brake servo was standardized on 1300GT and 1600 models (it was still optional on the 1300) and individual X and R dress-up options were withdrawn, though they were still available as part of the XL and XLR combinations.

1971

In the autumn, it was the turn of the V6 engine (but not the V4, whose days were already seen

Here's a minor puzzle, with a Brands Hatch 'Race Control' car liveried up with '1971 World Champion' around its modified boot area and Jack Brabham on board. But in that year, Jackie Stewart became World F1 Champion.

The 'Capri Special' of 1971, in bright orange, was the first of several limited editions that would be built over the years. Rear window slats and a boot-lid spoiler were very fashionable during this period.

to be numbered) to get a technical make-over. A new camshaft profile, re-worked cylinder heads and inlet manifolding, a viscous cooling fan and new ancillaries all helped to boost the peak power from 128bhp to a lusty 138bhp (at 5,000rpm).

That in itself was good news, but the provision of revised intermediate gear ratios and the raising of the final drive ratio to 3.09:1 (from 3.22:1) was much more significant. At a stroke, second gear (1.95:1 inside the box instead of 2.29:1) was much more valuable. New-style road wheels and larger auxiliary lamps also made their appearance at this time and the rear suspension was softened.

Somehow the latest 3000GT felt *much* faster than the original types – this being a combination of more power and torque, and a much more suitable set of gear ratios – and it showed up in the figures, with 0–60mph acceleration now taking only a little more than 8 seconds.

It can be no coincidence, surely, that sales of the 3000 leapt from 3,900 in 1971 to nearly 5,000 in 1972, that last figure being boosted by this version of the car going on sale in Germany for the first time.

But it was not all onwards-and-upwards. Disappointed by poor sales (though I have already pointed out the reasons for this), Ford withdrew the 1300GT.

Also in the autumn of 1971, the very first limited-edition car – rather mundanely titled the Capri 'Special' – was produced. Only 1,200 such cars, all based on the 2000 GT XLR, were built, solely for the UK market.

Painted in a lurid vista orange (such colours were very fashionable in this short 'flower-power' era), the 'Special' had a sheet of venetian blind slats over the rear window, a boot lid spoiler, a 3000E-type vinyl roof, cloth trim, a heated rear window and a radio. In many ways this reflected what was happening to Mustangs in the USA at this time.

1972

In June, a fresh trio of Capri 'Specials' were put on sale, these being 1600GT-, 2000GT- *and* 3000GT-based. Once again, there were no mechanical changes, for these cars merely offered dress-up packs – but with a difference. Here, for the first time, were British-built Capris with bonnet bulges, painted in black or green, complete with a heated rear window, cloth trim, opening rear quarter windows, hazard flashers, inertia-reel seat belts (it was still not compulsory to wear belts in the UK, only to fit them to cars) and a centre console.

Mid-Term Facelift

In September 1972, Ford rationalized all the changes and improvements that had gradually been building up in the previous year by introducing a much-revised range of 1973 models and a new flag-ship model, called the 3000GXL. Although the same basic body style/shell/layout was retained, the entire line-up had been refreshed, and Ford claimed that there had been 151 detail improvements, 194 on cars to be delivered to the USA.

From the autumn of 1972, the original 'flag-ship' E model was dropped in favour of the more sophisticated GXL derivative.

When the mid-term face-lift cars appeared in the autumn of 1972, they were treated to different front and rear lamp clusters. This was the tail lamp area of the 1973-model car, larger and more flamboyant that that of the originals.

Range

The basic models were: 1300L, 1600L, 1600XL, 1600GT, 2000GT, 3000GT and 3000GXL. Although the individual dress-up packs had

been abandoned, there was a sports custom pack for GT models, which included sports wheels, twin auxiliary lamps, a map-reading lamp light, a leather gear knob, and side stripes, though these were rarely ordered.

Style

All UK Capris now had the bonnct bulge, and all except the 3000GXL had much larger rectangular headlamps and tail lamp clusters, with new radiator grilles. The GXL had the four-

From late 1972, the original shape Capri was given a significant styling make-over, which included the use of much enlarged headlamps, and the bonnet bulge became standard on all models.

circular headlamp front style that was already familiar on USA-market Capris and also on the limited-production RS2600. Each and every Capri now got matt black paintwork on the sills under the door. The 3000GXL, which replaced the 3000E, retained the vinyl roof covering of that car.

Inside the car, as well as changes to the trim pattern and seat coverings, there was a completely fresh facia/instrument display, along with a two-spoke steering wheel. This, in fact, was what would appear, unchanged, in the Capri II of 1974. As before, there were two levels of instrument display, with the GT/GXL types getting a full six-dial layout; there was a glove box for the first time on a Capri; and a new type of centre console on GT and GXL models.

Engines

There had been a reshuffle, with the old-type 1.6-litre Kent engine being dropped in favour of the new overhead-camshaft 1.6-litre Pinto power unit (but not yet as a 2-litre – that would have to wait for Capri II), this being available in 72bhp, and 88bhp form on the GT.

Kent 1300, V4 Essex 2000 and V6 Essex 3000 engines continued as before, the V6 cars getting a more suitable variety of gearbox with a better-quality gear change, though the internal ratios were retained.

Chassis

The major change came at the rear, where in common with other Ford models, the original type of radius arms had been dropped in favour of a slim and rather ineffectual anti-roll bar. Spring and damper rates were softened up, though rebound travel of the wheels was increased at front and rear: the result was to give a softer-riding car than the original Capri. At the same time, all cars got new wider-trim 5in rims in eight-spoke 'sports' style.

Thus rejuvenated, the Capri carried on selling briskly, to reach its fourth anniversary in January of 1973. By this time, of course, the

The mark of the true Capri enthusiast is the ability to recognize, and list, all the different types of road wheels to be found on these cars. Introduced in the early 1970s, and described as 'sports road wheels' by Ford, these eight-spoke components were in pressed steel (though to some they looked like alloys) and – depending on the model and the year – came in a variety of finishes.

Capri I Specifications (1969–74): UK-build cars, except the RS3100

Engines

1300 Kent
Layout	4-cylinder, in-line, overhead-valve
Bore × stroke	80.96 × 62.99mm
Capacity	1298cc
Compression ratio	9.0:1
Maximum power	52bhp @ 5,000rpm (57bhp @ 5,700rpm from 1970)
Maximum torque	66lb ft @ 2,500rpm (66lb ft @ 3,000rpm from 1970)
Fuel system	Ford/Motorcraft GPD carburettor

1300GT Kent
Layout	4-cylinder, in-line, overhead-valve
Bore × stroke	80.96 × 62.99mm
Capacity	1298cc
Compression ratio	9.2:1
Maximum power	64bhp @ 6,000rpm (72bhp @ 5,500rpm from 1970)
Maximum torque	64.5lb ft @ 4,400rpm (65lb ft @ 2,500rpm from 1970)
Fuel system	Weber compound dual-choke carburettor

1600 Kent
Layout	4-cylinder, in-line, overhead-valve
Bore × stroke	80.96 × 77.62mm
Capacity	1599cc
Compression ratio	9.0:1
Maximum power	64bhp @ 4,800rpm (68bhp @ 5,700rpm from 1970)
Maximum torque	85lb ft @ 2,500rpm
Fuel system	Ford/Motorcraft GPD carburettor

1600GT Kent
Layout	4-cylinder, in-line, overhead-valve
Bore × stroke	80.96 × 77.62mm
Capacity	1599cc
Compression ratio	9.2:1
Maximum power	82bhp @ 5,400rpm (86bhp @ 5,700rpm from 1970)
Maximum torque	92lb ft @ 3,600rpm
Fuel system	Weber compound dual-choke carburettor

1600 Pinto
Layout	4-cylinder, in-line, single overhead-camshaft
Bore × stroke	87.65 × 66mm
Capacity	1593cc
Compression ratio	9.2:1
Maximum power	72bhp @ 5,500rpm
Maximum torque	87lb ft @ 2,700rpm
Fuel system	Ford/Motorcraft GPD carburettor

1600GT Pinto
Layout	4-cylinder, in-line, single overhead-camshaft
Bore × stroke	87.65 × 66mm
Capacity	1593cc
Compression ratio	9.2:1
Maximum power	88bhp @ 5,700rpm
Maximum torque	92lb ft @ 4,000rpm
Fuel system	Weber compound dual-choke carburettor

2000GT Essex V4
Layout	4-cylinder, in 60-degree V, overhead-valve
Bore × stroke	93.66 × 72.44mm
Capacity	1996cc
Compression ratio	8.9:1
Maximum power	92.5bhp @ 5,500rpm
Maximum torque	104lb ft @ 3,600rpm
Fuel system	Weber compound dual-choke carburettor

3000GT Essex V6
Layout	6-cylinder, in 60-degree V, overhead-valve
Bore × stroke	93.66 × 72.44mm
Capacity	2994cc
Compression ratio	8.9:1
Maximum power	128bhp @ 4,750rpm (138bhp @ 5,000rpm from late 1971)
Maximum torque	173lb ft @ 3,000rpm (174lb ft @ 3,000rpm from 1971)
Fuel system	Weber compound dual-choke carburettor

Transmission
Gearbox	All synchromesh manual 4-speed Optional 3-speed automatic with 1600, 1600GT, 2000GT and 3000GT engines
Final drive	4.125:1 (1300/1300GT); 3.90:1 (1600); 3.78:1 (1600GT); 3.545:1, 3.44:1 from 1970 (2000GT); 3.22:1, 3.09:1 from 1971 (3000GT/E/GXL)

Suspension
Front	MacPherson strut, coil springs, anti-roll bar, telescopic dampers
Rear	Live axle, half-elliptic leaf springs, radius arms, telescopic dampers Note: Radius arms were deleted, and an anti-roll bar was introduced from late 1972, at mid-life facelift time.
Steering	Rack and pinion
Brakes	Disc front, drum rear, optional vacuum servo on 1300, 1300GT, 1600 (to 1970); vacuum servo standard on all other types

Running Gear
Wheels	13in steel wheels, several styles including Rostyle, depending on model
Tyres	Cross-ply on 1300 and 1600 (to 1971), radial-ply on all other models

Dimensions
Wheelbase	100.8in (2,559mm)
Front track	53in (1,346mm)
Rear track	52in (1,321mm)
Length	167.8in (4,262mm)
Width	64.8in (1,646mm)
Height	50.7in (1,288mm)
Weight (unladen)	From 1,940lb (880kg) for 1300, to 2,380lb (1,079kg) for 3000GXL

hype had died down, so the latest cars were viewed more as conventional Fords, rather than as ground-breaking coupés. It is interesting to look back and see how little difference the arrival of the new overhead-camshaft Pinto engine actually made – Ford's accountants, of course, were delighted by the way that this engine was finding a home in so many Ford models of the day – but in performance terms it made only a limited impact.

When *Autocar* tested a 1600XL in its Christmas issue of 21 December 1972 (the other test in the same issue was of a Young's Brewery Dray, complete with two massive Shire horses!), they headed their report: 'New Heart for a Basic Sports Saloon', noting a top speed of 98mph (158km/h), and 0–60mph in 12.9 seconds, and also that:

> In its old form, the 1600 was a relatively leisurely car, but pulled strongly at low revs and had a good top gear performance. To a large extent the new version retains the punch, but it runs out of breath much less quickly, and is a good deal faster in consequence.

The suspension changes came in for much comment:

> The suspension changes have certainly altered the Capri's ride. In its original form, the car was very good on smooth surfaces, but gave up quite suddenly when the road became rougher. Now the smooth-road ride gives less of a feeling of rock-steadiness, but the Capri is much more willing to absorb the shocks from uneven or broken road surfaces. There is no longer a point beyond which the car is obviously unhappy. Roll angles in hard cornering remain very small, and overall we rate the ride as noticeably improved.
>
> Summing up: In many ways it is an admirable compromise car for those who do not wish to adventure into the GT field.

What we did not then know (but might have guessed, if Ford's strategy with other models, and their life cycles, had been studied) was that this original Capri, even in what many people call 'Mark 1?' guise, did not have long to live. Work on a completely new style of Capri – Capri II, which is described in Chapter 5 – had already been going ahead for some time.

Even so, demand for the 'Mark 1?' car was good. A total of 47,005 cars were produced at Halewood in 1972 and 152,120 in Germany, and in 1973 those totals rose to 49,392 and 183,933, respectively. When we consider that the Yom Kippur War and the resulting oil-supply Energy Crisis struck with real ferocity towards the end of the year, this is a real achievement.

By the end of 1973, however, the Capri I was almost ready to be retired. The RS3100 'homologation special', described in Chapter 3, appeared in November 1973, just as plans to completely re-equip the assembly lines to produce a new-style car were being finalized. Although the Capri II was not launched until the end of February 1974, the first pilot-built cars were produced just before the end of 1973.

For Ford, therefore, 'The Car You Always Promised Yourself' had been an enormous success, for in five years, no fewer than 1,209,100 of all original types had been produced. Would a new style prove to be as successful?

3 Capri RS2600 and Capri RS3100

Many years ago I asked a Ford top manager how often the production cars were sold at a loss. Was there such a thing, I asked him, as a 'loss-leader'? Looking at me as if I was an alien being, he raised one elegant eyebrow, and snorted: 'Good Lord, No. It's against our religion. My dear boy, Ford is many things – but it is not a charitable institution!'

All Ford projects, in other words, are expected to make money. Well – almost all of them. Occasionally, just occasionally, new Fords have been sold in small numbers for just one reason – they were 'homologation specials'. In the 1970s, cars like the Capri RS2600 and the RS3100 were two such machines. Those of you who lust after today's extremely rare Capri RS2600s and RS3100s should remember that one word – homologation. Why? Because without homologation – approval from the sporting authorities for use in international competition – no road car can take part in serious motor sport.

The most successful cars have always been the most special, and by definition the most special cars cost a great deal more to build and usually sell in smaller quantities. Therefore, although it might have been against their religion, because Ford had an urge to win races and rallies at world level, they sometimes had to approve the sale of special cars, take a smaller profit per unit and not worry too much about the bottom line.

RS2600 and RS3100 – Different Capris, Different Markets, Same Purpose

Although this chapter covers two closely related cars, their detailed engineering design was separated by several years, their production only barely overlapped, and they were built on different sites – one model in Germany, the other in the UK.

Before I even begin to examine their separate features, I ought to describe how the two types were interlinked in so many ways. Both cars were quite closely based on the original-shape Capri I coupé of 1969–74, and were intended to be vehicles from which the 'works' teams could develop race-winning competition cars, and both were originally planned and engineered by the Ford Advanced Vehicle Organization (AVO) at South Ockendon in Essex. Proving just how multinational Ford-of-Europe had already become, the engine work needed to make the RS2600 so powerful and so effective was carried out in Germany, while it was done at South Ockendon in the UK on the RS3100 that followed.

One basic difference, of course, was that the RS2600 appeared early in the life of the original Capri, while the RS3100 came along at the very end of the five-year career of the original-shape car.

The RS2600 was a German-market car with a German V6 engine, only ever built with left-hand drive, while the RS3100 was British, with a British V6. The RS2600 was never meant for sale in the UK, and accordingly it was never built with right-hand steering. The RS3100 was a home-market car, and was never built with left-hand steering. In that respect, the two cars could not have been more different.

They remained on the market for several years (the very last RS2600 was delivered at least a year after the model was discontinued),

---

The AVO Project

The idea for what eventually became the Ford Advanced Vehicle Operation (AVO) had been developing in Walter Hayes' fertile brain since 1965. Although cars were only built at South Ockendon (sometimes called Aveley) from 1970 to the end of 1974, this business is now legendary – and closed.

Hayes eventually gained approval to set up the AVO as a self-contained business in which specialized cars, many of them for use in motor sport, would be built. These would be supplied to a new breed of Ford dealerships, known as the RS (or Rallye Sport) chain. The AVO also spread its tentacles to Ford-Germany, where cars like the Capri RS2600 were to be produced.

On Hayes' behalf, product planner Bob Howe viewed no fewer than fifty locations in Essex before eventually recommending an in-house facility, where spare space had recently appeared. Originally a corner of a vast complex set up in the late 1950s by Ford at South Ockendon for engineering and other purposes, it had become redundant as these departments moved to the new technical centre at Dunton. Conversion work began in the winter of 1969–70, and the first complete car – an Escort RS1600 – was officially driven off the lines on 2 November 1970. In the meantime the Capri RS2600 had already been revealed, to be built in Cologne.

At its peak, the AVO employed more than 250 people and – officially at least – the 110,000sq ft plant (which cost £329,000) could produce twenty-three cars a day, or around 5,000 cars a year. In fact it was rarely at full stretch, and was never very profitable. One reason for the building of thousands of Escort 1300Es at the AVO in 1973 and 1974 was to help spread the financial overheads.

When early enthusiasm was at its height, the AVO's team considered making new projects as various as the mid-engined GT70, a 3-litreV6-engined Cortina, four-wheel-drive (FWD) Capris and Granadas, and even batch assembly of a turbo-Ford engined DeTomaso Pantera. For good commercial and manufacturing reasons though, the Capri RS2600 was always built at Cologne and the RS3100 at Halewood.

The Energy Crisis struck in the autumn of 1973, after which the mainstream factories found themselves on short time, the AVO was always in danger and was soon scheduled for closure. The last cars were built there in the winter of 1974–75. By the 1980s no trace of the AVO remained at South Ockendon. As Ford-UK downsized in the new century, the entire plant became redundant and was vacated in 2005.

---

but far more RS2600s than RS3100s were sold – the RS3100 was strictly a 'one-winter' wonder and very definitely only an 'homologation special'. Ford-Germany eventually built as many RS2600s as they could sell, whereas Ford-UK built only as many RS3100s as they thought they could get away with to secure homologation. The fact that RS3100 assembly (original shape) clashed with the early build-up of Capri II assembly (hatchback style) at Halewood did nothing to help.

As I have previously mentioned, when the RS2600 was new, and because right-hand-drive cars were never produced, it was never officially sold in the UK. The fact is, though, that a few cars were imported for the use of senior Ford managers in the early 1970s, and for the occasional contract car for 'works' race drivers to use on the road. In more recent years a small number of RS2600s (which are now

classics by any standards) have been imported, and they do say that one or two have even been converted to right-hand drive.

As I make clear in Chapter 4, in both cases the racing versions were as totally different from the road cars as was possible – the 'works' RS2600s eventually used special Weslake cylinder heads (up to 325bhp was finally squeezed out of the 3-litre derivatives), while the racing RS3100s used Cosworth-developed 3.4-litreV6 engines that might have been loosely based on the Essex V6 cylinder block, but had totally different twin-overhead-camshaft cylinder heads: these engines eventually produced up to 450bhp.

It is important to remember that in those days the Capri was manufactured at Halewood in the UK and at Cologne in Germany. I should also remind everyone that although the basic layout of the British and German cars was the same, there were big differences in the engines and transmissions that were employed. In Britain, as already related, the first Halewood-built Capris used the British range of 4-cylinder and 6-cylinder engines, while early Cologne-built cars used V4s and V6s of their own special variety, which were made entirely in Germany. It was not until the early 1970s that any kind of rationalization of the different nationalities of Capri took place.

Engineering Development

Like the mass-production Capris, all RS-badged derivatives had two-door coupé body styles, with long noses, short tails with a rather small boot, and very cramped rear seats. Somehow or other, Ford managed to convince the motor sport authorities that these were genuine four-seater saloons, which allowed them to be homologated into Group 2 and to go Touring Car racing.

When the time came for cars to be inspected (and measured) before they could be approved, a bit of 'massaging' of rear seat cushion shapes and trim panels took place. Ford felt no shame in doing this, for there was at least one illustrious precedent: in Germany, Porsche had already completed the same 'yes it really *does* have four seats' trick with the ultra-sporting rear-engined 911 coupé.

All Capri Is had MacPherson strut front suspension and their axles were suspended on leaf springs, so this basic layout was naturally retained by the RS derivatives. Early RS2600s also had twin radius arms to locate the rear axle, but most of them, and all RS3100s, lacked those items but were fitted with rear anti-roll bars instead. For motor sport use, where there was considerable technical freedom in the Group 2 regulations, the axles were sprung and located in a more sophisticated manner.

Except for the special parts developed for RS models, it is quite amazing to note how many totally mainstream Ford parts were used in these rather exclusive Capris, which probably explains why they still cost relatively little

to service and restore, and why the insurance ratings could be so reasonable. Except where I mention it, the RS Capris used the same parts as standard V6-engined Capris.

RS2600 – Very Rare in the UK

Although Ford-Germany always liked enthusiasts to think that it was their idea, the newly-founded AVO was closely involved at first. Rod Mansfield, who would later found Ford's Special Vehicle Engineering department (SVE), and would engineer the charismatic Capri 2.8i, once told me how it all started, and that:

In the beginning we did the original Capri RS2600s, where 50 cars had to be built for Ford-Germany to homologate, don't ask me how, for that was way under the official numbers required. It was a joint Anglo-German project – I had a three-man Performance Parts group in Cologne, including engineer Otto Stulle – and I'm sure we never thought of building Capris on the British AVO lines. We had to negotiate with German managers to get those cars built at Cologne – Albert Caspers, who was boss of the pilot plant, was very helpful there.

Jochen Neerpasch [Motorsport Manager, Ford-Germany] insisted on getting that car very quickly, and as light as possible. It had fibreglass doors, perspex side windows, no heaters, no carpets - the quality was appalling, and you could never get a car like that through Ford's systems today!

The properly-developed RS2600 followed that – it was the first-ever fuel-injected Ford, I think. We did a lot of work at Aveley [AVO] and in Germany on that. I was proud of the RS2600, it was a lovely car. At the start there were very few of us at AVO – by mid-1970, when the RS2600 came along, we must have had eight or ten engineers, running several programmes, plus three people in Germany.

Later I think it maybe rose to 18 or 20 as an absolute maximum. AVO was always the fashionable place to be, but not for those with career plans – other people at Ford regarded AVO as a cowboy outfit, peopled by mavericks. But it was a fantastically exciting place to work, at the time. The mentality of the average Ford person was to do everything by the book, so people like us weren't liked because of the way we wriggled round the system.

The 2.6-litre RS2600 was launched in March 1970, by being previewed at the Geneva Motor Show, and came complete with the characteristic four-headlamp nose. Not only did this style delineate it from the mainstream cars (in fact the assemblies were about to be used on US-market Capris), but it meant that more efficient, high-intensity, lights could be used for motor sport events where it was necessary to race or rally in the darkness.

Even so, the cars that would later count as production models (assembly would begin in September 1970) were very different from the originals, and altogether more civilized. The first fifty cars, built (or should I perhaps say 'thrown together'?) specifically to Ford-Germany Competition Manager Jochen Neerpasch's specific requirements, were very light and very crude, with carburetted engines,

magnesium Minilite wheels, glass-fibre doors, bonnets and boot lids, no carpets or heaters, no bumpers, and with perspex side windows. They weighed a mere 1,985 lb (900kg) and their general build quality was awful: racing drivers, though, don't complain about noise and vibration!

Proper production cars did not appear until the autumn of 1970, and were so much more civilized that they weighed much more – in fact they were heavier than the normal 2300GT/2600GT series. All had glass all round, carpets, heaters and all such up-market fittings that the price demanded. The V6 Cologne engine was a 2,637cc/150bhp unit with Kugelfischer fuel-injection (this had never before been used in a Ford road car of any type) and was backed by the heavy-duty (Taunus 26M, at first) gearbox and back axle: the final drive ratio was 3.22:1.

To alter the suspension geometry, and to provide more front negative camber, there was a specially-fabricated front cross-member,

Ford electrified all Ford enthusiasts with the launch of the stripped out, and very purposeful, RS2600 model in 1970. On the early cars there were no bumpers, very little decoration apart from the black bonnet and sills (and certainly no fake louvres on the rear wings), four headlamps, and specially styled alloy wheels.

The RS2600 had a 2.6-litre version of the Cologne V6 engine, complete with Kugelfischer fuel injection – a combination never to be found on any other European Ford. With 150bhp, and a very sporty state of tune, the RS2600 was the fastest-ever Ford when it first went on sale in 1970.

along with stiffened springs, while there were special single-leaf rear springs and gas-filled Bilstein dampers all round. Cast alloy wheels with 6J section rims and 185/70HR-13in tyres were standard.

Inside the car there were special bucket seats, while outside the quadruple headlamps were matched to front quarter bumpers, Escort

Twin Cam and RS1600 style. There was no rear spoiler of any type.

From October 1971 the latest Granada/Capri 3-litre gearbox was standardized (stronger, more robust and with more suitable intermediate ratios), along with a different style of Ford AVO four-spoke cast alloy wheel and 9.75in (247mm) ventilated front brake discs.

This was the interior style and equipment of the original RS2600 of 1970, a car intended to be fast and functional but without the trimmings. The steering wheel and the bucket seats were special, of course, but there was no centre console, and the radio seen in this car was an optional extra. All RS2600s, incidentally, were built with left-hand drive.

Not a pure RS2600 by any means – this car having rectangular headlamps, flared wheel-arches and ultra-wide after-market alloy wheels – but indicative of the way that Ford-Germany was marketing the car in the early 1970s.

Visually, a true RS2600 had a contrasting (usually black) bonnet panel, and from late 1971 RS2600 stripes and identification were added. At the end of the run, matt black bumpers were fitted.

A total of 3,532 such cars were built before the end of 1973. There is no official UK price to give any marketing comparisons – though in Germany it was priced at DM15,800, which should be compared with the DM9,980 of the existing 2300GT.

This meant that one had to pay nearly 60 per cent more for the RS equipment, and for the extra exclusivity and performance. It might not

For the Capri enthusiast, there was no mistaking the sheer presence of the RS2600. Here seen in action on gravel, this low-down, head-on view emphasizes the four-headlamp nose, which was not seen on any other European-market Capri until late 1972.

All by itself, in the deserted streets of a German city, this RS2600 looks as if it would rather be out on the open highway…

… as indeed the same car was, here, rushing past the camera car. From this angle, the twin exhaust pipes, twin built-in reversing lamps and the quarter bumpers all make their own fashion statement.

This 1972-specification RS2600, pictured in rather bleak test-track surroundings in Germany, shows off the black-painted bonnet that was a good recognition point, together with the RS-style four-spoke alloy road wheels.

This full side-view of the RS2600, taken from a low angle at a proving ground, shows that it was only really the wheels that gave the game away visually.

have been a bargain, but it did, for sure, deliver something unique that appealed to Capri enthusiasts. In standard trim, an RS2600 could reach 125mph (201km/h), and sprint from 0–60mph in around 8 seconds, so this made it the fastest Capri of all (and, naturally, the fastest Ford private car ever to be put on sale).

RS3100 – Last-Gasp Capri I

Commercially, of course, it never made any sense for Ford-UK to introduce the Capri RS3100 only a matter of months before the entire Capri I range was to be dropped in favour of the bigger, heavier, hatchback Capri

II. Commerce, though, had nothing to do with this – as the events listed in Chapter 4 make clear. For motor racing purposes Ford was beginning to suffer an assault from BMW's latest 'winged-monsters' – and needed to develop a counter for these. Something even more extreme than a full-race RS2600 would be needed (by 1973 the 'works' RS2600 race cars had reached the limit of their development, both aerodynamically and in terms of engine power). Just so long as sporting homologation could be achieved, such a car as the Capri RS3100 might be race-competitive for some years after its production had ended.

Although work on a special Cosworth-derived engine had been underway since 1972, the car for which this engine could be ideal, the RS3100, came together much faster. Thinking began in the spring of 1973, the project officially took wings in September 1973, and the end product would be unveiled

For the very limited-production Capri RS3100, these charismatic four-spoke RS-style road wheels were standard. Unhappily, such wheels were much coveted by thieves, and a number disappeared while cars were parked in unguarded streets.

This is a very well-known 'jumping' shot of the RS3100. Let us hope that the gas-filled dampers could cope with the crash landing that took place just outside the frame of the camera. The location? Probably Boreham, close to the loose-surface test track.

Mean, moody, and telling every possible story – this is the RS3100 of November 1973, as captured in Ford's own photographic studio. The features that stand out, of course, are the four headlamp/quarter-bumper nose, the big four-spoke alloys and the big rear spoiler.

in November 1973 – immediately *after* the British Motor Show had closed its doors, and unfortunately just after the Energy Crisis threatened to close down motor racing for years to come!

Motor sport personalities such as Stuart Turner, Peter Ashcroft, John Griffiths and Mike Moreton could all see that the racing RS2600 had reached its limit, and that a replacement, or a dramatic update, would be needed if Ford was to remain competitive in saloon car racing. A careful reading of the rules suggested that for production purposes, the engine should be over 3 litres (this would

Recently retired triple World F1 Champion Jackie Stewart poses alongside the rare Capri RS3100 model in November 1973. In many ways the RS3100 was 'son of RS2600', though it used a British type of V6 engine, which had less peak power but more mid-range torque.

allow it to be enlarged still more without it coming up against any capacity limit restrictions), but kept simple (as all types of top-end modification were authorized for racing), and that a sizeable rear spoiler should be added. That, in fact, was the spoiler that the 'works' cars used to go racing in 1974.

The RS3100, therefore, was one of many 1970s Ford models that was invented by motor sport, rather than by the marketing departments, and had only one purpose in life, which was to prove the grounding of an 'homologation special' that could be used in 1974 and beyond. Over the years, remarks dropped casually to me have made it clear that there was resistance to the launch of such a machine, especially from production engineers at Halewood, who did not wish to be bothered with it at a time when they were preparing to put the very different Capri II on to the market.

Stuart Turner, who counted Ford's Public Affairs supremo Walter Hayes as one of his most thoughtful supporters, probably came out with the clinching remark at a planning meeting when things were not going well: 'What you have to decide,' he said, 'is whether you want to back a winner, or get used to losing all the time' – it did the trick.

Accordingly the RS3100 came together very rapidly, really as 'son of RS2600'. Mechanically and structurally, this car had the late-model RS2600 chassis (the RS2600 was still in production when the RS3100 was being planned – more than 1,000 RS2600s were sold in 1973 alone), so it included that car's lowered suspension, the Bilstein dampers, the single-leaf rear springs, the rather ineffectual rear anti-roll bar, and the negative-camber front suspension geometry. One must not forget that dual-circuit brakes were also standard, and that the wheels now had 6in rim widths.

Visually it was easy to distinguish an RS3100 from an ordinary 3 litre, not only because the fashionable four-spoke Ford AVO cast alloy wheels were being employed, but because of the fitment of quarter bumpers, and because of the under-front-bumper air dam, allied to the presence of the large, rubberized, 'duck-tail' spoiler fitted across the edge of the boot lid. Unhappily, the RS3100 was never fitted with special figure-hugging front seats (these had been available on the RS2600 of course), but retained those being used in Capri 3-litres at the time: Motorsport (who invented the car) had no regrets about this omission, reasoning that anyone serious about boosting the performance of the RS3100 and using it in motor sport would automatically want to fit special seats as part of their 'package'.

That big spoiler, incidentally, was never to be seen on any other Capri, British or European, and proved to be extremely effective at high speeds (try one out on a motorway in blustery side-wind conditions if you are not convinced). Some early pictures show the RS3100 with full-width front bumpers that were never fitted to production cars, though striping around the bonnet bulge and on the flanks most certainly were. Figures show that the aerodynamic package worked well. We now know that the RS2600 production car had a drag coefficient of 0.40, whereas the RS3100 (complete with front chin spoiler and rear spoiler) had a coefficient of only 0.37. This might not seem to have been much, but represented a 7.5 per cent improvement.

For the RS3100, the Ford-UK Essex V6 engine was chosen, and for production fitting was modified only slightly. In the cylinder block, the maximum piston overbore approved by the service engineers was chosen (pistons of 3.75in/95mm) were freely available), the result being a swept volume of 3091cc instead of the usual 2994cc. There was no change to the downdraught Weber carburation, or to the exhaust system: it was too early in Ford's evaluation of Bosch fuel-injection for this to be seriously considered – and, in any case, time was extremely short.

According to the publicity surrounding this car, work was done on the cylinder heads, but this was minor, as was the rise in compression pressures due to the larger cylinder bore. The tappet covers, at least, were different – blue

Captured in later life when it achieved fame as a concours-winning machine, this particular RS3100 shows off the facia/instrument layout of the model, together with the flat three-spoke RS-type steering wheel.

Phil Boot's well-known concours-winning RS3100 shows off the styling details that distinguished this car from other Capri models, including the special badging on the front wings and the styling lines along the flanks and doors. Unlike RS2600s, RS3100s retained false louvres in the rear wings.

instead of black – though these did nothing for the performance of the car! The result was a claimed peak power of 148bhp at 5,000rpm, and along with the retention of the un-modified Capri 3-litre gearbox and 3.09:1 final drive ratio, this all helped to give the RS3100 a top speed of about 120–125mph (193–201km/h).

Assembly, as such, took place in a rush (if building such a limited number could ever be called a rush!) before and after Christmas at Halewood. Deliveries to UK dealers began in December 1973, but ended altogether in February 1974 when the Capri II came along, and except for a handful of factory demonstrators most of these cars would originally have been given 1974 – L registration numbers. To achieve Group 2 homologation for motor sport purposes, the regulations stated that Ford had to produce 1,000 cars, and although there seems to have been every intention for this to be done, in fact it was never remotely achieved. Homologation was forthcoming, but only after a few white lies had been told to the authorities. According to a set of AVO production figures that I inherited many years after that business had closed down, only 248 RS3100s were ever produced, of which 193 were sold in the UK, while 55 were sold to other ESOs (European Sales Operations), still with right-hand drive. To cloud the water even further, I am fairly certain that some of these ESO cars were retained in Britain by Ford, to be used by Ford-of-Europe top management based at Warley (HQ) or at Dunton (engineering HQ), having already been 'sold' to a variety of subsidiary Ford operations.

Although the RS3100 was carefully priced, not as a loss-leader, but not at silly money either – it was listed at £2,413 when officially launched in November 1973, which compared with the £1,763 asked for a Capri 3000GT at the time. It proved difficult to sell, and apparently a number had to be heavily discounted. The RS3100's reputation reached its low point in about 1981, when the new 2.8i Capri arrived, to make all other old Capris look out of date – the result being that not many RS3100s have survived.

From this description you will see that it is definitely possible for any crook to make any old Capri 3-litre look like an RS3100, so if you are shopping around these days, beware! Be sure that the negative-camber front end, the striping and the authentic rear spoiler are all present. And don't accept any excuses!

In 1974 Ford was still determined to wring the last amount of credit out of this model. Months after production had ended (six weeks, indeed, after the new-shape Capri II had been unveiled), *Motor*'s Gordon Bruce borrowed a Ford-owned car (NHK 282M), measured its performance, and commented on its behaviour. Having established a top speed of 123mph (198km/h), 125mph (201km/h) on the fastest quarter-mile timed and 0–60mph in 7.2 seconds (this compared with 119.5mph (192km/h) and 8.6 seconds for the outgoing 3000GT Capri I), he then had to grapple with its character:

> [Ford] took exception to their Capri being so soundly beaten by BMW in last year's European Touring Car Championship. Though not obvious at first sight, the Capri RS3100 is their way of trying to make sure it never happens again.

Writing of the handling, he concluded that:

> The result is a harsh and devastatingly knobbly ride, but very predictable handling. If anything, there is too much roll-stiffness and on grippy surfaces full power slides are prevented by premature spinning of the inside wheel. A limited-slip differential would, of course, cure this problem … As it is, the car corners very fast and safely though perhaps disappointingly for those who enjoy a little opposite lock. Fat 185/70 Klebers fill the 6in RS alloy wheels and give good dry but indifferent wet weather adhesion. The large offset of these wheels is responsible for the heavy steering that makes for difficult parking. However, it is full of feel for main road use.

Finally, Gordon made rather vague criticism of the big spoiler:

Capri RS2600 and RS3100 Specifications (1969–74)

Engines			*Suspension*	
RS2600 – Cologne V6			Front	MacPherson strut, coil springs, anti-roll bar, telescopic dampers
Layout	6-cylinder, in 60-degree V, overhead-valve		Rear	Live axle, half-elliptic leaf springs, radius arms, telescopic dampers. Radius arms deleted, anti-roll bar introduced, from late 1972
Bore × stroke:	90 × 69mm			
Capacity	2637cc			
Compression ratio	10.0:1			
Maximum power	150bhp @ 5800rpm (150bhp @ 5,600rpm from 1972)		Steering	Rack and pinion
Maximum torque	166lb ft @ 3,500rpm (159lb ft @ 3,500rpm from 1972)		Brakes	Disc front, drum rear with vacuum servo assistance
Fuel system	Kugelfischer mechanical fuel-injection		*Running Gear*	
			Wheels	13in cast alloy steel wheels, 6in rim width
RS3100 – Essex V6			Tyres	185/70-13in radial-ply
Layout	6-cylinder, in 60-degree V, overhead-valve		*Dimensions*	
Bore × stroke	95.19 × 72.44mm		Wheelbase	100.8in (2,560mm)
Capacity	3091cc		Front track	54.2in (1,377mm)
Compression ratio	9.0:1		Rear track	53.2in (1,352mm)
Maximum power	148bhp @ 5,000rpm		Length	164.8in (4,186mm) (166.9in/4,239mm from 1972)
Maximum torque	187lb ft @ 3,000rpm			
Fuel system	Weber compound dual-choke carburettor			
			Width	64.8in (1,646mm)
Transmission			Height	49.7in (1,263mm)
Gearbox	All synchromesh manual 4 speed		Weight (unladen)	RS3100 and early RS2600 2,315lb (1,050kg), late-model RS2600 2,381lb (1,080kg) from 1972
Final drive	3.22:1 (RS2600), 3.09:1 (late RS2600s and all RS3100s)			

Though we don't doubt that it is invaluable at 130mph [209km/h], we're not saying at what speed we think it starts to take effect. However, we can recommend it for two unclaimed properties. One is for keeping the rear screen remarkably clean, and the other is for retaining the filler cap when it was inadvertently left lying on the boot lid.

The fact is that by the time the RS3100 became available, it had already outlived its usefulness, for the Capri II had made it visually obsolete and the still-evolving Energy Crisis had made it politically difficult to sell. To move the metal, therefore, Ford made sure that many of their high-profile managers were issued with RS3100s in place of the Granadas that they normally drove. However, in the 1974 and 1975 seasons, as the next chapter makes clear, the 'works' RS3100s proved to be extremely effective race cars. In that, at least, they achieved exactly what Ford had set out to achieve in 1973.

4 Capris in European Touring Car Championship Racing

As I have already made clear, when the new Capri coupé went on sale in 1969, it was never intended to be a competition car, nor even a high performance car, for the largest engine on offer was a 2.3-litre V6. Like the Ford-USA Mustang on which many of its features were based, the style came first and the engineering came nowhere.

Zakspeed

Erich Zakowski set up his tuning business, Zakspeed, in Niederzissen, close to Nürburgring in Germany. Born in East Prussia (a satellite of pre-Hitler Germany), then moving to Schleswig-Holstein, and finally opening a truck dealership at Niederzissen in 1960, Zakowski started racing in 1968, using a self-prepared Escort 1300GT with a Broadspeed engine.

By 1973 Zakspeed was building and developing most of its own Escort parts, this being the year in which Dieter Glemser won the German Touring Car Championship. In 1974, with much help from Ford-Germany, Zakspeed effectively became the 'works' Escort team, its beautifully-presented RS1600s, led by Hans Heyer, winning the European series: the very same car (driven by Glemser) also won the German series.

More success followed in Germany in the late 1970s, but before long Zakspeed moved up to Group 5 racing, and to developing a series of highly modified Capris. At the same time, the company developed the special wheel-arch kit seen on so many other Mk II Escorts, along with a series of limited-production road cars for Ford-Germany.

In the mid-1980s, but with no conspicuous success, Zakspeed turned to F1 racing, and all links with Ford were lost.

Ford-Germany, however, had just opened up a new motor sport department. They concentrated on using British Escorts and on tuning-up the big-engined Taunus saloons at first, then set their sights on changing the Capri's image, by forging a completely new image in rallying and in racing.

Team boss Jochen Neerpasch, with Mike Kranefuss as his deputy and Martin Braungart as a talented young engineer, started in Cologne by assessing almost everything – Escorts for racing, Taunus saloons for long-distance rallying (Simo Lampinen so nearly won the London–Sydney Marathon, and there was victory in the 1969 East African Safari, which startled the rallying establishment), and Capris for racing and rallying. By mid-1969, however, Neerpasch's team had started serious development on the Capri range, initially by using the most powerful German-built Capri, which was the 125bhp V6-engined 2300GT.

At the same time, they learned from Ford-UK's proven methods at the Motorsport Centre at Boreham (who knew all about designing 'homologation specials'), and they inspired the birth of an ultra-lightweight version of the Capri. As I have already made clear in Chapter 3, what was at first a very rough-and-ready road car, but one with great potential for use in motor sport, was the fuel-injected RS2600.

Even so, at first the homologation authorities had to be convinced that an RS2600 qualified as a saloon car – with the necessary four seats, and appropriate minimum dimensions inside the cabin. That was never easy – if you have ever studied an original Capri, you will have realized just how cramped the original car actually was.

But in Germany there was already a precedent. Ford-Germany reasoned that if Porsche could get the 911 homologated as a saloon (have you ever tried to sit in the 'rear' seats of a 911?) then even with the somewhat more stringent regulations that had been applied since then, the Capri should qualify, easily. Well, perhaps not easily, but with a combination of presenting a car for inspection in which the seat cushions had gone on a diet (or the springs had collapsed!), and in which the car had miraculously gained shoulder width and rear-seat legroom, the trick was completed.

Because the Capri's chassis was really an amalgam of Cortina Mk II/Corsair, and Escort thinking, Ford-Germany was always confident that it could make the cars handle. Gaining the appropriate top speed was never going to be easy though, for the first cars had drag coefficients of about 0.44.

From 1969–73, therefore, great efforts were made to develop and improve the V6 engines, which including hiring Weslake (of Rye, in Sussex) to carry out much of the power-tuning, and also to make sure that Weslake's newly-designed light-alloy cylinder heads were eventually homologated as options. Then, as

---

Mike Kranefuss

Mike Kranefuss started as a Ford Motorsport departmental manager in Germany, became Ford's worldwide motor sport boss in the 1980s, and then moved out to run his own teams in the USA. He also presided over the famous 'works' motor sport team at Boreham and Cologne in the late 1970s.

Originally helping to run the first Ford-Germany rally Taunus cars, and then working on the Capri RS2600 race cars, he became Competitions Manager in 1972. When Stuart Turner moved out of Motorsport in 1975, Kranefuss then became Director, Motorsport, Ford-of-Europe, and apart from regular liaison meetings he left Peter Ashcroft, Ford-UK's engine build specialist, to run Ford-UK's motor sport efforts.

He was in charge from 1975–80, a period immediately after the 'works' Capris had been supreme at Touring Car Championship level. It was Kranefuss who imposed the closedown of the Capri's race-car activities at the end of 1975, but who encouraged Zakspeed to produce exotic versions of the Capri in the late 1970s.

In 1980 he was promoted yet again – this time to revive Ford-USA's motor sport programme in Detroit. After masterminding the building of a Mustang IMSA race car (which was mainly a Zakspeed Capri under the skin), he also took responsibility for the mainly US-financed F1 programme. It was at his insistence that Cosworth was invited to produce the turbocharged 1.5-litre V6 F1 engine of 1985, and the new-generation HB F1 V8 that followed in 1989.

However, in 1993 he walked away from Ford-USA, after a total of twenty-five years' service with Ford, to set up his own motor racing business – Penske-Kranefuss Racing of North Carolina – where he was in partnership with Roger Penske, running a stock car team.

Two important figures in Capri motor racing lore were Mike Kranefuss of Ford-Germany (right) and Erich Zakowski (left), who ran the Zakspeed cars.

'Works'-developed RS2600s used new cylinder heads developed by Weslake, and fuel-injection with individual butterfly controls in each inlet passage. This is a restored 1973 example.

later, the mass-production iron heads were positively asthmatic. It needed a mountain of practical input from Boreham Ford-UK's engine build specialist Peter Ashcroft before the power units became more reliable and race-worthy.

Racing of the 2300GTs began with an ambitious entry in the ten-day Tour de France – races, speed hill climbs and long-distance rallying all around that country – with a still unhomologated Group 5 version finishing sixth in the hands of Jean-Francois Piot/Jean-Francois Behra. Two other cars retired – one with fuel-injection problems, the other after an accident.

For 1970 a 'works' team was then sent out to work on the European Touring Car Championship, the entire season being tackled by slightly enlarged 2.4-litre 2300GTs, with the newly

One of the earliest 'works' racing Capris was this 2300GT, which competed in the Tour de France of 1969, complete with BP livery, and was crewed by Jean-Francois Piot and Jean-Francois Behra. It finished sixth overall.

developed ZF five-speed gearbox (the same basic box as used in so many rally-winning Escorts in the 1970s). This was ambitious, but the programme was a failure. As Kranefuss later admitted: '1970 was a complete disaster for us'.

The very first race cars looked purposeful but were not sophisticated, as wheel-arch flares were still bolted on (not moulded in), the spoilers looked (and were) tacked on and the engine bays still looked messy. Early in the year, the engines produced a little over 200bhp (though the ever-optimistic Weslake test bed showed 230bhp, Ford would learn to distrust the figures produced using 'Sussex air', and became quite vocally cynical about this) and used Kugelfischer fuel-injection.

From October 1970, however, the race team's fortunes began to look up, as the rather special Capri RS2600 had been homologated (Ford, somehow, had persuaded the authorities to accept that all the lightweight panels and other limited-production features of the original cars were suitable, and qualified, for homologation), and future prospects were brighter.

As we now know, the RS2600 was homologated at a weight of only 1,985lb (900kg), even though the lightest of the 'works' race cars was rarely measured, at scrutineering, at less than 2,095lb (950kg) – and as roll cages became ever more complex, and wheels/tyres larger, that weight would continue to creep up over the years.

The RS2600 could not come soon enough. Even though the first alternative cylinder heads – aluminium castings: machined, developed and carefully air-flowed by Weslake of the UK

– were fitted throughout the season, 1970 was an unhappy period littered with 2300GTs that retired with engine problems of one type or another. Even so there was a class win at Monza and a second overall in Budapest to celebrate.

However, for 1971, and with the possibility of glass-fibre panelled 2873cc (later 2933cc) RS2600s coming on stream, something would have to be done. Not only would the engines have to be tamed, and made more predictable, but the chassis and high-speed handling qualities would have to be improved.

Much against Weslake's wishes, and after brushing aside some resistance from Ford-Germany (there was a question of hurt pride here), Ashcroft was sent over to Cologne to analyse and, if possible, to sort out the mess. As my fellow author Jeremy Walton once wrote about this period: 'Ashcroft's six-month spell at Cologne ... was the stuff of which legends are created. He spoke not a word of German. He was English and meant to sort out the problems the Germans felt had been created by an English company [Weslake]...'.

Ashcroft found that at 7,000rpm the engines were suffering from severe internal vibrations, they were literally shaking themselves apart, and although he was not a qualified engineer, nor could he do the sums required to prove a point, he decided that the crankshaft design would have to be changed. A long telephone conversation with Keith Duckworth of Cosworth – literally, from his workbench, with an offending component on view as he spoke – and a master-class in crankshaft design and balancing was needed before a solution was found.

The 'works' Capri RS1600s carried a variety of liveries in early seasons – this is the way that Dieter Glemser's car looked throughout much of 1971. By this time the Capri was Europe's most successful touring car racer.

Ashcroft's recommended solutions (all of which had to be proved during the winter of 1970–71) – to fit a steel crankshaft of an entirely different design (so it was not Weslake's fault, after all), steel connecting rods, a dry-sump engine, and beefed up iron cylinder blocks – were all adopted:

> We started off with around 260bhp for the season,' Ashcroft later recalled, 'and ran a variety of Mahle piston compression ratios, maybe down to 10.5:1 for a long race like Spa, but 11:1 and more by the time we were searching for the target of over 300bhp.

By mid-season 275bhp was always available: by the end of the year the latest 2933cc engines were revving to 7,500rpm and producing 280–285bhp. All this and a more thoughtful, integrated, approach to chassis and aerodynamic engineering made the 1971 cars much more successful.

Winners in 1971

In 1970–71, the improvement in performance and reliability of the 'works' Capris was remarkable. This time around, the cars were Capri RS2600s instead of 2300GTs: cars that were lighter, more powerful, much more reliable, and handled a great deal better.

The chassis work eventually drew heavily on the proven advances of current British Ford race cars (Capris *and* Escorts), for a successful Ford MacPherson-strutted platform could usually be modified and refined to work well on a different, larger and heavier car.

This was the season in which what had almost become a corporate Ford racing rear suspension came to be adopted: location of the beam axle was by upper and power radius arms, with a Watts linkage pivoting on the rear of the axle casing. Although leaf 'springs' had to be retained to satisfy the Group 2 regulations, these could be in soft and quite useless plastic, the *real* springs being coils that were wrapped round the Bilstein dampers, forming sturdy-looking rear struts that fixed on top of the axle tubes themselves. If you think this looked similar to systems already seen on British Escort race cars, you are correct: at the time Ford-UK called it 'Escortisation', and were proud of this.

Four-wheel disc brakes, wider and ever wider alloy wheels (from Limmer, which by 1973 would eventually grow to a diameter of 16in and a width of 14in for the rear wheels), and ever-widening glass-fibre wheel arch extensions all became visible parts of the 'works' RS2600's appearance. Although front under-bumper spoilers were soon added, at that time the regulations would not allow a big transverse rear spoiler (desperately needed, to keep the rear wheels on the ground!) to be fitted.

Even so, in 1971, in the high-profile European Touring Car Championship (ETCC), the RS2600s were almost always race leaders, often race winners and (most important, this, for image reasons) usually beat the best that BMW could put up to race against them.

In the Championship of that season, the 'works' Capris started their renaissance by taking their first-ever victory in the Austrian Salzburgring event and taking second and third over all into the bargain, the driving heroes being Glemser, Helmut Marko and Alex Soler-Roig respectively.

All in all, in 1971 the 'works' RS2600s proved to be fast, stable and very reliable, winning no fewer than six of the eight long-endurance races outright. They also led the other two races before hitting engine problems, and notched up a load of seconds and thirds along the way, the result being that team leader Glemser ended the season winning the Drivers' Championship. Amazingly, because of a quirk in the Championship regulations, this was not quite enough to give Ford the Makes Championship, which went to the very reliable, but much slower, 1.3-litre Alfa Romeos.

Nor were these merely effective middle-distance cars, for among the wins were victory in

Dieter Glemser was the star of the 1971 Capri effort, winning five major international races.

Yet another sponsorship/colour scheme on a Cologne-built RS2600 during the 1971 race season. However, Castrol and Dunlop were the main, and consistent, trade supports when the RS2600 was in its glory days.

This high-speed study, impressive from a low angle, shows one of the RS2600s at the Spa circuit. Equipment for this 24-hour race included extra driving lamps.

the Spa 24-hour race (where Glemser/Soler-Roig averaged 113.51mph/ 182km/h), and in the Double 6-hour race (a total of twelve hours spread over two days) at Circuit Paul Ricard in France, when Glemser and Soler-Roig again shared the driving, all of which made victory in the Nürburgring 6-hour race for Glemser/ Marko) look positively routine.

At the end of the season, and just to prove the point, Jochen Mass was sent out to South Africa with just one of the cars and one mechanic, plus some spares, entered all six events in the Springbok Championship, won one of the six races and finished well up in several others – and gave Ford the Manufacturers' title in that series too!

Jochen Mass (left) and Gerard Larrousse were two of the important and successful 'works' RS2600 drivers in the early 1970s.

Better to be at the front of the queue than jostling for position in the pack. This was the first race of the 1972 season, at Monza, in Italy, with Dieter Glemser's car well placed – and with the other two Capris already through, and past the cameraman. Glemser's car eventually blew its engine, and victory went to the sister car of Mass/Larrousse.

1972 – Repeating The Trick

There followed a real upheaval, when vital team members Jochen Neerpasch and Martin Braungart both left the team early in 1972 (they were head-hunted to Munich, hopefully to do a similar rescue job for Ford's bitterest rivals, BMW!). Even so, this was a year in which the record of the still improving 'works' Capri RS2600 was even more startling than before.

Based on the same engineering as in 1971 and an extra winter's development, in which Ashcroft was once again sent over from Boreham to get involved, the engines settled firmly at 2933cc, with peak power pushed up to 285–290bhp at 7,500rpm. Structural changes

On its way to victory in the Monza qualifier of the 1972 European Series is the Mass/Larrousse RS2600 – with Gerard Larrousse ready to leave after a routine halt.

Model makers take note – for here are two views of the same RS2600 at the same event – Monza in 1972. Gerard Larrousse is at the wheel of the winning car on both occasions…

…with three yellow stripes on each side of the front spoiler, and the Dunlop decal symmetrically mounted.

saw the use of even more purposeful looking wheel-arch flares and a much more sturdy roll cage, along with wide-rim 15in wheels.

The Capri's continuing success was now as much due to immaculate preparation and perfect race craft, as it was to having a fast car – and of course to its team of very talented drivers. Not only were Mass and Hans-Joachim Stuck the regular stars, but there was even time

for a one-off appearance (in the French Paul Ricard 6-hour race) by F1 heroes Jackie Stewart and Francois Cevert.

The story is simple to tell – the 'works' Capris won seven of the nine European Championship qualifying rounds, a privately-owned British RS2600 won at Paul Ricard, and the 'works' cars finished second in the other event, the Nürburgring 6-hour race, when a lengthy

This was the anatomy of a 1972 Cologne RS2600 race car, which shows off the much-modified engine and the completely different type of rear axle location compared with production cars. These cars were good enough to win the European Championship in 1971 and 1972.

pit stop was needed to cure brake problems. Once again the team won the Spa 24-hour race (this time at 116.39mph/187km/h).

Mass ('Herman the German' as he was affectionately known by some of the media at this time) shared a winning drive five times and Glemser three times, which, along with minor placings, meant that Mass become the ETCC champion. This was also the year in which Stuck won the German Championship

in an RS2600. But not the team itself, for the manufacturers' title was taken by Alfa Romeo, who *always* won their 2-litre capacity class!

There was one oddity during this extremely successful season – in the French 6-hour race at the Paul Ricard circuit, 'works' team cars were beaten by the privately-prepared British RS2600 of Brian Muir and John Miles, not because their car was faster, but because the engine had been slightly modified, with a

Starting the race at the Nürburgring in 1972, on the legendary long circuit. The Mass/Larrousse car finished second overall after six hours.

Tyrrell F1 drivers Jackie Stewart (driving here) and Francois Cevert were obliged to use Goodyear tyres for contractual reasons, and took second overall in the Paul Ricard 6-hour race – beaten by a privately-prepared RS2600 from the UK.

different inlet manifold and fuel-injection supply arrangements. This gave noticeably better fuel economy, which meant that this Wiggins Teape-sponsored car (which had raced so successfully in the UK) was just as fast as the 'works' cars, but needed one less time-consuming pit stop to complete the six hours.

Even so, the Capris had been so dominant in 1972 – they had also performed well at out-of-formula races such as the Nürburgring 1,000km (for Group 5 sports cars!) and in the Le Mans 24-hour sports car race – that they were rarely troubled. Kranefuss, however, knew that this happy situation could not last forever:

Immaculate preparation, smooth driving and magnificent attention to pit-stop detail all helped Brian Muir and John Miles to win the 1972 Paul Ricard 6-hour race – defeating the entire fleet of 'works' RS2600s.

The Le Mans 24-hour race of 1972, when three 'works' RS2600s started the race, and two of them finished eighth and tenth, but first and second in their capacity class.

especially as his one-time employees were now working to transform the prospects of the BMW team … his fears were justified.

1973 – Wings and Horsepower

This was a season in which two major problems arose – one financial, the other a barrier against further homologation tweaks. Budget cuts imposed on Kranefuss were partly assuaged by PR boss Hayes, who helped by massaging the way in which superstar drivers' fees were paid to his stable of F1 pilots, who would steer these cars from time to time.

Technically, though, the team had a serious handling problem, for at high speeds the tail of the car would get very 'light' and over-steer would set in. In the Le Mans 24-hour race, drivers talked of getting rear wheel spin at maximum speed on the Mulsanne Straight.

By the time the RS2600 engine was fully developed in 1973, it was a full 3-litre power unit with at least 320bhp. This is what the engine bay of a late-model looked like. For 1974 it was would be superseded by the much more powerful Cosworth GA engine.

Fitting a large transverse rear spoiler would have been an easy and predictable cure (Ford-Germany had already developed one), but although Kranefuss tried to get an aerodynamic package homologated for 1973, the rules made this impossible unless Ford put the necessary spoilers into production (a move which was denied to him by Ford-of-Europe's sales force), so his efforts were pointless.

Unhappily BMW, under ex-Ford man Neerpasch, did precisely that. This, and the adoption of a new and super-powerful BMW 3.5-litre engine, meant that the RS2600s struggled to stay ahead.

Even so, looking far ahead (this was before the Energy Crisis erupted in the autumn of 1973), Ford was already preparing a riposte. Careful reading of Group 2 regulations showed that alternative cylinder heads could be used if 100 car sets (10 per cent of the homologated number of 1,000 being required) were first made, and put on sale. With that in mind, Ford commissioned a new engine, the GA, from Cosworth, which would be a full-blooded twin-cam, four-valves-per-cylinder 3.4-litre derivative of the British (*not* the German) V6 – though this would not be ready until the 1974 season.

For 1973, therefore, and only as a final measure, the original Ford-Cologne V6 cylinder block was stretched to its ultimate limit of 2995cc, where it developed a claimed 325bhp at 7,600rpm: this was now the absolute limit for an engine that had been under development for five years.

At the same time there was a new aerodynamic package of front spoiler and wheel-arch extensions, which cut the drag coefficient from the previous 0.45 to nearly 0.4. The radiator was re-positioned and there was new ducting to channel cool air into, through and out of the engine bay, and yet more changes to the roll cage. A big spoiler, though, would have helped even more, as Kranefuss later admitted: 'It was worth about 10 seconds a lap at the Nurburgring, almost exactly the amount we would have needed to stay ahead of BMW'.

If Ford-Germany could not make up the gap on BMW, they could always try to do it on driving talent. Stewart, Emerson Fittipaldi, Gerry Birell, Jody Scheckter, Mass, Heyer and John Fitzpatrick all figured in the line-up: even so, the entire Ford 'family' was shattered when Birrell was killed in mid-season, in a single-seater Formula 2 race that was quite unconnected with any of their programmes.

Although BMW's regulations-busting aerodynamic package (which instantly gave their 3.0 CSL the nickname of 'Batmobile') did not appear until mid-season, their existing cars were also very fast in early-season form, and the balance tipped just far enough to favour them. The result, at the end of an eight-event ETCC, was that the 'works' Capris won two races (both of them, significantly, early in the season) and took three second places. Heyer/Klaus

In the early 1970s, Ford-Germany used a galaxy of stars to race its RS2600s – left-to-right – Jody Scheckter, John Fitzpatrick, Gerry Birrell and Jackie Stewart in a pre-race discussion.

In September 1973, with the BMW 3.0CSLs enjoying the unfair advantage of using homologated aero kits, there was a titanic battle with 'works' RS2600s in the Tourist Trophy race.

Fritzringer finished second in the marathon Nürburgring 24-hour event (which was not in the ETCC), while Mass and Toine Hezemans won the non-championship Fuji international race in Japan at the end of the season.

This, though, was an expensive season, for the 'at-the-limit' engines gave a great deal of trouble, and no fewer than five cars were also badly damaged in accidents, some of them terminally. Over the years the handling of the RS2600s seemed to have got worse, not better, for the faster the cars went, the lighter they seemed to get at the rear.

Because of the ultra-wide tyres that were now being used, the cars could be seen to lift *both* inside wheels on dry corners, which made them look, and feel, quite unsafe. John Fitzpatrick, as brave as any Ford driver of his day, once commented that: 'The 1973 Capri was the worst handling racing car I have driven'. F1 World Champion Fittipaldi sometimes thought that the car was going to turn over on him! Even Stewart, that most analytical of racing drivers, found it difficult to wring any more out of what had become something of a brute of a car.

In the second half of the 1973 season, the Capris were finally overrun by the BMC 3.0CSL 'Batmobiles' – not on power, but because BMW had a new aero kit that provided more ground force, and more grip on corners. Ford would come back, with a real vengeance, with the RS3100 in 1974.

You had to sympathize with John Fitzpatrick when he expressed dismay over the way the final RS2600s handled. It was not that the body was not stiff but the tyres were very grippy, and Cologne needed to keep that inside rear wheel on the ground at all times.

John Fitzpatrick drove his heart out at Silverstone in September 1973 to take third place in the first of two TT race heats. Even so, in later years he would condemn the 'works' RS2600 as one of the worst-handling cars he had ever raced!

A quick listing of the Ford's ETCC season, with one telling note, is significant:

Monza 4-hour	2nd
Salzburgring 4-hour	1st
Sweden	1st
– BMW then homologated the 3.0CSL 'Batmobile', spoilers and all:	
Nürburgring 6-hour	No finishes
Belgium (Spa) 24-hour	2nd
Zandvoort (Holland)	3rd
Paul Ricard 6-hour (France)	5th
TT, Silverstone (UK)	2nd

The reason was clear. Before July, competition between Ford and BMW was close, but after 1 July, the new BMW 'aero' package proved to be worth 15 seconds *per lap* around the long Nurburgring, and more than 8 seconds per lap at the Spa circuit in Belgium.

Game over – or, effectively. Even though the RS2600s battled it out for the rest of the season (and managed to win several other non-championship races, especially in Fuji, Japan and Macau), they were no longer very competitive, and the team thought they were battling with regulations, not rival cars.

Spectators at Silverstone for the TT saw just how hard the rival teams of drivers were trying – and to just what extreme angles they got their cars – but Jochen Mass could only manage second place, three laps (nearly 9 miles/14.5km) behind the winning BMW, which proved a point.

For 1974, Ford homologated the new RS3100, which not only had Cosworth's magnificent four-overhead-camshaft GA engine but an entirely new aero package, including the big 'duck-tail' spoiler, and more elaborate cooling ducts under and around the rear axle and brakes.

This was the very first 'works' RS3100 to be completed, early in 1974, when Ford showed off the new aero package, which included a massive front spoiler, front and rear wheel-arch extensions and a full-width 'duck-tail' spoiler at the tail. Toine Hezemans, who would win several events in these cars, is at the wheel.

After only half a season, it seems, normal service was resumed. The Capri had beaten the BMW 3.0CSL up until the middle of 1973, lost out in the rest of that year, then started winning again in 1974 with the RS3100.

When the RS3100 race car was being shaped, lessons from wind-tunnel testing were well learned, though I have no doubt that Cologne design were also anxious that the completed car should look good. This, I think, is one of the most attractive aspects of the latest model.

RS 3100 – One Season Wonder

In the meantime, Ford-UK worked hard on a replacement for the RS2600. The crunch came in mid-1973 when BMW suddenly started winning races with the CSL, and Ford-Germany had no match. At a stroke, as a racing car the RS2600 had become obsolete. Although a replacement, to be badged RS3100, would look much the same as the RS2600, in racing *and* in road-car trim, its V6 engine would be totally different, while in race-car trim there would be many other changes and upgrades to the layout changes, and there would be new and better aerodynamic aids.

Totally? Well, how about a Ford Essex V6 engine instead of the entirely different Ford-Germany base? Peak racing power of 420bhp (455bhp later in the life of the engine) instead of 320bhp? 3.4-litres instead of 3-litres? Twin-overhead-camshaft cylinder heads instead of push-rod overhead-valves? Mountains more torque? Bigger brakes? Better aerodynamics? And more, and more.

This new car (and the GAA engine that would be central to its design) was conceived in 1972 when Ford's self-confidence was at its height. To make it happen, and to get approval for a basic production car on which race-car development could proceed, Ford would need

Engineers later admitted that the height of the front chin spoiler and its distance from the road (especially under braking) was critical to the balance of the racing RS3100. Any deeper and it would have grounded under braking, and any higher would have meant that high-speed down-force would have been reduced.

Cosworth's GA conversion of an RS3100 Essex V6 cylinder block included new cylinder heads with twin overhead-camshafts. Like all such Cosworth engines of the period, there was also a maze of drive belting, oil pumps and alternators to be accommodated. The result was that the initial engine produced 420bhp, a figure that became 455bhp by the end of 1975.

to evolve a new Capri derivative. Like various 'hot' Escorts that followed, what became the RS3100 was a typical 'why don't we...?' project, originally cooked up between AVO's manager Stuart Turner, and his Product Planner, Mike Moreton.

Based on the existing 3000GT, the RS3100 road car would have a slightly enlarged (3091cc) version of the British V6 engine, which normally measured 2994cc, a much larger rear spoiler – and Ford would only need to build the 1,000 cars necessary for homologation.

Making the engine bigger was a homologation wheeze to put the car into the over 3-litre category, which would enable Cosworth to enlarge it even further – as far as the cylinder block would allow (Ford had already pulled the same trick with the Escort RS1600). But there was more. By taking advantage of the regulation that allowed alternative cylinder heads to be homologated in Group 2, and by pushing every other interpretation to its limit, Ford got Cosworth to effectively design a new engine around the Essex cylinder block!

The RS3100 was launched in November 1973 (in the same week as the Energy Crisis

struck!), and Ford built the road cars at Halewood, among the last of the original-shape Capris. As we now know (but did not realize at the time), only about 250 such cars were ever produced, though homologation (Ford assured the authorities that they had produced 1,000 RS3100s!) was duly achieved from 1 January 1974.

Cosworth's four-cam GA engine, a total redesign of the Essex engine, in that it was based on the use of selected versions of the V6 cylinder block, used the classic twin-cam per bank, narrow-valve-angle layout of other contemporary Cosworth units such as the BDA used in the Escort RS1600. Although there had originally been provision for one, two or even three spark plugs to be used in each cylinder, only a single, central, plug was ever needed – and Lucas fuel-injection and ignition was chosen. Thus equipped, it produced more than 400bhp at 8,500rpm at once, up to 420bhp by the time it was race-ready in the spring of 1974 and a reliable 455bhp when it was at its peak.

Nor were these engines hand-built one-offs. One hundred engines (or kits of engines) had to be built before they could be homologated in Group 2, and these were duly and honestly produced by Cosworth in Northampton. About thirty complete engines were delivered to Ford-

There was plenty of space for the Cosworth GA engine to be inserted into the RS3100's engine bay for motor racing purposes. In this installation, the fuel-injection gear is mounted centrally, and far forward.

Although it still lifted a front wheel under extreme cornering conditions, the RS3100 seemed to be a better-balanced racing machine than the RS2600 it had replaced. Part of this, no doubt, was due to the extra down-force developed by the latest aero kit.

Germany (who needed a new, high-capacity, test bed to check them out!), and the balance went into stock at Boreham.

At £4,000 for a kit of parts, and an extra £750 for assembly, these were never likely to be quick sellers in the mid-1970s. Years later, on one of my regular visits to Boreham, I was shown shelves still stacked with GAA parts, and asked if I would like to buy a few!

Although the Energy Crisis, a temporary disruption in oil supplies from the Middle East, rigidly applied road car speed limits, and the threat of petrol rationing all hit hard at motor racing confidence during the winter, Ford-Germany pressed on with their new race cars for the 1974 saloon car season, no matter how truncated it was to be. Walter Hayes commented at the time:

> I think the two or three years of BMW and Ford battles have been very exciting, but of course BMW are going to withdraw completely. Ford is in danger of coming back with just hollow victories. Should we withdraw because other people have? We are going to play it by ear. We are sending 'works' cars to the first race. We may just end up by doing the major events in the series.

Once again, much of the chassis engineering design work was credited to Thomas Ammerschlager. For 1974, the RS3100 race cars were different from the last of the RS2600s in almost every way, for as 3000GT derivatives they could no longer use the plastic panels that had always been standard on original-specification RS2600s. The engine, and many other fittings, were more substantial than before, so the car's dry weight was about 2,315lb (1,050kg), about 154lb (70kg) more than it had been in 1973.

The suspension layout was much as before, including the use of the infamous 'plastic' rear leaf springs (which had no useful function, except to satisfy the scrutineers), for the actual rear suspension was by a coil-over-shock layout, with radius arms and a transverse Watts linkage to keep the solid Atlas-style axle in its exact as-developed position.

Disc brakes were fitted, all round: 12in (305mm) ventilated types at the front, and 10.5in (266mm) at the rear – the team being contracted to Dunlop for its tyres. Now that Stewart (who had been rigidly contracted to Goodyear) had retired, and was no longer available, there were not to be any supply problems there!

93

The new 420bhp 3.4-litre GA engine was mated to the well-known ZF transmission that had served so well over the years, but to make improvements to the weight distribution, the engine cooling radiators were relocated – in the boot, no less, at each side of the luggage container, and fed by air intakes ahead of the rear wheels. This moved a 26lb (12kg) mass all the way back from the nose to the boot area.

At the same time, there had been a reshuffle of auxiliaries, with the axle cooler now positioned behind the right rear wheel and the gearbox oil cooler behind the left rear wheel. The fuel tank itself had also been relocated, lower and further back, and the 1974 3100 had a very large and flamboyant transverse spoiler.

All this had been done because, in Kranefuss' words: 'On the RS2600 ... the Capri's rear end was always very light, while the front end stuck like hell. It was a difficult car to drive, and the star drivers we employed like Fittipaldi and Stewart were I think very surprised to find the job which the regulars like Mass and Glemser had to do.' In the same interview, Kranefuss also summed up what attracted him, and Ford, to running these monstrously fast, 180mph (289km/h), cars: 'With the Group 2 cars we on the Continent like to see – lifting wheels, drifting, sliding, etc., and looking exciting in themselves – I cannot understand why the British have gone to ordinary Group 1 cars – to us, that is *nothing*.'

Two Seasons – Eight Victories

Maybe the RS3100's success in 1974 and 1975 was slightly less emphatic because the 'works' BMWs had been withdrawn from the sport, but of course we must ask why the Bavarian cars dropped out. Were they frightened of being underdogs once again? Although they had been race-winners in 1973, with very special 370bhp cars, BMW realized that they could do little to make the cars any faster for 1974 (though there was an improved, twin-cam version of the engine on the way), and might be thought to have 'retired' as a precaution! However, to keep

up appearances, the very latest cars were made available to private teams, which explains why BMW beat Ford in the first three races, but not thereafter.

Except for early-season problems in 1974 (and the fact that they missed the first race, at Monza), by any standards the 'works' Capris RS3100s were very successful indeed. In two rather truncated seasons, they started in seventeen races, most of them of at least six hours duration, winning eight times, finishing second six times and third once. Not bad for a car whose engine was totally unproven before the first race, and for a department that was suffering seriously from budget and manpower constraints!

The programme started badly at Monza, with no RS3100s and with only one 1973-specification ex-works RS2600s driven by Hans Akersloot and Hezemans. That car started well, but retired before the end of the afternoon: the fact that the Zakspeed Escort RS1600 managed to finish fifth was a very significant result.

Things improved at the second race of the season, the Salzburgring in 1974, when Kranefuss sent two new RS3100s to do battle with one 24-valve/400bhp BMW. On the fast sweeping sections of the 'Ring', the Capris were geared to reach 178mph (286km/h) and did so, with great aplomb, for the new aerodynamic aids were remarkably effective. Unhappily, although the RS3100s soon got into the lead, and stayed there, both cars had to retire with broken (literally – for one car suffered a split cylinder block) engines. Cosworth's gloomy prediction – that their pieces would do the job, but that they were not happy about the strength of Ford's own V6 cylinder block casting – came true. It was not until some judicious modification was made to the casting cores at Dagenham that reliability was assured.

Ford then missed the Italian round of the ETCC at Vallelunga, preferring to go for local motor racing (and publicity) in the Nürburgring 750km sports car race instead, where Glemser and Hezemans won their Group 2

For 1974, the RS3100 was homologated for competition, complete with this extreme, but very effective, aero kit that included a massive front spoiler and large transverse rear spoiler. This was the first car seen at Nürburgring – the team would go on to win eight international races in the next two seasons.

class and took a storming eleventh place overall against full Group 6 prototypes from Matra, Alfa Romeo, Gulf and Porsche.

Then came the Nürburgring 6-hour race, the fourth ETCC qualifier of the year, and an obvious showcase for the Ford-Germany cars. According to Kranefuss's script, the RS3100s should have defeated the BMWs, but things did not quite work out that way, for one car retired with a broken axle, and the other was actually out-paced by the amazing 2-litre Zak-speed Escort RS1600!

Things then improved in the last events of the year, with Mass and Rolf Stommelen

winning outright at Zandvoort in Holland in a wet race, and the Klaus Ludwig/Hezemans/ Heyer RS3100 repeated that at Jarama in Spain at the end of the season. Although the factory was embarrassed to be beaten on two occasions in 1974 by the Zakspeed Escorts (the Radio Luxembourg-sponsored RS1600 won the non-championship nine-hour race at Kyalami, South Africa, in November, too!), it was a satisfactory season. Ford had taken maximum points in three of the six rounds and finished second overall in its division. This, though, was really the end of Ford's involvement at major (European, that is) championship level, for

Big front and rear wing extensions, a vast front-end spoiler and the large transverse rear spoiler – this could only be an RS3100 race car, seen diving into the notorious Karussel turn on the Nürburgring in 1974.

neither Ford nor their big rivals, BMW, took any interest in the 1975 ETCC, which sank to a very low, private-owners level.

In the aftermath of the Energy Crisis (and in the same series of cut-backs that saw the AVO factory in Essex closed down) Ford-Germany suffered a brutal closure at the hands of Ford-of-Europe's financial number-crunchers.

Nevertheless, Kranefuss's workshops somehow kept one or two of its RS3100 cars alive, entering Mass for the Norisring event in the German Championship, which he won, while Ludwig and an RS3100 were loaned to Team General Anzeiger of Bonn, and won two out of three races (both of them at Hockenheim) also in the same German Championship.

But that was that, the remaining cars were dispersed, and Cologne was never again to be directly involved in touring car racing. Even in the late 1980s, when the Sierra RS500 Cosworth began its 'destroyer' existence, Cologne would hire Eggenberger of Switzerland for its main assault.

In Britain, too, it was the same story, for Boreham was too far committed to the Escort rally programme to get deeply involved in Capri racing. However, as the next chapter makes clear, there was a cohort of private owners ready to do all the winning that was needed.

24-Hours at Spa – Great for Capris!

This event deserves special mention. For many years Europe's most gruelling saloon car race of all was the 24-hour event at Spa, Belgium, in July – on the original, classic, 8.76-mile (14km) public road, then from 1978 on the truncated, but still spectacular new F1 circuit.

Although different technical regulations applied from year to succeeding year, it offered a unique challenge, and required cars that were both fast and durable. As already noted, 'works' cars from Ford-Germany raced there from 1971–73, winning in 1971 and 1972 and finishing second in 1973, though the RS3100s were never committed to the Belgian circuit in 1974 or 1975.

For the rest of the 1970s, British-built Capri IIs and IIIs, with 2994cc Essex V6 engines, always turned up, always raced with honour, and often won outright. This was a fascinating sequence.

For 1974, the Spa organizers imposed its own special 'Group 1 3/4' regulations that automatically disqualified the Group 2 Capri RS3100s from taking part. Ford-UK, with cars built at Boreham, not Ford-Germany, sent two newly-built triple-Weber 200bhp Capri IIs (in fact these were the very first *and* last 'works' Capri IIs), with big fat wing extensions and 10in wide rear wheels, one of them being the car (though modified) that Tom Walkinshaw usually drove in the British Touring Car Championships of the period.

3-litre Capris were always competitive on the Spa circuit in Belgium. This was the Hermetite-sponsored 'Group 1¾' example, in wet conditions, with Tom Walkinshaw at the wheel in 1975.

'Kent' does not signify the type of engine being used in this RS2600 (which it wasn't – it was a Cologne V6) but was a brand of cigarette being promoted in Belgium at that time. The occasion was the Spa 24-hour race, with two other 'works' RS2600s close behind.

Although the Walkinshaw/Fitzpatrick car led the race in the early hours – it had a top speed of more than 135mph (217km/h) – it eventually retired with a broken drive shaft, the other car never even figuring in the top positions before it blew a cylinder head gasket.

There were no official factory-built Capri IIs at Spa in 1975, which was run to the brand-new Group 2 regulations, though Holman Blackburn's Hermetite-sponsored cars had a good deal of support in that year. Although the Walkinshaw/Fitzpatrick car held a solid second place for many hours, the engine eventually let go, and the sister car (driven by Holman Blackburn and Mike Crabtree) finally finished third overall, behind two BMWs.

Near, but not near enough – just as it would be in 1976, when the Blackburn/Crabtree car retired, once again due to engine failure. Gordon Spice and CC Racing Developments (of North Yorkshire) preparer Peter Clark, on the other hand, finished fifth with a damaged Group 1 car (the same machine that they were using in the UK), starting a personal obsession with the event for Spice that would eventually pay off.

The Spice/Clark/Chris Craft car led for more than twelve hours in 1977 before Spice crashed the car in very slippery conditions. However, Vince Woodman and Jonathan Buncombe took third place in an Esso-backed machine.

The same car, at the La Source Hairpin in 1975.

In 1978 Spa had become a Group 1 race, which was ideal for the Spice/Teddy Pilette CC-prepared Capri III (four circular head-lamps instead of two rectangular units, but precious few other differences), this car being sponsored by Belga, the national cigarette company, and was demonstrably quicker than anything else in the race.

After what Spice described as a 'steady' run – even though the Capri averaged 111mph (178km/h), and spent up to an hour in the pits for repeated fuel stops, for repairs after an accident due to a blown tyre, and to change a radiator following a shed fan belt – the Capri won the last race ever to be run on the old full-length Spa circuit: 'The great joke', Spice commented afterwards, 'was that they [the organizers] obviously weren't expecting a British win – and they didn't have "God Save The Queen" to play at the finish. So they made up for this by playing it twice at the prize giving.'

A year later the CC team repeated the trick for Belga, with the Belgian brothers Jean-Michel and Philippe Martin winning the race, with Craft/Jeff Allam fourth and Spice/Alain Semoulin fifth. Almost a parade demonstration, really, though the combination of a new, tight, short circuit, several crashes which held up cars, and appalling weather limited the winning speed to an average of just 79.83mph (128km/h).

Time for a hat-trick? Indeed, for in 1980 the Martin brother's Belga-backed Capri III won once again, with Woodman/Buncombe/Clark in fifth place and Spice/Semoulin ninth, the last car needing a complete gearbox change to keep it going at all. Running his own car, Andy Rouse/Thierry Tassin) finished seventh.

That, however, was the end of the Glory Days for the Capri in Europe, for the Woodman/Buncombe/Clark car could finish only third in 1981, and Spice/Tassin were down in eighth. By this time, and as in the UK, the Fords were technically obsolete, and more modern rivals were about to take over.

Gordon Spice and Teddy Pilette drove this 'Group 1½' Capri III 3000GT to victory in the Spa 24-hour race of 1978. All over the world, Capris excelled in long-distance events.

5 Capri II – New Style and a Hatchback Body

Even at Ford, it took a long time to get new models into production in the 1970s. Maybe this explains why first thoughts about a second-generation Capri came along in 1970, but production cars were not available until the beginning of 1974? In other words, it took more than three years to produce the new model – in a period when the automotive world was rocked by the Energy Crisis that struck with rare ferocity in the autumn of 1973.

Even so, this came too late to affect the launch of the new car, though the building of pilot-production cars cannot possibly have been carried out at a more traumatic time. If ever there was a time at which new-model programmes might be cancelled, this was it: Fiat, after all, froze much of its development for two years after the shock – but not Ford.

Producing a new car, after all, is always a very measured process. In a company that was not only the most profitable in Britain's motor industry but had a large and burgeoning market share, there were procedures at Ford that had to be followed. First of all, a small group of product planners – not engineers at that stage – would settle down, survey the market place, look at the success or otherwise of a car to be replaced, and decide how this should be done. Then, and only then, would management approve the start of design (styling and feasibility engineering), and detail development would follow.

The first common sense move was to wait long enough after the original Capri had been launched, to weigh up the reaction to all its features. How would the great motoring public react to the Mustang-like style and the Mustang-like character? Would they warm to the idea of sitting back in a chair, brochure in hand, to work out which of the myriad extras and option packs to order? Would they like the long bonnet/small cabin layout?

This meant that for 1969, at least, very little thought was given to the make-up of a successor to the original Capri, but from 1970 onwards things began to get more serious. Ford, of course, never tackled such projects without considering what else was going on around them and inside the company. Accordingly, before a Capri II (as it would finally be called – and badged) could be built, the company had to get new-generation Cortina and Consul/Granada types on to the market – both of them representing colossal investments in new machinery and factory facilities. Not only that, but there was the high-profile Advanced Vehicle Operation (AVO) to be considered, and this was also the time at which the biggest Ford-of-Europe investment decision of all – connected with a new small front-wheel-drive car to be called the Fiesta – all had to be made.

When decisions were finally made, in 1971, it was always clear that the next-generation Capri would be built on at least two sites – Halewood and Cologne. However, the third assembly factory at Saarlouis might have to revert to building only Escorts in the mid-1970s. As far as the economists and planners were concerned, too, the idea of using British-built and British-sourced engines in British Capris, with German-built engines in German Capris, was still compelling, and would be adopted once again.

Style and Structure

When work began on what we later knew as Capri II, it carried the in-house project name of 'Diana'. Diana? Who was she? No one now recalls, except that she was reputedly one of the most attractive secretaries at Ford at the time, someone who apparently made a big impression on everyone who met her!

Even at this stage, it seems, it was decided that a new car would be based on the existing body platform. For Ford, who were accustomed to using the same platform under at least two generations of any mass-production car they made, this was conventional thinking – and was sure to save untold millions in engineering, development, and of course in investment capital. The stylists and designers, accordingly, knew that they would be encouraged to produce a mostly new superstructure, but that they had to wrap their new shapes

around the existing 100.8in (2,560mm) platform, with the same front bulkhead/firewall/windscreen (which had only recently had a new-generation facia grafted into place), choice of engines and transmissions and suspension/steering layouts.

All credible, and forward-thinking, design studios react unerringly to public tastes and opinions before finalizing new shapes, and in the case of the Capri there was much early reaction to be sifted. Having studied what the public was saying, Ford identified three principal problem areas – one was the criticism of restricted interior cabin space, another was the lack of luggage accommodation, and the third was lingering complaints about the lack of all-round vision (particularly towards the three-quarter rear aspect).

Because design had already had to accept the existing platform/running gear architecture, it must have been logical, I suppose, to see

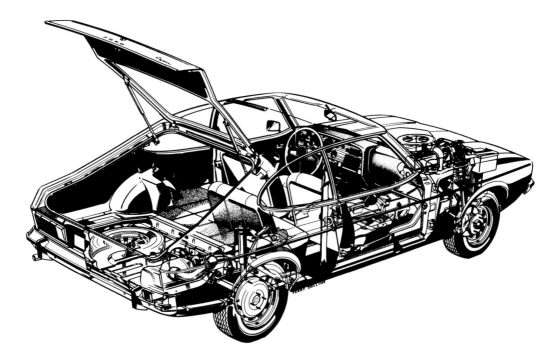

Look carefully at this cutaway drawing of the original Capri II, and it becomes clear that the entire platform/running gear was a carryover assembly from the last of the original types. All Capri IIs, of course, had a rear suspension with an anti-roll bar, just as the Capri Is had had since the autumn of 1972.

that the only way to increase the luggage space and the cabin volume was to increase the bulk of the 'cube' itself, but Ford design did not want to destroy the coupé-style looks of the Capri while doing that.

Sketches, small clay models, larger clay models and finally full-size clays gradually homed in on the shape that we now know today. Gradually – very gradually – it became clear that the glass area should be increased, the sides should become slightly more bulbous and that the original notchback style, with a small boot lid, should be abandoned.

The big decision, not made until 1971, or finalized until 1972, was that the new car should have a hatchback feature. This was not included as a mere fashion feature, nor to match what rivals already had on sale, but was partly done in response to what the market place was thinking. It was also a way of cheating a little over luggage space.

By 1971 there was nothing new about hatchbacks. Such features, indeed, had already begun to appear in the USA, not only on cars imported from Europe, but in cars like Ford-USA's home-grown Pinto and in its deadly rival, the Chevrolet Vega. Although there was going to be a slight weight penalty in adopting such a feature, this problem was outweighed by every other advantage.

Purely as a guide, it is worth listing the other coupés and hatchbacks that were the most obvious rivals to the Capri when serious development work got under way in 1971:

Audi 100 Coupé	1.9-litre, front-wheel drive
Fiat 124 Sport Coupé	1.4/1.6-litre
Lancia Flavia Coupé 2000	2-litre, front-wheel drive
MGB GT	1.8-litre
Opel Manta Coupé	1.6/1.9-litre
Reliant Scimitar GTE	3-litre hatchback
Volvo 1800E	2-litre

The Opel Manta, as a coupé built in Germany, and the Fiat, built in Italy, were the

---

Sporty Hatchback Coupés – Who Was First?

Although Ford's Capri II hatchback was stylish and fashionable, it was not the very first to combine two great ideas. Except for one-offs and styling-studio specials that may have appeared at earlier motor shows, the Aston-Martin DB2/4 of 1953 was probably the pioneer. Not that Aston Martin had the courage of their convictions, as they dropped the hatchback feature when the next-generation car, the DB4, came along five years later.

Jaguar, on the other hand, revived the hatchback on the E-Type Coupé of 1961, MG refined it for the MGB GT of 1965, and Reliant adopted an even more practical derivative for the Scimitar GTE. So, as far as the Capri II was concerned, there was nothing new – it was merely made available at a thoroughly attractive price, and in many varieties.

---

most significant competitors. There was only one hatchback among them, though a hatchback Volvo was known to be imminent, and the MGB GT had a vast lift-up rear window that doubled as a hatchback.

This was the time when several designers came to realize that the volume of air behind a rear window of a conventional saloon or coupé, but above the boot lid, was effectively 'dead'. By carrying on the sweep of the line of the roof to the rear of the boot lid, and by making most of that line in glass, the 'dead' air could be swept into the overall package. If that glass could then be arranged to fold up, access to the luggage area was at least as good as before and the hatchback feature was born.

Of course it was not as simple as that, but the overall effect was the same. As far as the Capri II was concerned, adding a hatchback to the evolving shape of the new car was a stroke of genius that helped solve several problems in one package.

For the Capri II the result, that had to go all the way to the top for viewing and approval (even Henry Ford II had a look at the clay model at one stage), was a body style that looked altogether smoother, larger and somehow less

This was one of several design sketches released by Ford in 1974 to show how the styling had developed.

aggressively sporting than the original. In character, indeed, this was a somewhat 'softer' car than the original Capri. As already stated, the basic platform/wheelbase dimension was not changed, nor was the front track and position of the front wheels, but the rear track (and by definition, the width of the axle itself, that on some models was the Atlas variety found under several other Ford products of the period) was increased by no less than 2.5in (63mm).

Although the complete car was only slightly longer (by 0.8in/20mm) and the windscreen was not only the same as before, but in the same position 'in space', the body was higher (by fractions of an inch, that gave marginal improvements in headroom) but it was no less than 2.1in (53mm) wider.

In packaging terms, this meant that the interior of the cabin was significantly wider than before, at shoulder height, and, along with the slightly higher roof line and the way that the roof/glass hatchback swept smoothly towards the tail, the cabin volume felt more spacious than before.

All cars had the same frontal aspect, with big rectangular headlamps (though there was still a four-headlamp nose on US-market versions), all had the same rather bulbous sides, from which every trace of the old 'hockey stick' panel features and the false air intakes had been

expunged. There was a big increase in glass area – 30 per cent extra at the rear and 14 per cent along the sides. This increase was mainly concentrated around three-quarter windows, though the waistline was also slightly dropped. Because glass is heavier than sheet steel, and because of the reinforcement needed to stiffen up the upward opening hatchback feature, the body shell itself weighed 45lb (20.4kg) more than before. Because much work had gone in to stiffening up the shell to make it a rigid base for the large hatchback, Ford also claimed that the new body shell was 30 per cent stiffer in torsion.

All in all, the Capri II was considerably heavier than the original Capri had ever been, though there had been a gradual increase during the life of the original car, which was almost inevitable in view of the extra equipment that had been standardized. As an example, and according to Ford, a Capri II 3000GT was 200lb (90.7kg) heavier than the 1969/70 3000GT. Since the new car was certainly no more aerodynamically shaped than the original, this meant that the fuel consumption was likely to be inferior, even though the new Pinto engine was more fuel-efficient than the old Kent that it replaced in some cases.

This, then, might be the appropriate moment to quote a few dimensions. Working from the drawings published in *Autocar* road tests, it has been possible to compare the original Capri 1600GT of 13 February 1969 with the Capri II 1600GT of 30 March 1974. Although the overall length changed only marginally, it was interesting to see that although there was really no more headroom in the Capri II, it was 4.5in (114mm) wider, at shoulder level, across the front seats, with a much larger luggage/stowage

area in the rear – the boot floor being 39in (990mm) long, front to rear, compared with 28in (711mm); and 18in (457mm) deep, to the hatchback glass, instead of 14in (355mm), to the boot lid pressing. According to the factory, if the rear seats were folded down, the Capri II could swallow up to 23cu ft of baggage, compared with only 7.8cu ft on the Capri I.

Maybe this did not suit everyone – certainly not the drive-it-flat-out brigade who were only interested in top speeds and 0–60 times – but it suited a new class of customer, one who needed to carry more than two people, and quite a lot of kit. Time, then, for the author to own up. Having had Triumph Dolomite 1850s and Hillman Avenger GLS saloons, I bought my first new Capri in 1976.

Looking to carry wife, two growing children and, would you believe, two bulldogs, I bought a brand-new Capri II 2000GL in 1976, and followed it up with a brand-new Capri III 2000S in 1978. Great cars, driven hard, and used for business and pleasure – and eventually succeeded in 1982 with a brand-new Capri 2.8i.

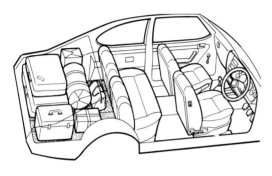

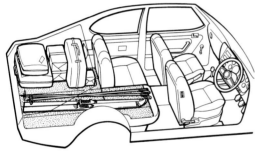

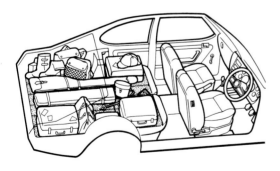

By building in a hatchback and folding rear-seat arrangement, Ford made the Capri II into an exceptionally versatile machine. In 1974, GT and Ghia types could be used as two-seaters, three-seaters and four-seaters because the rear seat back-rest was split into two squabs. Ls and XLs had a one-piece fold-down squab instead.

Stand by for the subliminal message in this promotional picture – you can use your Capri GT as a sports coupé, but it is still a versatile family car too.

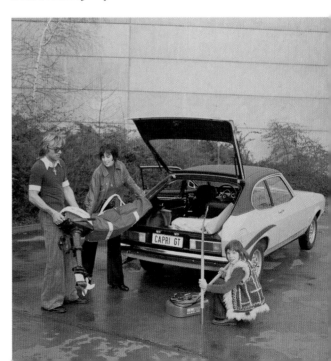

'Oh darling! You bought the new Capri II just for me? You shouldn't have!'

Maybe the wide-angle lens distorts this a little, but this study certainly shows just how much of the Capri cabin could be opened up to stow people, animals, luggage and almost anything else inside. Ford hoped that the hatchback feature would be welcome – and all the sales figures suggest that they were right.

Even in the mid-1970s, it was still rare for a Ford Capri customer to order a car with automatic transmission – but when he or she did, the badge on the hatchback made it known to everyone else on the road. Note the 'Capri II' badges – neither Capri I nor Capri III ever had a similar badge.

Engines, Transmissions and Chassis Components

Although the Capri I's line-up of engines had been re-shuffled as recently as 1972, when the Capri II came along there would be another upheaval. The truly significant change was that the British V4 Essex had been abandoned, and was replaced by a 2-litre Pinto engine. German-built Capri IIs, of course, still went their own way in terms of engine line-up, the details being quoted in the panel on pages 115 and 116.

Although the British V4 had done a good job in some models – the Transit, for which it was originally developed, the Corsair family car, and the Zephyr V4 models of the 1966–72 period – it was always just a bit rough and ready for sporty usage. Not smooth (in spite of the use of the balancer shaft), certainly not free-revving, and not at all tuneable, it had only been used in the Capri, rather in desperation, to fill a yawning gap in the range between the 86bhp/1600GT type and the 138bhp/3000GT model. When supplies of an alternative power unit – the overhead-camshaft 98bhp/1993cc Pinto became available, that problem was solved.

Accordingly, from the start-up of Capri II, this was the range of engines made available:

1,298cc	Kent/ 4-cylinder	57bhp
1,593cc	Pinto/4-cylinder, overhead-camshaft	72bhp
1,593cc	Pinto/ 4-cylinder, overhead-camshaft	88bhp
1,993cc	Pinto/4-cylinder, overhead-camshaft	98bhp
2,994cc	Essex/ V6-cylinder, overhead-valve	138bhp

Automatic transmission was available as an optional extra on all but the smallest engine (1.3-litre) Capri IIs, but the customer take-up was very limited on all but 3-litre models.

All except the 3000 were mated to new-type four-speed all-synchromesh gearboxes, with more suitably spaced intermediate ratios. As before, automatic transmission was an optional extra on all except the low-powered 1300 variety. Here, too, there had been a change. Whereas earlier Capris had used a proprietary Borg Warner Type 35 transmission, for the Capri II Ford now specified their own, new, in-house C3 automatic, which was being built in increasing numbers at a factory in Bordeaux.

As to the rest of the running gear, the chassis of the 1973–74 Capri I was carried over more or less intact, though the suspension was much softer than it had been on the original-specification Capris of 1969–72, which made this breed of Capri more 'touring' than the Capri I had ever been. Power-assisted rack-and-pinion steering soon became optional on V6-engined cars. Once again, the engineering of hydraulic pumps, and installation details on the engine, had already been carried out for the Consul/Granada models, which had appeared in 1972, so this was a well-proved (and popular) extra. In fact it was standardized on the Ghia model from late 1975. Elsewhere in the chassis, there were larger brakes on the 3000 models.

Models and Trim Packs

Compared with 1969, times had certainly changed. All pretence of allowing the customer to specify his or her own Capri by mixing and matching the equipment by adding in a variety of trim packs had been swept away. Now, for 1974 (but there was more to come!), only six models were immediately available: the 1300, 1600L, 1600XL, 1600GT, 2000GT and 3000GT

As before, there were two levels of facia – the GT cars getting a full six-dial instrument layout (one of which was a large rev-counter, placed ahead of the driver's eyes), while other models only had two big dials (one of them a combined unit) and no rev-counter.

On all but the basic L model, there was a carpet covering the loading surfaces of the rear hatchback, which also incorporated seven brightwork metal slides to make the loading of big bags more convenient. On GT models, the rear seat featured split folding, though lesser types incorporated a bench type.

As ever, trim levels were very carefully graded. The L model was what we would now call the 'entry-level' car with things like the one-

The 1600GT of 1974 was absolutely typical of so many Capri IIs that began to pour out of the Halewood and Cologne factories. Dress-up packs were no longer available, but the range itself was widened. This pattern of sports road wheels were standard on the GT at this time.

piece rear seat back rest, no carpet in the boot, the lowest equipment level and no radio as standard equipment. XL was next up – adding a vacuum brake servo, heated rear window in the hatchback and carpet on the floor in the hatchback area, while G models had all this, plus the six-dial facia/instrument panel and individual fold-down rear seats.

Even at XL level, a factory-fitted radio was still extra (a Ford radio cost £47.44), while a flexible plastic rear tonneau cover (£23.85) was optional on all types (this covered up what was being carried in the hatchback area, which could otherwise be seen by peering through the glass). This, for the prudent, was an essential fitment, as there was quite a high theft rate.

In addition, there was the option of a £63.01 Custom Pack (Ford was strong on capital letters at this time), which could be built into cars on original assembly. This included sculptured steel sport's road wheels, a rear wash/wipe fitment, a flexible map-reading lamp, bumper over-riders and an extra coach line painted on the body flanks.

The first pilot-build cars were completed before the end of 1973 (while Halewood was also trying to build some old-shape RS3100s), but true series production began in January 1974, and the launch followed at the end of February 1974, when the full range was already available, from stock, in most Ford showrooms. This was a real boost for dealerships as car sales all over Europe were suffering badly from the effect of the post-Yom-Kippur

War Energy Crisis. In the UK, at least (where coupons were actually issued), there was the threat of petrol rationing, and so-called 'temporary' open-road speed limits were imposed.

A measure of how hard the British motor industry was hit at this time becomes obvious from these figures:

Year	UK Car Sales	UK Car Production
1973	1,688,322	1,747,321
1974	1,273,814	1,534,119
1975	1,211,658	1,267,695

If you couldn't afford to buy the RS-type alloys, or other alloy wheels that were available from many specialists for the Capri II, then Ford's own sports road wheel, in pressed steel, but with eight spokes, was a very reasonable alternative.

In other words, in two years, UK car sales plunged by 476,664 and related production by 479,626, a truly massive slump about which the government of the day did precisely nothing. The Capri II, even so, got off to an encouraging start, and in spite of the rather frigid economic climate it managed to sell 185,361 cars in 1974 alone, the majority of these being built in Germany, although 38,932 were produced at Halewood.

When *Autocar* came to test one of these cars – a 1600GT registered PTW 459M – it seemed to be in a nationalistic cheer-leading mood, for it opened with the thought that:

> All-new body shell results in much greater versatility and more generous glass area ... With over a million units sold since its inception five years ago, the Capri already has been a huge success. Part of the secret lies in Ford's policy of offering trim and engine options to suit a wide variety of pockets and tastes.

After a great deal of factual analysis – in which the magazine recorded a top speed of 104mph (167kmh), 0–60mph in 11.4 seconds and an overall fuel consumption of 27.4mpg (10.3ltr/100km), this *Autocar* summary told its own story: 'There is no doubt that the Capri II range in general represents a vast improvement on earlier models. Almost entirely, this is attributable to the improved luggage-carrying capacity and the larger glass area.'

New Name, New Trim Level

Only weeks after the new-shape Capri had been introduced, Ford topped it out with a new flagship model – the Ghia-badged 2000 and 3000 types, which went on sale on 1 May 1974. Although these were mechanically unchanged,

Ghia versions of the Capri II had interiors that looked and were comfortable (at least in the front seats!). There's no getting away from the fact, however, that rear seat leg room was always quite restricted.

Boys will be boys ... and this also proves that although the Ghia was quite softly-sprung, it hung on when cornered hard.

The Capri II Ghia became the flagship of the range when it went on sale in mid-1974, replacing the GLX, which had itself replaced the E model. Nothing stayed the same for long at Ford in that period!

they offered a completely new level of trim, fittings and equipment for a Ford of this size and type.

Why Ghia? This, in fact, was the name of the Italian styling house that Ford had purchased in 1973, and which was rapidly being transformed into Ford's own 'skunk-works' for new styles and to investigate new trends. Ghia was not, of course, equipped to build cars in numbers, but it was an ideal conduit for styling jobs. As far as Ford-of-Europe was concerned, Ghia replaced the E model, and although not

all the features used in the Capri Ghia were developed there, it certainly gave that badging policy a flying start – for Ghia went on to be used on almost every other Ford range in the next decade.

New touches to the exterior included a vinyl roof, with a tilt-and-slide sun-roof as standard, tinted glass all round, rear wash-wipe, new-style aluminium alloy road wheels, a moulded rubbing stripe along the flanks, halogen headlamp bulbs and a choice of unique paint finishes.

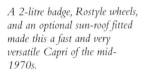

A 2-litre badge, Rostyle wheels, and an optional sun-roof fitted made this a fast and very versatile Capri of the mid-1970s.

Although the vinyl roof covering and special alloy wheels made a difference, the Ghia version of Capri II was really quite an understated car when launched in 1974.

Inside the car, there were high-back front seats (which therefore had integral head restraints), thick cut-pile carpeting, a vinyl-covered six-dial facia panel (colour keyed to the choice of upholstery), a radio as standard equipment, while seat upholstery was in a fab-

ric named Rialto, which was a velvet-finished type of nylon.

Such luxuries did not come cheap, and since Ford was never in the business of giving features away, the Ghia-badged cars were much more expensive than any other Capri II of the

Here is an early-type Capri II Ghia (sales began in mid-1974), complete with a tobacco-shade vinyl roof and with its hatchback raised, showing the much larger space for stowage.

Neat and tidy radio/ventilation/minor-control layout in Capri II/Capri III guise. No cassette in those days – haven't in-car entertainment systems come on a lot since the late 1970s?

day. When it was launched, therefore, the 3000 Ghia retailed at £3,109 – but there was a brisk demand. Almost all such Ghias, incidentally, would be built in Germany, for they never featured strongly at Halewood.

My good friend Stuart Bladon, then a distinguished staffer on *Autocar* magazine, took delivery of a 3000 Ghia (with optional automatic transmission) almost as soon as it was available, subsequently completing 17,000 miles (27,353km) in just nine months, and writing at length about his experiences. What was interesting was that he, like other Ghia customers, did not like the high-back seats which were originally standard, arranging with Ford for them to be replaced by conventionally sized 3000GT seats in a matter of weeks. In addition, his car, an early example, did not have power-assisted steering, which proved that the standard, manual, steering, was really too heavy to be acceptable.

As he wrote:

I could not help a smile or two at the Ford advertising when the Ghia Capris were launched in

May, with the comment :'The first thing Ghia had to do was to change the seats; the Ford seats came out and the new Ghia-designed ones came in'. In my case, exactly the opposite took place.

Although Stuart clearly did not enjoy the soft ride of this, the most expensive of Capris, yet :

So far – up to 16,500 miles [26,548km] – it has provided remarkably little source for comment, except for complete satisfaction at its consistent unflagging reliability and total freedom from faults of any kind, plus great pleasure in driving the car. Points which particularly appeal are the excellent driving position; the good ventilation with an efficient, responsive air-blending heater; the convenient three-door body style, which recently made it possible to transport a piece of glass 4ft [1.2m] long and 42in [1,066mm] wide; the ease of locking and unlocking (front doors can be locked without the key), and the rear door can be left unlocked when required, and particularly the excellent performance…The highest praise is due for the neat way in which the standard inertia-reel seat belts are built into the side trim. They are both comfortable and easy to use … In summary, our Capri has given excellent service so far.

The Arrival of the S and Comprehensive Updates

Only a year after the launch of the very first and, as it happened, the only special limited-edition of the Capri II, Ford chose the Geneva Motor Show to flaunt a new derivative called the S (it was available in 1600, 2000 and 3000 varieties), but because of its flamboyant black colour scheme it was also known as the Midnight Capri.

The colour scheme – all black paintwork, blacked out bright-work and blacked out bumpers, was set off by gold coach-lining (plastic strips, not paint, by the way), badging and special alloy wheels. It was no coincidence that the latest F1 championship car – the Lotus 72 – was decked out in black and gold John Player Special livery, though the ever politically

Only a year after the Capri II had been introduced, Ford launched this startlingly attractive special edition, dubbing it Capri S (or Midnight), which was painted in black with Lotus F1-style gold leaf detailing. The release was made doubly striking by the use of this extremely elegant model, complete with a black and gold dress.

correct Ford machine did not mention such things, or the tobacco connection! Just a few cars, they say, were also finished in white, with white bumpers, but these were neither as successful nor as visually attractive.

Inside the car, the black theme was carried forward – black headlining, black seats (with sizeable gold inserts) and epoxy-coated black on the brightwork of the interior fittings. Other fitments included heavy-duty suspension, wash/wipe features on the windscreen *and* the rear hatchback glass, and halogen headlamp bulbs. Even the jack in the tool kit was painted black to match the overall effect! A flat alloy

From the end of 1975, the special edition S became a mainstream model, and was available in a variety of colours.

three-spoke steering wheel was standard, though tinted glass, a laminated windscreen and a tilt/slide sunshine roof were all optional extras.

Much ado about nothing? Ford enthusiasts certainly did not think so – the 2,000 cars built at Halewood were soon snapped up, and the car almost immediately took on iconic status. On sale from June 1975, prices started at £2,330 for the 1600S to £2,543 for the 3000S, but as this was a period of high UK price inflation, those prices soon began to look remarkably cheap.

Later, from the autumn of 1975, Ford made the S a regular production-line option, though the John Player Special striping was deleted and a full range of body colours became available. In fact, so many development and equipment changes were made to all UK Fords from the start-up of the 1976 model year assembly that Ford gave the process a new acronym – VFM (Value For Money). The company claimed that it was effectively giving away £14 million in added value in the coming twelve months.

Updates were comprehensive, so what follows is just a summary of how the Capri changed. For 1976, a 1300 base model was added, XLs became GLs, and the GT became the S, with the Ghia continuing as the flagship model:

1300 base	plain steel wheels, cloth seats with fixed backrests and a rubber mat in the boot space – but radial-ply tyres were standard.
1300L/1600L	now with sports road wheels, a brake servo, reclining front seats and a divided-fold rear seat backrest.
1600GL/2000GL	replaced the 1600XL/2000XL types, and were given halogen headlamps, tailgate wash/wipe, inertia-reel seat belts and a centre console.
1600S/2000S/3000S	replaced GT derivatives, and retained almost all the 1975 model year fitments, including alloy wheels as standard, and power-assisted steering now standard on the 3000S.
2000/3000 Ghia	the specification remained as before, this car now being based on the 3000S.

This was the 'hi-line' layout of facia/instrument panel used in the GT, S and Ghia versions of the Capri II. Note the very 'touring' type of steering wheel that would give way to a much more sporting design before the end of the 1970s.

The Capri II came in only one shape – a three-door hatchback, but in many different colours and models. This was an 'entry-level' type (you can recognize it by the simple wheel covers), either a 1300L or a 1600L.

Although costs were still rising alarmingly fast at this time in Britain's history, at the time of launch (September/October 1975) the Capri 1300, for example, cost £1,717, the 2000S £2,383 and the 3000 Ghia £3,211. Even so, the gilt seemed to have gone, finally, from the Capri's reputation, for world-wide sales slumped considerably in this year. Whereas 185,361 cars had been produced in 1974, only 100,051 followed in 1975, and no more Capris were ever assembled at Saarlouis: worse, as far as Ford-UK was concerned, was that only 21,225 Capris were produced at Halewood, just a quarter of that achieved when the Capri was fresh in 1980.

Original Capri II Prices – March 1974

Model	Engine size/power	UK Retail Price
1300L	1298cc/57bhp	£1,336
1600L	1593cc/72bhp	£1,416
1600GT	1593cc/88bhp	£1,633
2000GT	1993cc/98bhp	£1,688
3000GT	2994cc/138bhp	£1,932
3000 Ghia (from mid-1974)	2994cc/138bhp	£2,444

Mid-1970s Struggle

For the next two years Ford then allowed the Capri II to coast along, with few innovations – either mechanically, or visually – to lift the gloom. US sales had stagnated, there seemed to be no long-term future for the Capri in that vast market, and for the first time there were doubts about the future of the entire project in Europe. This was the time at which Ford-of-Europe was spending zillions on completing a new factory in Spain, so that its first modern-generation front-wheel-drive car – the Fiesta – could go on sale, and there seemed to be little time, or interest, in developing the Capri, which was something of an old concept by their standards.

This was the period in which the financial idiocy of running two Capri assembly lines, neither of them flat-out, neither of them fulfilling a unique need, became clear. Early in the 1970s it had been good to see Halewood producing more than 80,000 Capris a year, with more than 180,000 being produced in Germany – but times had changed, and it was decided to concentrate Capri assembly in Germany, which would therefore begin to build right-hand-drive cars for the first time.

114

German Market: German-Built Capri IIs – 1974–78

By the time that Capri II hatchback assembly began at Cologne and Saarlouis in the first weeks of 1974, the specification of UK-market and German/European-market cars had been brought much closer together. The style of both types of car was identical – all having the same big-headlamp/hatchback body shape – and the mechanical specifications gradually came closer and closer together.

Interestingly enough, the 1.3-litre Pinto-engined package that had featured in 1972 and 1973 was dropped, to be replaced by the traditional type of overhead-valve Kent power unit.

Compared with the British version of the Capri II, the only special-to-Germany engine option was the use of the 2293cc derivative of the Cologne V6 engine. Although this unit was at once bulkier and less technologically efficient than the British version's 2-litre overhead-camshaft Pinto engine, it probably made good economic sense to use it in the Capri II, especially as larger versions of 2.8-litres were also figuring in US-market Capri IIs.

This was the original German Capri II line up, as launched in March 1974:

1300	1298cc, 4-cylinder, overhead-valve,	55bhp @ 5,000rpm
1600	1593cc, 4-cylinder, overhead-camshaft,	72bhp @ 5,500rpm
1600GT	1593cc, 4-cylinder, overhead-camshaft,	88bhp @ 5,700rpm
2300GT/S/Ghia	2293cc, V6, overhead-valve,	108bhp @ 5,100rpm
3000GT/S/Ghia	2994cc, V6, overhead-valve	138bhp @ 5,000rpm

This time around, of course, there was no RS2600 derivative, nor even a close approximation to one such car. The following development changes took place.

Capri II assembly at Saarlouis closed down in 1975, as facility engineers needed to rejuvenate the equipment and assembly lines to build the new front-wheel-drive Fiesta family car, which would go on sale in mid-1976.

From May 1976, yet another engine supply reshuffle saw the 88bhp/1600GT Pinto version of the car dropped in favour of the 90bhp/1998cc Cologne V6 type. This restored the drive line to what it had been in 1970–73 on Capri Is, where the same V6 engine had been used. Even though the V6 had more torque than the abandoned Pinto, Ford claimed no improvements in performance, with the top speed remaining at 106mph (170km/h).

From the autumn of 1976 (*see* this page) assembly of Capris finally ended at Halewood on Merseyside, and henceforth right-hand-drive British-specification cars and left-hand-drive German-specification cars shared the same production lines at Cologne. Incidentally, even though Cologne was now the home of the Capri, sales in the UK were much more buoyant than in Germany – this being a classic case of filling up a factory, while having to spend much more money on transport and trucking facilities to take new cars back to their appropriate showrooms.

As mentioned elsewhere, US-market Capris were built at Cologne until mid-1977, but there never would be a US version of the Capri III.

Accordingly, from the summer of 1976, Halewood was progressively emptied of Capris, the last of all being produced in October. From that point, Halewood would only build Escorts, a situation that persisted until 1990, when the last of a long line of family saloons was finished off. All in all, 398,440 Capris had been produced at Halewood, which all but a hard-nosed Ford economist would hail as a great marketing success.

In the meantime, Ford had rather belatedly reacted to the straitened economic climate, the high (and rising) cost of fuel and the need to look more environmentally aware (doesn't this all sound very familiar, thirty years on?), by introducing economy versions of two of its engines. As far as the Capri was concerned, this meant that the 'entry-level' model received a 50bhp version of the 1298cc Kent engine, which had less torque throughout, though more at low engine speeds.

This was done by fitting an 1100 head to the 1300 block, and using Ford's latest carburettor, called the sonic idle type, and at the same time the final drive ratio was raised from 4.125:1 to 3.89:1.

Engines Available, All Capris, 1969–86

In an amazing seventeen-year career, no fewer than eight different families of engines – 4-cylinder, V4, V6 and V8 types – were used in three generations of Capri body shell, these spanning eighteen different capacities. All fitted, without changes being necessary, inside the same capacious engine bay:

Engine	Sizes	Years
Ford-UK Kent	1298cc	1969–82
(4-cylinder overhead-valve)	1599cc	1969–72
Ford-Europe Pinto	1293cc	1972–74
(4-cylinder overhead-camshaft)	1593cc	1972–86
	1993cc	1974–86
Ford-USA Lima	2301cc	1975–77
(4-cylinder overhead-camshaft)		
Ford-Germany Cologne	1305cc	1969–72
(V4-cylinder overhead-valve)	1498cc	1969–72
	1699cc	1969–72
Ford-Germany Cologne	1998cc	1969–78
(V6-cylinder overhead-valve)	2293cc	1969–84
	2550cc	1970–73
	2637cc	1970–74
	2792cc	1974–77

and (1981–86):

Engine	Sizes	Years
Ford-UK Essex	1996cc	1969–74
(V4 overhead-valve)		
Ford-UK Essex	2994cc	1969–81
(V6 overhead-valve)	3091cc	1973–74
Ford-USA	4949cc	1970–73
(V8 overhead-valve)		

If Ford thought that this would appeal to a grateful public, they were wrong, for there seemed to be little attraction in a Capri that had less power than any version produced in the seven years of the car's life. Although the sales decline of the Capri 1300 was halted for a year or so, it was only temporary – for in fact it was the 1600 and 2000 types that continued to capture the majority of all European sales.

Independent road tests confirmed that the economy Capri 1300 was not a car that was likely to appeal to many drivers, for here was a machine with a top speed of only 86mph (138km/h), 0–60mph took 18.8 seconds (that felt – and was – a very long time !), with over-all fuel consumption of around 28–32mpg (10ltr/100km–8.8ltr/100km).

Even so, it was not all gloom and doom at Ford. With the company still heading every sales chart in the UK (where the brand regularly took more than 30 per cent of all registrations), and with the Capri 3000 still recognized as one of the most successful saloon car racers in the business, dealers were still happy to have such a car in their lists.

X-Packs for All – Including the Capri

This was a time when a great deal of work went into preparing X-packs for every Ford model and range. Consequently, in mid-1977, Ford's publicists began to bang the big drum. X-packs, anyone? Tune-up kits? Body kits? Making good cars even better, all with the approval of Uncle Henry? These days it doesn't sound likely but in August 1977 it all became possible. The original publicity picture – a sweep of five different models – told it all. Not just Escorts, but Capri IIs, Fiestas and Cortina IVs as well … those were the days! When Ford still made Rallye Sports (RS) models. When Ford still had RS dealers. And when those RS dealerships had staff who really knew their stuff. There were no limits, really, to what we enthusiasts could achieve.

But – and here was the clever bit – someone at Ford had been very thoughtful. Maybe

the brochure wording was ever so slightly wide of the mark, and though all the leaflets talked about kits, each item was individually priced, and it was always possible to add, or subtract, from what Ford initially recommended. The advertising made that very clear:

> New 'Series X' kits – you specify as much or as little change as you like … you can, depending on model, specify more power, bigger brakes, stiffer suspension, lightweight alloy wheels, air dam, spoiler, wheel arches – with Series X you make as much or as little improvement as you like … How much Series X should you add to your Ford – the one you own or are about to own? Your approved Rallye Sport dealer is the man to consult.

It didn't matter whether you were adding X-pack to a Fiesta, an Escort or a Capri, the offerings were mainly split into these areas:

- Body dress-up kits
- Interior seating kits
- Engine tune-up items
- Transmission kits
- Wheels
- Suspension/handling/steering kits

The ever-modest rallying superstar, Bjorn Waldegard, who drove for Ford's 'works' rally team and became World Champion in 1979, poses alongside one of the very first Capri X-pack models in 1977.

Engine
3.OL V6 – bigger valves and carburettor give 170 smooth tractable horse power. Bags of torque and performance. 0-60 in 7 seconds.

Suspension
Gas filled front struts and rear shocks. Stiffer front springs, single leaf rear springs. Overall effect: 1" lower and stiffer.

'Spa' wheel arches
manufactured from high quality fibreglass add the finishing touch.

7½ x 13 lightweight alloy RS wheels
give outstanding roadholding when combined with wide, low profile tyres. Good looking too.

Car illustrated is a 3 litre Capri 'S'.

Anti Dive kit
For greater stability throughout the braking period.

Ventilated disc brakes
Radial ducts help cool the discs under continuous application – help reduce brake fade.

"With Ford's new 'Series X' or as little change
Kits you specify as much as you like" Bjorn Waldegard

The new 'Series X' kits from Ford Rallye Sport are the most flexible way to improve all these fine cars: **Capri, RS 2000, Cortina, Escort or Fiesta.**
You simply decide which of these departments you want bringing up to 'Series X' specification – performance,

handling, roadholding, or appearance – and Ford trained technicians do the fitting. You can specify as much or as little as you like.
How much 'Series X' should you add to your Ford – the one you own or are about to own? Your approved Rallye Sport Dealer is the man to consult.

Final word from Bjorn Waldegard: "I liked the 'Series X' Capri 'S' so much I've recorded my impressions in a two page road test. You can read it in this magazine next month".

New Rallye Sport 'Series X' Kits

[Ford] [RS]
RALLYE SPORT PARTS

This was how Ford advertised the features that could go into turning a normal Capri II into a full X-pack model in 1977.

Maybe this is not the most attractive of all the colours made available on a Capri II, but it shows that Capri specifications, fixtures and fittings could still start from a very modest base.

Capri II Specifications (1974–78): UK-Market Cars

Engines

1300 Kent

Layout	4-cylinder, in-line, overhead-valve
Bore × stroke	80.96 × 62.99mm
Capacity	1298cc
Compression ratio	9.2:1
Maximum power	57bhp @ 5500rpm (50bhp @ 5500rpm from 1976 for base/economy version)
Maximum torque	67lb ft @ 3,000rpm (64lb ft @ 3000rpm from 1976 for base/economy version)
Fuel system	Ford/Motorcraft GPD carburettor

1600 Pinto

Layout	4-cylinder, in-line, single overhead-camshaft
Bore × stroke	87.65 × 66mm
Capacity	1593cc
Compression ratio	9.2:1
Maximum power	72bhp @ 5,500rpm
Maximum torque	87lb ft @ 2,700rpm
Fuel system	Ford/Motorcraft GPD carburettor

1600GT Pinto

Layout	4-cylinder, in-line, single overhead-camshaft
Bore × stroke	87.65 × 66mm
Capacity	1593cc
Compression ratio	9.2:1
Maximum power	88bhp @ 5,700rpm
Maximum torque	92lb ft @ 4,000rpm
Fuel system	Weber compound dual-choke carburettor

2000GT Pinto

Layout	4-cylinder, in-line, single overhead-camshaft
Bore × stroke	90.8 × 76.95mm
Capacity	1993cc
Compression ratio	9.2:1
Maximum power	98bhp @ 5,200rpm
Maximum torque	112lb ft @ 3,500rpm
Fuel system	Weber compound dual-choke carburettor

3000GT Essex V6

Layout	6-cylinder, in 60-degree V, over-head-valve
Bore × stroke	93.66 × 72.44mm
Capacity	2994cc
Compression ratio	9.0:1
Maximum power	138bhp @ 5,100rpm
Maximum torque	174lb ft @ 3,000rpm
Fuel system	Weber compound dual-choke carburettor

Transmission

Gearbox	All synchromesh manual 4-speed Optional 3-speed automatic with 1600, 1600GT, 2000GT and 3000GT engines
Final drive	4.125:1 (1300), 3.78:1 (1600), 3.75:1 (1600GT), 3.44:1 (2000GT), 3.09:1 (3000GT/Ghia/S)

Suspension

Front	MacPherson strut, coil springs, anti-roll bar, telescopic dampers
Rear	Live axle, half-elliptic leaf springs, anti-roll bar, telescopic dampers
Steering	Rack and pinion (power-assisted optional on 3000 at first, standardized on 3000 from late 1975)
Brakes	Disc front, drum rear, optional vacuum servo on the 1300, vacuum servo standard on all other types

Running Gear

Wheels	13in steel wheels, several styles, or cast alloy wheels on GT, Ghia and S models
Tyres	Radial-ply on all models from 165-section (1300) to 185/70 section (3000S)

Dimensions

Wheelbase	100.8in (2,559mm)
Front track	53.3in (1,353mm)
Rear track	54.5in (1,384mm)
Length	168.8in (4,288mm)
Width	66.9in (1,698mm)
Height	51.1in (1,298mm)
Weight (unladen)	From 2,227lb (1,010kg) for the 1300, to 2,580lb (1,170kg) for the 3000 Ghia

Some RS dealers still employed parts specialists who truly knew their stuff. Secret documents shown to me many years later indicate that in those days Tricentrol alone, a Ford RS dealership with just two outlets, in Dunstable and Chelmsford, was supplying 35 per cent of *all* RS parts, and that Tricentrol was selling hundreds of X-pack Capris in a year. This car, along with the Mk II Escort, was much the most popular car to benefit from the X-pack treatment.

On the Capri, it wasn't just that X-pack customers could add flared front and rear wheel arches and an extra-sized front air-dam in body colour, but that they invariably added those magic four-spoke aluminium alloy RS wheels with 7.5in wheel rims and fat 225/60-13in tyres.

That was a start, but only a start, for it was then possible to added the X-pack front and rear springs (the rear leaf springs were of the fashionable single-leaf variety), along with gas-filled front suspension struts and rear shock absorbers. The X-pack Capris not only looked wider, but were lower too.

You may never have driven an X-pack Capri, but many of you will have sampled a Capri 2.8i model in the 1980s. Maybe some of the Finis Codes (part numbers) of the later car look different, but the road-holding balance, the stance and the handling of both cars were much the same. Think of the 2.8i's handling, allied to the grunt and bellowy torque of an old-type V6's engine, and you will get my drift.

X-pack Capri customers, though, didn't usually stop there, for Bill Meade, Boreham's rally engineer, had also evolved two different types of 3-litre engine conversion. The Group 1 tune (which referred to the type of Capri that Gordon Spice and others made so famous in British Saloon Car Championship racing) included a larger-throat downdraught Weber carburettor and larger inlet and exhaust valves, which, if the heads were also flowed and cleaned up during the rebuild, could result in a 170bhp power output.

Then, if you were really determined to out-sprint a Dino Ferrari, there was the triple Weber kit, where three downdraught Weber 42 DCNFs and a unique manifold sat atop the otherwise standard-looking Essex V6 engine. Worth another 20bhp, it was a kit that cost only £496.86 at the end of the 1970s.

Unbeatable value? It might sound like that today, but at the time that was about 10 per cent of the cost of a new Capri, which rather knocked back the demand.

Even so, by the early 1980s – and for the first time since 1970 – Ford had turned its back on the RS brand, in favour of the softer XR image. With no more rear-drive Escort RS models to sell, and with the old Capri 3.0S shouldered aside in favour of SVE's Capri 2.8i, Series X sales fell rapidly away. And they never came back. Which means that, today, the pristine survivors we see at enthusiasts' days are worth more, and treasured more, than when they were new.

This was what went into the kits of the Capri II:

- 7½in rim × 13in RS four-spoke alloy wheels
- 225/60-13 tyres
- Anti-dive front suspension
- Flared front and rear wing (fender) extension kit
- Rear spoiler
- Group 1 engine – 2-litre Pinto – 3-litre V6 (carburettor/inlet and exhaust valves)
- Triple-carburettor engine conversion for 3-litre V6 (*c.*170bhp)
- Limited-slip differential
- Lower/stiffer front and (single-leaf) rear springs
- Gas-filled MacPherson front struts
- Gas-filled rear shock absorbers
- Ventilated front disc brakes, including Granada calipers

Time for a Change

By the end of 1977, the Capri range seemed to be coasting along, maybe with retirement only one or two years away. However, Ford had another significant face-lift in mind.

6 Capris in National Motor Sport

The original Capri was not an obvious choice for saloon car racing in the UK – especially as Ford's own Escort was so dominant at that stage. The German-assembled RS2600 did not go on sale until late 1970 (and could therefore not go racing until 1971), and the British 3000GT, that had been available from the start of 1970, was not then considered suitable for use in motor racing.

In the UK, in any case, there was much resistance to what was really only a 2+2-seater taking part in saloon car racing. Even though the necessary interior measurements were taken, and marginally proved that the cabin dimensions of this compact car complied with the FIA's saloon car requirements, this was enough to delay the first serious British-based Capri race programme until 1971.

This was the season in which Ford spread its bets in British saloon car racing, for while John Fitzpatrick was racing the stunningly fast Broadspeed Escort RS1600 in 1971, Gerry Birrell drove a British-maintained Capri RS2600 that had originally been prepared for him by Ford-Germany. Originally the Ford-Cologne V6 engine was a 2873cc unit, but this was soon enlarged to 2933cc and about 285bhp, which made it the same as those being used in the victorious European Touring Car 'works' Capris.

Gerry Birrell's programme of 'works' events in Europe was so intense that he rarely managed to race an RS2600 in Britain – but in 1971 he brought this example to Brands Hatch to compete in the 'Jackie Stewart Tribute' weekend.

However, because of Birrell's commitments to racing for Ford in even more important long-distance events in Europe, he was not always able to compete in every British qualifying event. In the British series, too, Birrell's problem was that he had to compete for outright victory against the 5- or even 5.7-litre Chevrolet Camaros. This and the fact that it took time to get the car's handling right meant that he did not achieve great success.

In seven of the RAC British Championship rounds, he won outright only once (at Brands Hatch, the last race of the season – and that was due to a massive shunt that took place immediately ahead of him on the last lap!). He inherited another win when the Camaros that beat him were later disqualified on technical grounds, finished third twice (Brands Hatch and Silverstone) and fifth once, but his engine blew twice, and on one occasion he was nudged off the track in a first corner multiple accident.

It was all change for 1972, when Wiggins Teape, which was also the British Touring Car Championship (BTCC) series sponsor at the time, chose to support Brian Muir, who drove a fully works prepared Ford-Cologne 2.9-litre Capri RS2600, which had all the latest homologated pieces and more than 300bhp, sometimes with a particular Weslake-built engine which was already one step ahead of the units being provided to Cologne from the same source. Except that it still had to battle against the big-engined American cars, it was the most competitive car in the entire field.

Muir's season, unfortunately, was ruined by a series of engine failures (Weslake's reputation was, rightly, under attack at this stage). There were three major blow-ups, usually when he was leading, or fighting for the lead, so he had to settle for just two outright victories (one at Oulton Park, the other at Crystal Palace) and two second places. On the other hand, the self-same car won a prestigious 6-hour race at the French Paul Ricard circuit (Muir and John Miles sharing the driving), in which they beat the 'official' Ford-Cologne cars, this causing considerable loss of face on the part of the

Germans, and a great deal of bad feeling too.

For 1973 there were further changes, for with Broadspeed no longer running the big-engined Escort RS1600s, they elected to run a brand new Capri RS2600 car in Group 2 trim, with the very latest Ford-Germany 3-litre V6 Weslake engines – supposedly with 310–320bhp. David Matthews, who had performed so well during 1972 in the Broadspeed Escort RS1600, was hired to drive it.

Although this was an immaculately prepared race car, it had been fitted with founder Ralph Broad's own design, controversial (and scrutineer-challenging) suspension layouts. At the front, what was effectively an auxiliary coil-over-damper arrangement was linked to the MacPherson struts, where the original spring was replaced by something entirely ineffective, while at the rear, similar coil-over-dampers were positioned well behind the line of the rear axle, this being located by trailing arms and a Watts linkage.

All this, added to the use of a ZF five-speed gearbox, Can-Am sized disc brakes front and rear, plus 12in wide front wheel rims and 14in wide rear rims, along with newly-homologated flared front and rear wheel arches, presented the ultimate expression of what Ralph Broad thought a Group 2 car could actually be. It was almost bound to confront the series scrutineers – and it did!

'It's part of the fun, trying to beat the regulations,' Broad quipped at the time. 'If I don't do it, some other bugger will – and beat me.'

Even before a huge accident claimed the car at Silverstone, in the GP meeting (fortunately Matthews, the driver, recovered well), by previous Broadspeed standards this was an unsuccessful campaign. In the first four races there were two engine failures, a third place over all and a sixth over all – all this being enough to convince Ralph Broad that he would not try to repeat the exercise.

In the meantime, Broadspeed had built up a similar sister car for Claude Bourgoignie to use in Belgium, where it had a good deal of success and won the Belgian Saloon Car

Championship. Later in the season, Andy Rouse was entrusted with it in the British Tourist Trophy race (where the 'works' Capri RS2600s fought a day-long battle with the BMW 3.0CSLs), where it performed equally as well as any of the Cologne cars. In the race, unhappily, not only did Rouse come into contact with Dieter Glemser's 'works' car (exit one Cologne Capri), but the engine crankshaft later broke – and that was that.

By the end of 1973, with the Energy Crisis bringing a temporary halt to motor racing, and with Ford temporarily having to cut its motor sport budgets, there was no longer much support in the UK for the Capri RS2600s, especially as they could not run in Group 1 form in 1974.

Tour of Britain – Group 1 Cars

Now, in any case, it was time for a diversion – and one which race organizers hoped would make competing cars more recognizable to the spectators. Proposals for trying to run a Tour of Britain – something like that already held in France – had been floating around for years, but no entrepreneur had yet managed to find the right combination of cars, available circuits and backing.

In July 1973 the problem was finally solved. The BRSCC ran the first of its own Tour of Britain events, which, like the Tour de France, was to be an arduous multi-day mixture of circuit racing, rally stages and road mileage: in the first year it totalled 1,000 miles (1,609km) – which might sound a lot, though this was quite dwarfed by what the French event imposed.

Ford entered three Boreham-built Capri 3000GTs, complete with British Essex V6 engines: these engines having improved dramatically since the days when ace mechanic Mick Jones had once famously described them as having cylinder blocks made out of 'f★★★★g Weetabix!'.

Roger Clark and Matthews drove the leading machines (Prince Michael of Kent drove the third of the 'official' Capris), while other privately-entered cars for Gordon Spice, Adrian Boyd and Mike Crabtree all had access to the recommended specification, and all were potentially competitive. Blueprinted engines were tested and prepared at Boreham, and developed around 160bhp.

Although this first event was quite unexpectedly dominated by F1 driver James Hunt's 5-litre Chevrolet Camaro (he had never driven the car before the start of the event, and had never before tackled such a road/race competition of this character), the Capris were always close to him, and battling for victory. In fact Clark's 'works' Capri led, on the second day, at half distance, but an engine electrical failure (the distributor) in the race at Oulton Park spoilt that.

At the end of the event, it was Spice's privately-financed Capri 3000GT that finished a

Except for James Hunt's magnificent effort in a Chevrolet Camaro, 'works' Group 1 Capri 3000GTs nearly swept the board in the 1973 Tour of Britain. This was Roger Clark at Brands Hatch, well in the lead at half-distance, before engine trouble let him down.

very close second to Hunt, just 26 seconds (in 114 competitive minutes) behind the bellowing American car. Other Capris driven by Boyd (fourth) and Matthews (fifth) were well placed.

A year later, it was the blue and white 'works' Escort RS2000s that beat all comers in the Tour of Britain, for somehow the Capris (still Mk Is, though such cars had not been on sale for months) did not seem to be as competitive as before, the highest placed car being sixth, with Boyd and John Davenport driving.

For 1975, victory once again went to an RS2000, but Spice urged his Capri 3000GT Mk II (as in regular use in the BTCC) into fourth place over all, close behind rally driver Tony Pond's Escort, while Stuart Rolt was second in class behind him, but this was increasingly an event where rallying expertise on the special stages seemed to count for more than race craft on the circuits. Although the Capris were very fast in the races, it was cars like the RS2000 that were so nimble on the stages, their drivers being so much braver on sections that they had tackled in previous rallies.

There was little point, the race drivers thought, in even trying to win the 1976 race, for this time there were to be only four races and no fewer than twenty-six special stages. Of the competitive Capri racers, only Spice turned up in his regular 3000GT Mk II, and finished very bravely in thirteenth place.

Group 1 in the Later 1970s

For 1974, in the meantime, the British Saloon Car Championship was re-jigged, henceforth to run to Group 1 (more strictly, to 'Group 1½' regulations), which severely handicapped the Ford Capri, as neither the RS2600 nor the RS3100 had ever been homologated as Group 1 cars. Nevertheless, since the new rules promised stability for some seasons to come (and there were other events overseas in which the same regulations applied), Ford concluded that they should be supported. This, then, was the point at which a steady development programme for the British 3-litre Essex engine began – originally for use in old-shape Capri 3000GT Mk Is, and later with the re-styled (and rather heavier) 3000GT Mk IIs.

At this point it is interesting to quote homologated weights. In 1970 Ford had persuaded the authorities to accept that a 3000GT weighed only 2,040lb (925kg), which meant that race car preparers could strip out a lot of sound-deadening and extraneous material without breaching the quoted lower limit. Later the Capri II appeared, according to Ford as an 'evolution' of the original, which meant that it could still race at the same minimum weight even though the real road cars were significantly heavier than before.

All this eventually ended in tears, when rivals began to protest about unfair weight

Just for fun, Ford let Timo Makinen loose to go racing on snow in Finland. Good fun, and spectacular, but not likely to beat the engine-over-driving-wheels cars that dominated in that country.

advantages, and from 1978 the new Capri IIIs were obliged to run at 2,341lb (1,062kg), which was nearer, if not quite actually, the truth!

In 1974, there was only one 'works' backed programme, for Tom Walkinshaw's car was supported from Boreham. This was one of the ex-Tour of Britain 1973 machines, refurbished and with another year's development behind it, yet confusingly it originally ran in Ford-Cologne colours, which made some people assume that it was an RS2600! Several other privately-prepared cars seemed to be equally as potent when it came to homologation and the provision of engine tuning expertise, Ford was

always open with its findings, and by this time Walkinshaw could enjoy the use of 175bhp.

Except on one isolated occasion, when Walkinshaw won a race in his native Scotland, on the serpentine Ingliston circuit, he was never able to keep up with the 5.7-litre Chevrolet Camaros that totally dominated the season, in fact he often had to struggle to match the pace of Peter Hanson's 2.8-litre Opel Commodore GSi. Not only was the engine difficult to tune (and suitably homologated pieces rare), but the internal gear ratios were appallingly spaced, with a yawning gap between second and third ratios. It was not until 1975 that someone 'happened' to discover

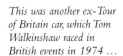

This was another ex-Tour of Britain car, which Tom Walkinshaw raced in British events in 1974 …

… as seen here at Brands Hatch.

than certain Hewland gears could be fitted into the same casing!

At the end of an exhausting thirteen-round season, where much of his support came from Castrol, Walkinshaw had taken one second place overall, along with three thirds and three fourth places, and easily won his 2.5–4-litre capacity class. Ford, it seemed, had immediately been able to turn general expertise into detail achievement.

Then came a more important change. For 1975 Ford not only homologated the smoother-styled (though heavier) Capri II; they also made a determined attempt to homologate all the right pieces for the latest 3000GT, though this did not seem to make the cars much more competitive than before. As in 1974, they could obviously not match the vast American cars (some of which had 7.4-litre engines!) that were always up front.

All in all this was a most unsatisfactory year for the BTCC, for although the series had a flamboyant new sponsor – Southern Organs – the owner of that company, Sidney Miller, disappeared in mysterious circumstances towards the end of the season, taking his company funds with him, and the promised sponsorship was never apparently handed over. As far as the Capri IIs were concerned, Walkinshaw had moved on, the result being that there was no official 'works' car in 1975, the most impressive of several private entries including Spice (who also used his car in the Tour of Britain), Rolt and Holman Blackburn.

Even so, this was a season that was dominated by rumbling American V8s, and for the Capri there would only be a sprinkling of third places overall to be celebrated. Spice, running a car sponsored by Wisharts (a Ford dealer in the north-east of the UK), won the 2.5–4-litre capacity championship class in spite of missing several races after he was badly injured at Mallory Park in a crash in another type of race car. For 1976 things could only get better.

Which, indeed, they did. Stunned by the apathetic response of the paying public to the

earlier series, which was quite overshadowed by ill-handling but ferociously fast American cars, for 1976 the RAC re-wrote its own rule book. This time round, the organizers found themselves a new sponsor (Keith Prowse, the theatre bookings specialists) and set the top engine size limit at 3 litres.

This, of course, effectively banned all American cars from competing (can this have been purely accidental?). Happily, this was an ideal situation for the Capris, which could also enjoy another package of newly homologated items (including a different camshaft profile, a closer-ratio gearbox inspired by Hewland, and bigger brakes), and a full year's racing experience on which to build.

Somehow, too, homologation specialist John Griffiths managed to get a higher performance engine (high altitude territories) approved, this having a nominal compression ratio of 10.25:1 with a tolerance of +/- 0.5!

Their main competition would come from the 'works' Triumph Dolomite Sprints, and from anyone who could gain backing for an Opel Commodore Coupé.

This was a season, in fact, in which the Capris always seemed to be the best cars for the job. Each and every race was won by one or other of the privately financed Fords (there was no longer an official car from Boreham), although Rouse's well-developed 'works' Triumph Dolomite Sprint often disputed the Capris' lead in the early laps.

Spice and Walkinshaw each won four races, the other two rounds going to Vince Woodman and Colin Vandervell. Ten races, ten Capri victories – Ford was certainly not complaining, though the organizers began to wonder if they were promoting rather predictable motor sport. Spice even used the same car in the Tourist Trophy race, which was run to more open Group 2 regulations, and finished fifth over all.

Once again, because of the marking system that favoured a driver who won his capacity class the most times, it was a 1.3-litre machine (Bernard Unett's Hillman Avenger) that won the 1976 series, though Spice won his

Tom Walkinshaw, still making his way as a race driver before being a constructor, was a formidably successful Capri racer in the mid-1970s. In this Hermetite-sponsored car he won four BTCC races in 1976.

championship class narrowly, by five points, from Walkinshaw, with Vandervell and Woodman trailing behind him.

With no changes for 1977, except that the enthusiastic Tricentrol Group, whose operations not only included Ford Rallye Sports (RS) dealerships but a stake in new North Sea oilfield exploration, came on board as series sponsors, the Capri II 3000GT was the odds-on favourite to win most of the races. Perhaps not all of them, though, for the 'works' (Broadspeed) Triumph Dolomite Sprint, driven by Tony Dron, and Walkinshaw's privately-supported BMW 530i saloon, were both likely to be formidable competition.

With seven or eight Capris at each of the twelve races, Ford fanatics expected a walkover, but it did not quite work out like that. In the event, the 2-litre Dolomite had become so well developed (though some of the items homologated were of truly doubtful validity) that it won no fewer than five of the races outright – though in every case it was closely followed by one or other of the fleet of Capris. The other seven races were all won by Capris, driven var-iously by Spice, Vandervell, Woodman, Stuart Graham and Chris Craft.

Because of the well-known points-scoring system – which favoured consistency by one driver in his class – once again it was Unett's 1.3-litre Hillman Avenger that became Champion!

To quote *Autosport*'s seasonal survey, the 1977 series had been: 'the most competitive year since the National Series went Group 1'. Even so, the 3-litre Capri was still not a very fast car – and by no means as fast as the RS2600s that had been used earlier in the decade.

The Capri's problem at this time was that it had no more than 225bhp, though at least a new front spoiler, high-ratio steering rack, anti-dive front suspension kit and a brake balancer-bar had all been homologated for this most individual of championships.

There were no 'works' cars, though Spice, Graham and Craft were so impressive as private owners that they would be guaranteed some help for the following season. Using his CC-prepared machine, Spice took two outright victories and four class wins, which guaranteed him success in the class, with Craft close behind him.

127

Ford Rallye Sport (RS) club promoted one-model races at their motor sport weekends. Here, at Brands Hatch, a fleet of near-standard 3000GTs – eight in the picture and at least another eight still to follow – rush round what we used to call Bottom Bend. Famous race drivers came along, just for fun, so who is leading in this shot?

By the late 1970s, British touring car racing was dominated by Capri 3000GTs. Here is Gordon Spice, ahead of two other Capris, in the British GP support race of the period.

Chris Craft was a formidable Capri racer in the UK, not only in this Capri II 3000GT but in the rebuilt Capri III that followed it. Hammonds, by the way, was a concern making food products in Yorkshire, its owner being a motor sport enthusiast – in this way are sponsors made!

Gordon Spice won more British races in one of his Capri 3000GTs than any other driver. This was Silverstone in the mid-1970s …

… and here again in the self-same car, but with a subtly different livery and advertising job.

In one of the Ford Capri celebrity races, famous race drivers paired with team managers in two-part races. Here Emerson Fittipaldi (who would become twice World F1 Champion in Lotus-Fords) races a car that he will soon hand over to his team boss, Colin Chapman.

1978: High Tide

By 1978 the V6-engined Capri 3000GT was as dominant as it was ever likely to be, for Walkinshaw's BMW 530i (which was too large and too heavy if run in homologated condition) finally proved to be uncompetitive in the category, leaving the Fords to fight among themselves. More importantly, further development meant that in 1978 they were now always quicker than the 'works'-backed Triumph Dolomite Sprint, and took almost every outright victory.

Compared with 1977, the only important Capri change was a visual one – with the Capri III taking over from the Capri II early in the year. The new style (complete with four

circular headlamps instead of two rectangular ones and a small, but useful, boot lid spoiler, along with even wider wheels) was speedily homologated – there were distinct advantages to running the new layout. It was typical of Ford that the moment this was done, they issued a series of conversion kits so that the teams could immediately update the looks of their existing cars.

In 1978 *Autocar*, who part-sponsored Spice's car, spilt the beans on many details of a successful Capri's preparation. Noting that it took at least 500 man-hours (more than ten working weeks for one mechanic, or maybe a month by a team, always assuming that there was no 'down time' while the special parts arrived), the engine (developed by Neil

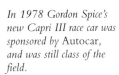

In 1978 Gordon Spice's new Capri III race car was sponsored by Autocar, *and was still class of the field.*

The car looked even better in the developed type of livery, when Ford's Motorcraft division had topped-up the budget.

Brown) was quoted as producing 220bhp at 6,500/7,000rpm, running on a near-11:1 compression, special camshaft grind, gas-flowed cylinder heads and larger inlet and exhaust valves. Even though they only produced 73bhp/litre, these V6s ran at no better than 7mpg (40ltr/100km), and had to be rebuilt every 500 racing miles (unless they were sent to the Spa 24-hour race, when fingers were firmly crossed).

Complete with a full roll-cage, plumbed-in fire extinguisher, big brakes, racing wheels and tyres, and a special fuel tank, Spice's racing Capri III weighed in at around 2,536lb (1,150kg) – at least 194lb (88kg) above the minimum homologated weight limit.

As widely forecast, Spice's car was consistently faster than almost every other Capri in the country, winning the 3-litre category six times (out of twelve races), while team-mate Craft won once and rival Jeff Allam won twice – one of those two occasions being when Spice was disqualified from the Donington Park race because of cylinder head illegalities. Gerry Marshall and Muir also won the class on one occasion each.

This was all very satisfying for Ford (though they rarely did much to advertise this dominance), but not necessarily uplifting for the paying public. By 1979, and the end of an eventful decade, British 'Group 1½' racing seemed to have got itself thoroughly into a rut, which did not worry the Ford racers at all, as their Capris remained at the top of the ratings. In almost every event of the 1979 season – twelve championship races in all – a fleet of Capri 3000GT III 3-litre cars fought it out for the outright victory, with Spice (six wins) much the most consistent of them all, though Allam, Craft and Woodman were always competitive.

To prove that development rarely stands still - even of so-called simple 'Group 1½' cars like these – Spice's team acknowledged that they had managed to reduce the weight of their 1979 cars to no more than 2,359lb (1,070kg), and because this was now less than the minimum class weight for this type of racing, they were obliged to add ballast in the rear seat-pan area. They also had 230bhp at 6,600rpm/7,000rpm, and with slight regulation changes favouring the Capri engine for 1980 this was eventually increased to a final total of 255bhp at 7,500/7,600rpm.

Gordon Spice, at Oulton Park in 1978, on his way to winning yet another touring car race.

As *Autosport*'s seasonal survey commented: 'Such is the standard of preparation of these hatchbacks, and so complete the necessary homologations that the 3-litre class often seemed like very expensive one-make racing'.

As ever, because of the vagaries of the points scoring system, outright wins were not enough to win the title or even the manufacturers' crown, so, as in 1978, the actual championship winner was Richard Longman in a Mini 1275GT, a car much slower, but more consistent in its class, than the Capri.

Even so, there was evidence – rarely spelled out, and never admitted to – that the RAC MSA was beginning to turn against the Capri, if only to ensure that some other make and model of car won a few races. Rear anti-roll kits that had been approved for more than a year were suddenly banned by the scrutineers, front strut modifications of equal longevity were soon picked out and banned, and it wasn't long before the Spice/CC onboard air jacks (like those of Penske) were also declared sporting-illegal.

Was the Capri's dominance soon to end?

1980 – V8 Challenge

All this was bound to change for 1980, as the championship organizers had come under pressure from British Leyland. For the new season, the rules were changed to admit 3.5-litre cars, which (by a bit of judicious massaging of engine sizes) admitted the Rover 3500s, even though their showroom engine size was actually 3528cc!

This change meant that the racing would certainly be more varied than before – and in fact no fewer than thirteen marques and twenty different models of car appeared from time to time during the season. To quote *Autosport*: 'It has been a vintage year for the Tricentrol series, with rounds being dubbed the "best race of the day" at each meeting … the Tricentrol series has become a real crowd puller and a crowd *pleaser*'.

Even so, it took time for the bigger-engined and heavier Rovers to become competitive –

or, let us say, to start homologating the appropriate pieces that would let them be competitive. Capris won nine out of the ten rounds, being defeated only once – at the British GP meeting at Brands Hatch, in a wet race where ex-Capri driver Allam won in a Rover 3500.

Once again it was Spice (his car, as ever, being prepared by CC) who was the most outstanding driver, winning six times out of ten, and easily capturing the 3.5-litre category. His team-mate, ex-Dolomite-driver Rouse, in the other CC-prepared car, won three of the other four races.

Once again, need I say it; the championship points-scoring position made a nonsense of the entire series, for although the Capri had dominated almost every race, it was a much slower and smaller-engined Mazda RX-7 (a Wankel-engined machine driven by Win Percy) that won its class in every event, and therefore lifted the crown at the end of the year.

But this had all been too good to last, for even though no fewer than eleven Capris were prepared for the 1981 season, they were no more effective than before. By this time the larger-engined Rovers had assembled all the appropriate gear, the Capris were, frankly, ageing and getting no faster – and the balance was tipped. In an eleven-event Tricentrol-sponsored series, Capris won four races early in the season, but from mid-June there seemed to be no stopping the larger-engined Rovers.

In the end, Rouse's Capri (originally backed by the *Daily Mirror* and by Broadspeed, later by Charles Sawyer-Hoare) finished third in the class. (When Broadspeed went into liquidation early in the year, Rouse took some of the redundant staff with him, set up Andy Rouse Engineering in Coventry, and proceeded to build up an impressive race-car operation.)

Among the others, Spice's car finished fourth and Woodman's car fifth – but the writing was now well-and-truly on the wall. The Capri 3-litre had already dropped out of production, the Rovers continued to improve, and it looked as if the Capri's long dominance of British tin-top racing was over.

For 1982, the RAC announced that this would be the final year for what had become an increasingly specialized and unique 'Group 1½' formula – and that for 1983 the new Group A category would be introduced instead. Ford-UK, which was itself in transition, showed little interest in this development. The Capri 3-litre, after all, had dropped out of production in 1980–81, while the Capri 2.8i that took over was not a promising replacement.

There were several reasons for this. Although, as every enthusiast surely knows, the Capri 2.8i was a much faster road car (160bhp compared with 138bhp), there seemed to be very little point in evolving all the extra homologated equipment for one season of 'Group 1½' motor sport. The teams, in any case, would soon have had to throw away their well-honed 3-litre cars and start again – something that they made clear they were reluctant to do.

Not only that, but Ford's top management made it clear that in marketing terms they now saw the Capri as *vieux jeu* (out of date, and out of fashion), so the trusty old cars were cast aside to do their own thing in lesser categories of motor racing. But not before one last season, in which some of the 1980–81 Capri fleet appeared again, suitably re-prepared.

The Rovers, on the other hand, were prepared and managed by the redoubtable Tom Walkinshaw/TWR organization, already had torquey 290bhp engines, and were destined to improve still further as the 1980s progressed with much effort (and money) being put behind them.

All things considered, therefore, the miracle is that in 1982 the venerable Capri 3-litres (and some of the individual cars that had never been crashed were surprisingly old) won no fewer than five races.

Ford dealer Woodman, by then forty-four years old, and a veteran of saloon car racing, once again teamed up with CC Developments (that had previously been linked with Spice) and won four of those races outright, only narrowly failing to beat Allam's Rover for the category prize, and for a possible third in the Championship.

Group A – Not for Capris

When Group A and Group B arrived in 1983, the motor sport industry breathed a sigh of relief, for the sport's world organizing body, the CSI, which had been talking about this for years, made a long overdue attempt to rationalize the way that cars were to be homologated, and to define more accurately what could, and could not, be homologated.

In broad terms, Group A replaced the old Group 2, and Group B replaced the old Groups 4 and 5, but there was a much more significant change of emphasis than that. Group B, for which only 200 cars needed to be built, would rapidly evolve into a no-holds-barred 'supercar' formula, in which four-wheel drive (FWD) was essential, and there was no question of running any saloon car racing to these rules.

Group A was meant to cover saloons. First of all, 5,000 cars had to be built within a year, and although a great number of transmission, suspension and braking options were to be authorized, manufacturers were no longer to be allowed to homologate any alternative cylinder heads, carburettors, or fuel-injection.

Group A racing was first imposed on the European Touring Championship in 1982 (where no Ford cars were involved), and then imposed on the British series from 1983. Although there was also an overlap period where old Group 2 cars could be used in Group A events, this did not favour Ford either – the result being that the ancient Capri 3-litres were seen, but were simply not competitive.

In 1983, therefore, the 3-litre Capri breathed its last, for only four cars ever appeared during the season, and all were totally outclassed. This was the season, in any case, when the series descended into farce, with protest and counter-protest surrounding the eligibility of the 'works' Rovers.

(As an aside, some parts of the Rovers were said to be running with what was known as Third World specification pieces, but no complete cars were ever seen to be delivered to the Third World. It wasn't long before the initials of Third World were seen to be the same as Tom Walkinshaw, who prepared the cars.)

If Ford had been as determined to bend the rules as TWR demonstrated that they were, the Capri 2.8i might have been made competitive, but no one (certainly not Ford) seemed to care for the challenge. To quote *Autosport* in its end-of-1982 survey:

> Although the 2.8i Capri is eligible for the series, there seems to be a marked reluctance from either the Spice or Woodman camps to take over the project. Ford themselves are not keen on promoting the vehicle as the Capri's [future] life is limited. But development work on the 2.8-litre engine must be allowed to start if the Sierra XR4i is to have any hope of a competition life.

Ford, however, chose to ignore all such pointed remarks – especially as they realized that the 2.8i engine was not a very promising unit to transform into a racing engine. This, then, was a temporary end to Ford's dominance of British saloon car racing. But not for long – a series of ferociously fast turbocharged Sierras was already on the way.

Silhouette Racer – the Zakspeed Capri

It was almost as if Zakspeed's body designers had been sampling mind-expanding chemicals, or fiercely-potent booze. In their sober moments they must have studied a Capri or two, but none of those could ever have been like this. Wider, lower, faster and more powerful – you've never seen this sort of Capri before. And neither, in 1978 when they appeared, had anyone else!

It's difficult to know where to start when describing Zakspeed's near-unique Capris of the late 1970s. Capris, or not? Saloons or racing

The Zakspeed Capri Turbo looked astonishing from any angle, and needed tyres that wide to transmit the huge power developed.

Although the Zakspeed Capri Turbo looked something like a Capri road car, it was totally different under the skin. Here, as launched in 1978, is the multi-tube space frame that formed the ultra-rigid structure.

This was the head-on view of the original Zakspeed Turbo race car of 1978.

By mid-1974, Dave Brodie had completed this stunningly beautiful 'silhouette' Capri II, that not only featured a bodyshell supported by tubular reinforcements, but was powered by a 3.4-litre Cosworth GA power unit (like the 'works' RS3100s of the period). Although it looked wonderful from every angle …

… it was not lastingly successful. However, it gave Dunton Design quite a lot of pointers for their future.

sports cars? Modified production cars or race cars with familiar styling? But one thing was certain – no one but Zakspeed ever built faster or more successful cars carrying the Capri title.

Group 5 Monsters

In the 1970s, motor sport was run according to a long list of FIA categories, from Group 1 (showroom standard machinery) to Group 7 (two-seat racing sports cars). Later in the decade, when the technology – and the regulations – had moved on, the Germans embraced Group 5 for their own national sporting categories.

Start with a standard shell, Group 5 regulations stated, but feel free to alter almost everything else, which explains why non-original fittings such as engine transplants, massively reinforced monocoques, turbocharged engines, composite bodywork and extrovert aerodynamics all swept past the scrutineers without challenge.

In Germany, BMW and Porsche had Group 5 racing all to themselves at first, as Ford and Zakspeed were still committed to Touring Car racing, in which more restrictive Group 2 regulations applied. By the mid-1970s Ford's 'works' Capris RS3100s were fastest of all, though it was Zakspeed's RS1800s that had

won the European and German Championships. One morning, it seems, Erich Zakowski of Zakspeed woke up, decided that he was bored with Group 2, that Group 5 racing was spectacular and that he wanted to be part of it. Ford-Germany, curiously somnolent since their own Capri RS3100s had retired, offered technical, material and moral support. The result, unveiled in mid-1978, was the most astonishing Capri that the world had ever seen.

The Capri elements that survived were the front-engine/rear-drive layout, and some features of the style, plus the much-improved MacPherson strut front suspension – but that was about all. Chassis, engine and component layouts were all very different. Vastly wider and longer than the road car, stuffed full with an aluminium roll cage that did more for chassis stiffness than the body shell had ever done, and with a turbocharged version of the Escort RS1800's BDA engine, this layout made a mockery of the lax regulations that applied.

Those were the days, incidentally, when turbocharged engines ran to regulations that effectively multiplied their actual capacity by a factor of 1.4:1 – which in effect limited the turbo engine to 1428cc, so that it could compete in the 2-litre class. Zakspeed, like Porsche and BMW before them, concluded that they could

For German Championship racing, where Group 5 regulations applied, the Zakspeed Capri Turbo was able to run with this colossal rear wing.

When the new Zakspeed Capri Turbo was unveiled in 1978, everyone – including every rival – wanted to see just how Erich Zakowski had packaged his new monster. Once out on track, this car did not disappoint them.

produce better than 1.4 times the power by turbocharging an engine, decided that this really was 'power for nothing', and chose to do it!

The performance was colossal. Capri 3-litre road cars had just 138bhp, but even the very first of the 1.4-litre Zakspeed cars boasted 380bhp. By 1980, when a larger 1.75-litre

BDA had been installed (which made this a '2.5-litre' car), there was no less than 560bhp–600bhp. Four times the power of the road car, in a lighter machine that handled like a thoroughbred !

They won races, many of them, of course. For the 1.4-litre car, the first victories came in 1978, Hans Heyer using one to win its 2-litre championship division in 1979, and in 1980 it was Klaus Ludwig who won no fewer than six races in the larger division in the latest 1.7-litre machine.

Once the BDA turbo engine of the Zakspeed Capri was installed, the technicians immediately bolted a stiffening brace into place on top of it. The turbocharger was huge, and that is an air/air intercooler immediately behind the front grille.

Every detail of the Zakspeed Capri Turbo had been carefully thought out.

137

Because it was a race car that just happened to have a passing resemblance to a Capri, the Zakspeed racer cornered like a thoroughbred.

By 1979 the Zakspeed Capri Turbo was running a 1.7-litre turbocharged engine, and had a new sponsor to help support its progress.

Having spent time in previous seasons in Zakspeed Escorts, which were quick, but not that quick, and certainly not as brutish, Hans Heyer found himself on a steep learning curve, but succeeded.

Then came 1981, and the most emphatic victory of all – when Ludwig used the 1.4-litre-engined car to dominate the 2-litre division, going on to win the German Championship overall. Since this was to be the last season of Germany silhouette racing, it was the right time for the extrovert machines to bow out.

Technicalities

So, how was it done? The original secret, of course, was that engineer Thomas Ammerschlager read the regulations extremely carefully, proposed a truly radical solution, and persuaded Zakowski, Ford-Germany and a raft of enthusiastic sponsors to back a truly radical rc-statement of the Capri theme.

The whole design was based on a hugely complex roll cage, which doubled as a multi-tube chassis frame. According to Zakspeed's own data, no less than 262ft (80m) of tubing – some round-section, some square-section – was involved, this being augmented by some (but not much!) of the original Capri sheet steel panelling. The screen and side glass was standard Capri, and there was a near-standard bulkhead/front firewall, but much of the rest of the bodyshell was in composite material.

Wider than standard and lower – 10in (254mm) wider and 8in (203mm) lower – this was also a car with much extended rear wings (as with the RS3100s, the cooling radiators were located ahead of the rear wheels, and there were oil coolers mounted nearby), a massive 'snow-plough' front spoiler and a colossal rear spoiler. Those spoilers, incidentally, were not there for visual effect (or to provide somewhere for sponsors' logos to be located), but were diligently and carefully tested on wind-tunnel models. The rear spoiler was so effective that in 1980 the authorities found an excuse to ban it, and a narrower spoiler then took its place.

The size and shape of the front 'splitter' was critical, and the high transverse rear aerofoil had an adjustable blade. Although the regulations would have allowed full underbody 'ground effect' channels, there never seemed to be time to evolve these to their ultimate limit.

The detailing of these cars never stood still, by 1980 they had also grown longitudinal air-smoothing strakes along the bonnet (rather like the BMW 3.0CSLs of 1973 that had given the old Capri RS3100s such a hard time), and the front-splitter had also become adjustable for length. This, don't forget, was a Capri – honestly!

Power? Right from the start, Zakspeed chose to develop their own turbocharged versions of the famous Cosworth BDA rather than using the RS3100's normally aspirated 3.4-litre Cosworth GA. And why? Because Zakspeed knew that the GA could only achieve 455bhp (and was heavy), while they had every hope of beating that figure with the smaller, lighter, turbo-BDA.

And so they did. Not all alone, but with help from the German engine specialist Dr Schrick, and many rugged reliable pieces from Cosworth. By modern standards not much boost was used, only 1.1 bar at first, and 1.5 bar later – but these were always meant to be high-revving, high-output engines.

The motor sport development of these cars (there were only four chassis – none being written off, or sold off while the programme was running), of course, was intense. Early 1.4s produced 370bhp, and by 1980 that had been pushed up to 460bhp: it finally rose to 500bhp. Then, for 1980, a 1.7-litre derivative was produced, this producing no less than 560bhp at first, and up to 600bhp when evolution was finally over. These, let us not forget, were 'sprint' engines that needed a rebuild after every outing – but by any standards they were remarkable figures.

Dispersing all that heat from conventional front-mounted water-cooling radiators would have produced blasts of hot air, both through the engine bay and into the cockpit, so Zakspeed's decision to mount the radiators behind the cabin was very wise indeed.

Even in a Capri road car engine bay there would have been space, and to spare, but in this larger, wider, 'look-a-like' machine, the engineers could make even more of their own

Developed from the Cosworth 16-valve BDA engine, the original Zakspeed Turbo used a turbocharged 1.4-litre derivative, complete with iron cylinder block, which produced a massive 460bhp and helped deliver 174mph (279km/h). A later car used a 1.7-litre version, produced 560bhp and a top speed of 186mph (299km/h).

decisions. The squat BDA engine – based, incidentally, on a 1.3-litre iron block – sat vertically, and well back towards the bulkhead. Long inlet tracts were on the right side, stainless steel exhaust manifolding was on the left, and the bulky KKK turbocharger was towards the front left of the compartment, feeding pressured air to the largest air/air intercooler that Zakspeed could find, which was up front where a water radiator might normally be located. By 1980 not one, but two, intercoolers were fitted.

The ubiquitous ZF gearbox, and the broad-beamed live axle were familiar Capri stuff, as was the general layout of the suspension – MacPherson strut at the front, and a live axle located by radius arms and a Watts linkage at the rear, along with the adjustable height Bilstein strut and damper bodies that every serious Ford competition car seemed to use in the 1970s and 1980s – yet almost every component of every installation was updated, made more specialized, and idealized for the occasion.

The cast alloy wheels, centrally-locked German BBS as on the earlier 'works' RS2600s and RS3100s, were colossal. Fronts were 16in diameter with 10.5in wide rims, while at the rear they were no less than 19in diameter with

14in rims. Goodyear, which supplied the tyres, had a hard time, not in dealing with road holding demands, but in coping with up to 600bhp.

The same, too, went for the brakes, disc all round of course and originally evolved by Ate for use on the Porsche 917s of the early 1970s, and using four pistons per calliper. Water cooling for the brakes was used for some of the high-speed circuits where slowing the car from high speed for slow corners was regularly needed.

High speeds? Oh yes! Even with the 'small' 1.4-litre engine there was so much power, and such an aerodynamically efficient style, that this Zakspeed monster could be geared to reach more than 170mph (273km/h). Later, when the 600bhp/1.7-litre version of the engine was employed, that top speed could be well over 180mph (290km/h).

And where in Germany could these cars even approach such speeds? Think of the extremely long straights at the Hockenheim circuit (where today's F1 cars exceed 200mph/ 322km/h) and at the Norisring, and this becomes very clear.

They were incredibly quick in all conditions of course, and if you can't get your minds around the bald figures, try this for a comparison. Everyone on this side of the English Channel knows about the Rouse/Trakstar/Eggenberger style of Sierra RS500 Cosworth – yet the 1.7-litre Zakspeed Capri had at least 50bhp more power, weighed about 660lb (300kg) less, had effective front and rear aerodynamic aids *and* had a much lower drag coefficient. Around the old Nürburgring circuit, all 14 miles (22.5km) of it, the ultimate development of the 1.7-litre Zakspeed was 51 seconds faster *per lap* than a 'works' RS3100.

Even so, a bare description of the mechanical layout doesn't tell the whole story, for these were machines that were almost alive, and definitely had a character of their own. So much more powerful than any race car that Zakspeed had ever before produced, they needed to be tamed, and mastered, to give of their best.

Heroes who regularly drove them to their flame-spitting limits included Harald Ertl,

Heyer, Klaus Ludwig, Klaus Niedzwiedz and Manfred Winkelhock. Since it was the two Klauses who later got together to make the Eggenberger Sierra RS500 Cosworths into such formidable saloon car racers, perhaps we now know where they got their high power output training!

600bhp Capris! Have you ever seen faster ones?

Two Types

Two different types of Zakspeed Capri were produced in 1979 and 1980. Because a 1.4 multiplier 'factor of comparison' was applied to turbocharged engines at this time, a 1.4-litre car was produced to meet the '2-litre' category limits, and a 1.7-litre car to act as a '2.5-litre' machine:

1.4-litre: Iron block BDA, 1427cc (80mm bore × 71mm stroke), KKK turbocharger, 1.5 bar boost. 460bhp at 9,000rpm. Top speed – up to 174mph (279km/h)

1.7-litre: Iron block BDA, 1746cc (87.4mm bore × 72.75mm stroke), KKK turbocharger, 1.5 bar boost. 560bhp at 9,000rpm. Top speed – up to 186mph (300km/h)

Long, Wide, Flat

This is how the Zakspeed Capris originally compared with a normal 3-litre Capri III of the period:

	Zakspeed race car	Capri 3-litre road car
Length	197.34	172.29
(in/mm)	(5,012)	(4,373)
Width	78	66.9
(in/mm)	(1,981)	(1,699)
Height	44.85	53.2
(in/mm)	(1,139)	(1,351)
Weight	1,740	2,578
(lb/kg)	(790)	(1,169)
	(1.4-litre)	

Four-Wheel-Drive Rallycross Cars

Do you remember those monstrous 'works' rallycross Capris of the early 1970s? The ones that always beat the opposition off the line, but which struggled to get round the first corner?

Henry Taylor, Ford's competition manager, 1965–69, takes most of the credit. Although the four-wheel drive (FWD) was still specifically banned from rallies, he wanted, at least, to start working out what it could do for him. In rallycross, where millions of people were currently watching TV's *World of Sport* races, there were no restrictions at all.

Well before the end of 1968 – and this was before the public even knew that the Capri was about to go on sale – Taylor somehow got his hands on a pre-production Capri 1600GT – 'just for a look-see'. Taylor recalls:

> I knew Tony Rolt very well … he was the managing director of Harry Ferguson Research – so I arranged for the Capri to be sent to him, in Coventry. Although we knew his four-wheel-drive system, with Dunlop Maxaret anti-lock braking, was bulky, and too heavy, we wanted to see what it would do.

By this time Harry Ferguson Research had already built about thirty Zephyrs with a FWD conversion, and had also supplied Dunton with two prototype Capris, complete with V6 engines and FWD (at a piece price, they say, of around £2,000 for the conversion job). During the winter of 1968/69, the very first competition V6 3-litre engined Capri took shape in Coventry, and in January it was returned to Boreham. After the 'works' mechanics had finishing preparation, the new car's engine had Weslake-modified cylinder heads and about 160bhp, though it still ran only on a single twin-choke Weber carburettor.

These Capris used what we call the 'classic' Ferguson Formula/FF layout. Behind the main gearbox, a step-off/transfer chain case moved the drive sideways, to a centre differential, from which the rear prop shaft pointed backwards as normal, while the front prop shaft led alongside the right of the engine to a front differential mounted alongside the sump.

Amazingly, the front and rear final drive ratios were slightly different – that at the rear being 4.63:1, that at the front being an Escort crown-wheel-and-pinion set of 4.71:1. The difference, actually of 1.7 per cent, did not seem to matter at all, especially on loose surfaces where there was wheel spin all the time.

Although several different torque splits could be used, Ford eventually settled on a 40:60 split, front to rear, as providing the best balance. This, in fact, was at the drivers' request, because it allowed them to start spinning the rear wheels before the front end broke traction – all the better for getting a Capri sideways on loose stuff.

The whole installation was heavy – Ferguson reckoned that there was an extra 171lb (77.5kg) of 'clobber' – and Boreham's mechanics had to design their own new front sub-frames to hold everything together. They also had to carve away at the floorpan to make space for the bulky centre transmission.

On 8 February 1969 – just days after the new Capri range had been unveiled – Boreham sent Roger Clark to contest a rallycross meeting at Croft, near Darlington. A year earlier, Clark had shown off the original Escort Twin-Cam at Croft. Now he would do the same with the Capri.

Quite simply, this appearance caused a sensation. The Clark/Capri/FWD combination won all three races that it started. Where there was good traction, this monstrous Capri was no quicker than its rivals – but on muddy going, where traction mattered, it was uncatchable.

Even so, apart from the FWD installation, this was still a very simple machine. Specification details included a 160bhp 3-litre V6, complete with Weslake cylinder heads and a different camshaft, rough-treaded Goodyear tyres on 7in-wide Minilite wheels, plastic side and rear window 'glass' and a glass-fibre bonnet, plus Taunus (front-wheel-drive type) front struts. Taunus? This was because the Taunus was then the only front-wheel-drive Ford in existence.

Four weeks later two Capri FWDs turned out at two different events. Ove Andersson drove the original Clark model at Croft (where he couldn't match a white-hot 'works' Mini-Cooper S), while at Lydden Hill Barry Lee was entrusted with a brand-new car, with automatic transmission. It was unfair to ask much of Lee, who had not driven the car before he met it in the paddock before practice. Unhappily, he crashed it when the system kicked-down at an inappropriate moment!

Only weeks after the first car had run, the FWD Capri had won its first rallycross race. Now with side exhaust pipes exiting under the driver's door, and with Roger Clark wearing his crash helmet, it looks altogether more purposeful.

Roger Clark couldn't wait to test the original FWD Capri rallycross car when it was finished. This first-day testing shot, taken at Boreham, shows Clark still in a business suit, and without a helmet …

… but he still had the commitment to get it all sideways …

… and corner it very hard indeed.

Four-Wheel-Drive Capris

Capris with FWD and smooth V6 power? Nowadays, with the technology tamed, that would be an exciting prospect, but in 1969 little was known about such installations, and things were very different. Ford Motorsport at Boreham decided to build such machines, but the results were not totally successful. The best way to summarize the FWD Capris that were used in rallycross is for me to quote Roger Clark from his best-selling autobiography *Sideways to Victory*:

> If ever there was a legendary beast it was the four-wheel-drive Capri, and if ever there was a car that didn't live up to its legend, this was it. The theory behind four-wheel-drive for a rallycross car was obvious – there ought to be that much more traction for starts and to sling you out of a muddy corner. That was the theory – the problem was that I don't think anyone had told the cars about it, and they didn't always behave themselves.

The original idea for making Capris FWD came from Competitions Manager Henry Taylor in 1968, and the first example was seen in early 1969. In rallies and in rallycross everyone knew that the Escorts and Cortinas of the day were all slow to get off the start line, with bad traction on muddy surfaces. This was about the time when Ferguson Research (which became FF Developments) had started co-operating with Ford, by building a handful of FWD Ford Zephyrs for possible use by the police and other emergency services.

Rallycross had become a popular TV sport, with excellent ratings, but the Escorts were sometimes being humiliated by the front-wheel-drive Minis. Even before the Capri was introduced, therefore, Henry Taylor got together with his colleagues at Dunton, approached Tony Rolt at Ferguson Research, and commissioned some rallycross 'Specials'. Since the Capri 3-litre used the same engine and manual gearbox as the Zephyr, not a lot of new engineering was involved. The basic layout, but none of the detail, would become familiar to XR FWD and Sierra/Escort Cosworth owners worldwide.

In the end, Ford built up three rallycross cars from bits supplied from Ferguson. All had 3-litre Essex V6 engines, two of them with 212bhp engines and Weber carburettors, which Clark's brother Stan usually drove, but one – specifically built for Roger Clark to tame – ended up as a 3.1-litre, with Weslake-modified cylinder heads, a high-stack Lucas fuel-injection system and something like 250bhp. It also had a large and unsightly bulge in the bonnet, which surrounded the inlet stacks.

To tame the power, Boreham then decided to use an early-type ZF five-speed gearbox to which the Ferguson FWD system (giving a familiar torque split of 37 per cent front, 63 per cent rear) was grafted. Modified front uprights from the front-wheel-drive German Taunus 12M were fitted – and later experience showed that it was the front drive shafts that broke so often to cripple the cars. The front axle had a 4.7:1 Escort ratio, while the rear axle had a slightly different axle ratio of 4.63:1. The slight difference in ratio wasn't important for as Roger Clark wrote:

Roger Clark's younger brother, Stan, drove another of the FWD Capris in 1970–71 – and was very successful …

… sometimes having to battle it out, wheel to wheel, with Escorts like John Taylor's Haynes of Maidstone car.

For 1970–71, Boreham built the ultimate FWD Capri, with fuel-injection and long inlet trumpets. Here it is seen testing without protection for those trumpets …

… and here with a simple sheet metal protective tower round the trumpets. This was a very fast car, with problematic handling.

… it didn't matter much because all of the wheels were spinning all of the time. Actually we did try a rather different front ratio once, but that soon led to disaster. We had a limited-slip rear diff, but for some reason there was no limited-slip in the front. The Ferguson centre diff also had its own spin limiter as usual.

Although the cars were lightened as much as possible, with glass-fibre panels and with all the interior ruthlessly gutted, they were a lot heavier than standard. Even in racing form a typical car weighed 2,604lb (1,181kg). The traction was phenomenal, but the handling was problematic and, once again, to quote Roger Clark:

The record shows that the cars were competitive enough for Stan and I to drive fast, and in fact we won a championship in them. [This was the TV Rallycross Series of 1970–71, where Roger's car was sponsored by the *Sunday Express*]. But after just one season they were put away … basically we ditched them because they were an enormous amount of trouble, not just in reliability, which was dreadful enough, but because they were absolute pigs to handle. Four-wheel-drive was splendid from the start line, but in muddy conditions it was a different story. I hesitate to say it, but I never mastered those Capris, not even after a full winter with them. They had minds of their own, and they changed their minds far too often.

You could also get into a situation, sometimes, where the front wheels were sliding about on mud, and you just didn't know which way to turn the steering wheel for the best. Sometimes everything happened beautifully, and we could get out of a corner in a full-power four-wheel-drift with big silly grins on our faces. There was that tremendous noise too, but get it wrong and – Oh boy!

For Capri lovers this was a short and exciting period, but after 1971 Ford ditched the project and sold off the remains to Rod Chapman who tried hard to recapture the excitement, but somehow never made it. At least one car survives to this day.

Interlude

Everything then went quiet at Boreham. Clark complained loud and long about the car's handling and its brakes, demanding that the crude anti-lock mechanism be disconnected. Henry Taylor soon accepted that the performance of the much-vaunted Dunlop Maxaret braking system – an anti-lock system that was being used on aircraft – could easily be beaten by skilled drivers.

Because rallycross was essentially a bad-weather, winter activity, this meant that the very special Capri would not be able to shine again before the end of 1969. In the meantime, prototype Capris shown to the world's press had also previewed Cosworth's all-new 16-valve 1.6-litre BDA engine. Amazingly, at that stage, Boreham had had little to do with the evolution of the BDA, and Hayes's original hope was to see it used in the Capri in due course.

Team Entry

By the autumn of 1970, the original Capri FWD rallycross cars had been joined by others. During the winter of 1970/71, three FWD Capris were prepared and further developed for use in the ITV/Castrol rallycross season and at Lydden Hill. One of these, certainly, was the original car that had appeared briefly in February 1969.

All three cars now used fuel-injected Essex V6 engines on which a lot of power-raising development work had been carried out: both Lucas and TJ systems were employed. Two cars, for Stan Clark and Chapman to drive, had about 212bhp (this was later massaged up to nearer 230bhp), while Roger Clark's ferocious machine used specially designed aluminium cylinder heads, straight-tube Lucas fuel-injection – and boasted a very healthy 252bhp. This car needed a massive 'tower' on top of the bonnet to hide the inlet trumpets, which rather spoilt the styling of the car itself.

The ever-inventive Mick Jones (who, by this time, had taken over from Bill Meade as Boreham's rally engineer) would eventually have many rude things to say about these cars, but did a great job with what was still a very crude FWD installation. By this time it was mated to an early version of the ZF five-speed main gearbox that had been adopted on the 'works' Escorts.

Interestingly enough, these were apparently the first FWD systems ever to use an FF viscous coupling limited-slip device. Nothing was ever admitted about this at the time, and it would not be unveiled for some years. These, by the way, were the first 'works' cars from Boreham to use Dunlop tyres for some years, for this was a separate Stuart Turner-inspired contract, and the rally team's contract with Goodyear was still in force.

It was a troublesome campaign. Cars were entered in two different TV series, which ran to different sets of rules. In the six-round Castrol-sponsored ITV series at Cadwell Park, in Lincolnshire, the Capris usually won if they did not hit mechanical trouble, because their FWD system was not handicapped. If they could harness their superior traction off the line (and this was usually possible) they could arrive at the first corner in the lead, then control the races.

In this Championship, the result was a perfect 1-2-3 in the standings, with Roger Clark leading the list, narrowly from Chapman, and with Stan Clark ('my fat little brother') bringing up the tail.

At Lydden Hill, in the Thames Estuary AC series, the Capris were always obliged to start 5 seconds behind their rivals, which was a grave handicap. This meant that there was always an unseemly overtaking battle to be tackled. Not easy, particularly in awful visibility! This, along with the fact that all three cars were unreliable and it was obvious to us, from the sidelines, that they were difficult to drive, meant that they struggled. In the end, Chapman's car could only finish fifth in the Championship, with Roger Clark eighth and Stan Clark tenth.

The records, therefore, show that if there was no unfair organizers' attempt to cut away at their advantage, then the cars did what they were asked to do, but none of the drivers really enjoyed them and there were many mechanical dramas to cope with. If it wasn't overheating due to mud blocking up the radiators, it was a tendency to break front-wheel-drive shaft joints, and all the engines suffered repeatedly from fuel-injection problems. Those were the days when Essex V6 cylinder blocks were none-too-strong, and when revved very highly, several units were destroyed.

After one very hectic winter the Capris (and their drivers!) were virtually worn out, and Ford sold off the remains to Stan Clark and Chapman during 1971.

As Roger later commented: 'It's vital to get the car into the right attitude way before a corner. If you can get that right, it's perfect, but more often it'll be wrong and you'd just wind up with more and more understeer lock'.

In addition they were heavy, and there was a lot of friction in the transmission system, so they were not as fast as the original forecasts had suggested. Monsters? Oh yes, and like all monsters, they eventually became extinct.

7 Capri III, From 1978

Maybe it was time for a change, but all except Ford insiders were surprised to see that a new version of the Capri – universally known, if not badged, as the Capri III – came along in March 1978. It was, after all, only four years since the original hatchback Capri II had been launched, and sales of that car had always been good

No matter. At this point in history, Ford's market share was booming as never before (in the UK the brand was easily the market leader, regularly taking more than 30 per cent of registrations), and although European cost inflation was still too high (soaring energy costs had much to do with this) Ford thought it could afford to invest in significant changes to all its models

Not that this happened in a haphazard way. This brief summary of major new private-car models which poured out of Ford-of-Europe in the mid- and late 1970s emphasizes just how busy the company actually was:

February 1974	Introduction of the new Capri II
January 1975	Introduction of the Escort Mk 2
Spring 1976 (Europe)	
October 1976 (UK)	
	Introduction of the Cortina Mk IV
July 1976	Introduction of the all-new front-wheel-drive Fiesta range
September 1977	Introduction of the new Granada/Scorpio range
– then, six months later:	
March 1978	Introduction of the Capri III

As ever, Ford's product planners, stylists and engineers had thought long and hard about the changes they wanted to make to the Capri. Stylists, naturally, would have liked to produce yet another completely new hatchback shape, but those who did all the investment calculations vetoed that idea at once. Accordingly, the recently knighted Sir Terence Beckett (aided and gleefully abetted by his sales director, Sam Toy) sent them all away to think again. The brief, apparently, was: 'Do as much as you can, but don't spend any money!'

In the end, the emphasis was on trimming the style so that the car looked different (a four-headlamp nose would help but more of that later), along with subtle aerodynamic changes to bring down the drag coefficient that should, by definition, help to provide better fuel economy. After 1973, when the Arab nations had shocked the world by applying oil embargoes, which precipitated the first Energy Crisis, wind-tunnel testing to achieve that end had always been a priority at Ford.

What became known as 'Carla' – the Ford project code for the Capri III and, as before, a name borrowed from one of the secretaries who worked within the management hierarchy – therefore began to take shape in people's minds, even before the building of prototypes started. By 1976 everyone at Dunton really knew where they wanted the development to lead, this being signalled by a front and rear spoilered project version of the Capri II that appeared at the Geneva Motor Show in March that year. This, in fact, was too angular to be considered as a production possibility, but at least it showed that Ford was thinking.

Generally accepted as the show car that influenced changes made to the Capri II to turn it into Capri III was the Modular Aerodynamic show car, which first appeared at the Geneva Motor Show in March 1976.

By modern, twenty-first century standards, the drag coefficient of early Capris had been quite appalling, though Ford was not ashamed of it at the time. The coefficient figure usually quoted for the Capri II was, of course, 0.428, and the aim for the Capri III, which became an official project in 1976–77, was to get it down below 0.400.

Kitting Out the New Range

By this time, Ford-UK was reasonably happy with the range of engines and transmissions that it had finalized in the Capri II. As ever, it was preparing to launch the Capri III with engines as small as the 57bhp/1298cc Kent, and as large as the brawny 138bhp/2994cc Essex V6. Automatic transmission was to be optional with most engines.

Many trendy, sporty-minded people still sneered at the idea of a 1.3-litre Capri, but the sales figures continued to prove them wrong. In 1976 (when the Capri III was being finalized) no fewer than 9,691 such cars had been built. On its own, of course, this could never make such a range profitable, but it contributed

10 per cent of all sales, and was therefore justified.

Similarly, it had always been fashionable to talk up the attraction of the big 3-litre engined cars, yet in the mid-1970s these were the slowest-selling of all types. The best-selling Capri at this time, no question, was the 1.6-litre Pinto-engined type, while sales of 2.8-litre V6-engined cars purely to the USA were also very healthy.

Visually and mechanically, therefore, much of the work that went into turning the Capri II into the Capri III was concentrated on making detail style and shape changes to the bodywork. Not only did design engineers led by Uwe Bahnsen want to update the looks of the car (though they were not being allowed to make sweeping changes to panel shapes), but they wanted to reduce the aerodynamic drag too.

Fortunately for Ford, this did not mean starting from scratch. In the early 1970s an active and very successful high-profile motor racing programme (using earlier type RS2600s and RS3100s) had already proved that the hoary old cliché about 'racing improves the breed' was true. An enormous amount of basic aerodynamic development and wind-tunnel work on the 'works' race cars, which were of course based in Cologne (I have described them in Chapter 4) had already shown just what worked and what did not. Accordingly, when a programme of road-car wind-tunnel work got underway in late 1974, Ford already thought they knew what work would be worthwhile.

At the same time, too, the marketing specialists were beginning to press for changes to the front-end style – in particular for four circular headlamps to take the place of the big rectangular lamps found on most previous Capris. To summarize, all Capris sold in the USA had always been fitted with four circular headlamps, while the same feature had appeared on RS2600 and RS3100 models, plus the 3000GXL from late 1972–74. Although these always looked smarter than the same cars fitted with two big rectangular headlamps, they were also considerably more expensive and did not provide dramatically better lighting.

Also, by the mid-1970s there was growing customer resistance to rectangular headlamps (which were, let me remind you, fitted to *all* European-market Capri IIs), so the big decision for the new car was therefore taken. All Capri IIIs, for every market, would have the same four-headlamp nose, and even though the accountants apparently complained about this, their concern over increased prices was over-ruled.

At the same time as specifying four circular headlamps, what we then recognized as the new corporate grille structure was also adopted. Whereas Capri IIs had used mesh grilles between the headlamps, the new car was to have what Ford described as a louvred aerofoil radiator grille, which comprised a number of horizontal aerofoil-profile slats fixed on top of each other. Looking neat in black plastic, this created less drag than before. Not only that, but at the same time the front edge of the massive front bonnet pressing was lengthened, being

Although this 3.0S appears to have two-tone yellow paintwork, this is merely a quirk of the studio lighting. Compared with the Capri II, the only basic visual changes were to bumper profiles and tail lamps, while the transverse spoiler was now standard on all models.

pushed slightly forward so that it not only made the entire style look that important bit more sleek, but it provided enough cover over the headlamps to eradicate any upwards dazzle.

In and around all this style innovation, two other features were developed and eventually adopted. A chin spoiler was added under the front bumper and a rubberized transverse rear spoiler was added to the rear edge of the hatchback.

It was not enough, however, just to decide that these were needed, to shape some in the studios, and then to fit them without further testing, for badly-detailed spoilers could increase the drag – which was absolutely not what Ford wanted to achieve!

At the front of the car, the object of using a chin spoiler was to divert any air that would otherwise have gone underneath the car, where it would become turbulent and add to the overall drag. As RS2600 and RS3100 motor racing experience had already shown, it had been tempting to provide a very large spoiler, which worked, but which brought ground clearance problems with it and, if executed badly, would actually increase the drag by acting as an air-plough.

Much patient testing was needed before Ford arrived at an acceptable shape – acceptable, that is, to the design and styling experts and the body and mechanical engineers. Once finalized, the same nose – four headlamp, spoiler and big front bumper – was standardized for

each and every version of the Capri built from 1978–86. Previous Capri II S types had used plastic add-on spoilers, but in this case the steel pressing was to be standard on all types, and welded into place on initial assembly.

Once again, it was not ostensibly as easy as it looked to develop a rubberized transverse spoiler on the rear edge of the big hatchback panel. However, Ford, at least, had become expert in this area – not only in developing the spoiler for the RS3100, but also in producing a similar component for the Escort RS Mexico, RS1800 and RS2000 models.

For Capri III, incidentally, the spoiler would only be standard on S models, and not even optional on other types. However, since no changes to the hatchback lid were needed (except for the piercings), it was easy enough for a private owner to buy a spoiler from his Ford parts stockist and to have his car updated into an S 'look-alike' and many did just that.

Makeover at Front, Rear and Sides

Accordingly, when the Capri III made its bow in March 1978, it looked much the same as before, though from every aspect there had been changes, which, Ford expected, would make it all the more saleable for the next few years.

At the front end, the combination of four circular headlamps (instead of two rectangular slabs), a lengthened and subtly re-profiled bonnet panel that slightly overhung the headlamps

To launch the Capri III, Ford invited journalists to drive the car in picturesque surroundings in France. This 3-litre S is quite overwhelmed by the chateau behind it.

The author sampling a 2000S on the press launch, in France, in February 1978. It was as a result of this session that he ordered a new car for business use.

themselves, the horizontally-slatted front grille, the new under-bumper chin spoiler and full wrap-around black bumpers all made this car look different from the Capri II. Even so, by Ford standards, these were low-investment changes and easy to make: this was proved by the way that Ford Motorsport provided easily fitted conversion kits for race car competitors, to turn competitive Capri IIs into Capri IIIs without changing the chassis or running gear.

There were two different new treatments along the flanks – and visually neither of these was particularly successful. S types – 1600S, 2000S and 3000S – got a brash new sticker that visually linked front and rear bumpers, with a

letter 'S' in place just ahead of the rear wheel-arch cut-out. All very well and good, except that the new sticker was truly horizontal, whereas the existing body shell crease along the same flanks was not.

Other models in the range got a wide, black plastic rubbing strip on the flanks, which linked front and rear bumpers. This, at least, lined up well, but was not the prettiest styling feature of the car. Laminated windscreens, incidentally, had now been standardized on all types.

At the rear, the only important change was to the tail lamps, which had the then-fashionable horizontal ribbing on the plastic lenses (Ford called these self-cleaning, but, as a Capri owner

The changes made to update Capri II to Capri III were most obvious, and most pleasing, when viewed from the front of the car. On the S models, the decal along the flanks was always a controversial feature.

151

Ford made much of the conversion to four headlamps on the Capri III – which were carefully positioned to hide under the front end of a lengthened bonnet pressing.

Styling studio detail of the Capri III, showing the paired headlamps, the longer bonnet pressing, the more massive bumpers, and the turn indicators now recessed into those bumpers. This was the most integrated solution so far found on this ever-popular Ford coupé.

of the day, I can tell you that was wishful thinking!) and, as already noted, a horizontal spoiler was fitted to S-types.

All this, indeed, had combined to reduce the overall drag. Ford claimed an average improvement of 6 per cent, and no less than 12.6 per cent on S/spoiler-equipped types. The very

best Capri III had a Cd rating of 0.374, the rest of the range 0.403, while we now know that the Capri II figure (without front spoiler) had been 0.428. Naturally Ford claimed that this would improve the fuel consumption and/or the maximum speed figures, but these changes were only marginal.

Capri III S models all had this broad decal along their flanks, which never seemed to sit quite right with existing panel creases. Die-hard Capri enthusiasts tended to have them removed, but the author costed this out on his own car and decided against it!

On the Capri III, Ford claimed that the new, larger, tail lamp clusters were 'self-cleaning'. In fact they paid homage to a style recently introduced by Mercedes-Benz.

As ever, there were two different types of facia on the Capri III. This was the 'entry-level' type, with only two main dials, a three-spoke steering wheel and a simple centre console …

… while S and Ghia models used this more completely equipped six-dial panel. Note the optional automatic transmission on this S model, still a rarity, but at least very suited to the 3-litre V6 engine.

Some called them 'tennis racquet' front seat head-rests – but Ford's practical reason for fitting them to the Capri III was to improve visibility for rear-seat passengers. Personal experience on the author's car proved the worth of this fitting.

Inside the car, the changes and improvements were mainly visual – which is to say that the facia/control layout was still the same

as it had basically been since 1972–73. However, the RS-style sports steering wheel on all except Ghia types was of a smaller diameter than before, and the seats had been re-shaped and made more comfortable. Head restraints now featured mesh-type inserts (so that rear visibility was marginally improved), Recaro seats were optional on S models, and a fold-up parcel shelf/luggage stowage cover had been standardized on GL, S and Ghia types: at a stroke, this seemed to discourage casual vandalization by opportunists who had been able to see what was being carried in the back.

A sliding steel sun-roof was optional, and proved to be very popular. Other long-established accessory manufacturers marketed roofs too, which involved brutal surgery being applied to the roof panel after delivery. How do I know? Because in 1978 I had a Webasto roof fitted to my own 2000S.

As on the last of the Capri IIs, the Capri III came with a choice of five different engines, the option of Ford C3 automatic transmission on all but the 1300 type, and with power-assisted rack-and-pinion steering on the 3000S/3000 Ghia types. This was the line-up:

Did you like the tartan seat cover style on the Capri III? It was very fashionable at the time, and certainly brightened up an otherwise conventional interior.

1300/1300L	1298cc Kent, overhead-valve	57bhp @ 5,500 rpm
1600L/GL	1593cc Pinto, single overhead-camshaft	72bhp @ 5,200 rpm
1600S	1593cc Pinto, single overhead-camshaft	88bhp @ 5,700rpm
2000S/Ghia	1993cc Pinto, single overhead-camshaft	98bhp @ 5,200rpm
3000S/Ghia	2994cc Essex V6, overhead valve	138bhp @ 5,000rpm

Each engine was matched to a familiar manual gearbox (the 1300's box was Escort-related, the 3000's box was Granada-related, while other types used the German-built type of gearbox whose ratios had originally been seen on Cortina III/Escort RS2000 types early in the 1970s). The Ford C3 automatic transmission (still an option) was fitted to an increasing proportion of V6-engined cars. Cast alloy wheels were standard on S and Ghia types.

Note that in a rather humiliating climbdown, Ford had abandoned the economy setting of the small 1.3-litre Kent engine that had been imposed on Capri owners in 1976. This had always been a sales flop, and was not continued – Ford's customers, it seemed, might have understood what the Energy Crisis was all about, but they were not about to give up a little bit of performance, even at this level!

Compared with the last of the Capri IIs (there was no overlap on the assembly lines), prices of the Capri III were very slightly increased. In the absence of any ground-breaking mechanical innovations, Ford made much of the way they had increased service intervals (12,000 miles/19,300km instead of 6,000 miles/9,650km on the Capri II). It was because the cars still looked so familiar to seasoned Capri-watchers, with running gear that was mainly unchanged, Ford could not offer them with any new type of whiz-bang advertising.

Plenty of under-bonnet space for the overhead-camshaft Pinto engine in Capri III types. The Capri was always an easy car to service and maintain.

V6 engines also slotted comfortably into the Capri engine bay, which was long and comfortably wide, too. The alternator sticks out towards the top right of the engine.

S derivatives of Capri III had this new style of eight-spoke cast alloy road wheels.

Original Capri III Prices in the UK –
March 1978

Model	Engine size/ power	UK retail price
1300	1298cc/57bhp	£2,848
1300L	1298cc/57bhp	£2,997
1600L	1593cc/72bhp	£3,178
1600GL	1593cc/72bhp	£3,446
1600S	1593cc/88bhp	£3,916
2000GL	1993cc/98bhp	£3,644
2000S	1993cc/98bhp	£4,035
2000 Ghia	1993cc/98bhp	£4,697
3000S	2994cc/138bhp	£4,422
3000 Ghia	2994cc/138bhp	£5,337

(Automatic transmission extra (standard on the 3999 Ghia) optional at £253.)

Instead, the display advertising campaign was led by the headline: 'The difference between driving and just motoring'. Not only this, but the copy emphasized the versatility of the car by stating: 'With the two rear seats folded down there is a massive 22.6cu ft of luggage space between you and the wide rear door. We've even seen a wheelbarrow in the back of a Capri. There can't be many more awkward shaped objects than that'.

Hatchback open, rear seats folded forward, and all the loading space on view. The Capri III really was a very practical machine – the author regularly used to carry his wife, two growing children and two bulldogs in the Capri III without feeling too overcrowded!

Capri III on the Road

No sooner had the Capri III been introduced than every UK-based dealer seemed to have cars ready to sell. This was wise, for annual British Capri sales had usually seemed to potter along at the same sort of rate – between 35,000 and 40,000 – though a low point had come in 1975. Once again, however, a combination of novelty, and the fact that insurance companies still treated the Capri as a saloon car rather than a sports model, gave the new model a boost, for in 1979 no fewer than 49,147 Capris would be registered, which was an all-time record for this model.

Writing about the 2000S (the same model that the author was just about to acquire, incidentally) in the week in which it was launched, *Motor* magazine noted that the: 'Third generation Capri benefits by aerodynamic aids and subtle mechanical modifications which have made it faster and more economical than before. Engine noise mars an otherwise likeable entertaining hold-all'. 'Faster' translated as a top speed of 107mph (172km/h), which was maybe 2mph better than before, while the car returned 26.8mpg (10.5ltr/100km) over the entire run of the test, which the magazine thought was good. Testers clearly liked the front-end style because: 'Night visibility is much improved by the adoption across the range of a four halogen headlamp system which was most effectively cleaned on our test car by bumper-mounted pressure jet washers costing £56'.

In the very same week, *Autocar* published its thoughts on a 3000S, writing that it offered 'fantastic value for money', but that this particular car suffered from poor fuel consumption. The conclusion, though, was more upbeat:

> It would be difficult to find an excuse for not buying one or other version of the 3-litre Capri if one is seeking value for money and close-on 120mph [193km/h] performance. It is at least £1,000 cheaper than any comparable car and, disregarding the extrovert exterior finish and strangely poor fuel consumption, has the advantage over its rivals of being totally practical and unfussy transport … It remains a hard act for anyone to follow.

No, don't get too excited – the '220' markings on this Capri III speedometer are in km/h.

Simple, reliable, front-wheel disc brakes on the Capri III. Few people had any cause to complain about the braking performance of their Capris – unless, of course, they super-tuned the engines to go racing.

Even so, it was interesting to see that Ford still liked its customers to load up their new cars from the lengthy options list, for the 3000S came equipped with a remote control driver's mirror (£22.70), a tilt-and-slide sun-roof (£146), a pair of Recaro front seats (£75.84)

and pressure headlamp washers (£56.14). All of which was very easy and very tempting for a Capri customer to do.

Perhaps the Capri had now been around for too long for anyone to expect any worthwhile mechanical changes to be made in the months and years that followed. Capri customers were obviously moving slowly, but steadily, up-market, for demand for the 'entry-level' 1300 was falling right away. Only 3,070 1300s of both types would be built in launch year, 1978, and well before the end of that year the 'base' 1300 was dropped completely: thereafter the range started from the base of the 1300L.

However, Ford's ever-astute marketing staff always seemed to have something new to talk about in terms of new equipment, as season followed season. Chronologically, therefore, it's worth noting what happened and when – though I have held back a description of the handful of special/limited-edition types that arrived during the 1970s, which are described separately in the following pages:

- In 1979, 1300L/1600L models gained a radio as standard, 1600S/2000S types got rear fog lamps and the 2000/3000 Ghia types got upgraded radio-cassette players.
- From April 1979, there were more up-grades, the most noticeable of which was

This was what Capri motoring was (or should have been) all about – fast touring, in fine weather, in fabulous scenery. More than 1.9-million buyers eventually subscribed to that dream.

Ford continued to promote the X-Pack add-on equipment for the Capri III. This was a typically-equipped 3000S, complete with flared arches, big front and rear spoilers and special wheels.

the standard fitting of twin-door mirrors, a sports (three-spoke) steering wheel, and high-pressure headlamp washers for the 2000/3000 Ghia.

- From October 1979, there was one significant mechanical change, when a viscous cooling fan was standardized on all the 4-cylinder cars. This was done to rationalize the engines, to bring them in line with the changes being made for the arrival of what we now know as the Cortina Mk V (though Ford never advertised it as such). The result, a minor improvement worth having, was that the 1300 gained 3bhp, the 1600GL just 1bhp, and the 1600S and 2000S types gained 3bhp. Over in Germany (but not sold in the UK, of course), the Capri 2300 was boosted from 108bhp to 114bhp, a really worthwhile improvement, though internal engine changes were also made for that power unit.

- In February 1980, the 1600S was dropped at the same time as the GT4 limited-edition car (*see* below) arrived.

- In January 1981, the 1600LS was introduced, in equipment this effectively being a halfway-house between the 1600L and the 1600S, with the same engine as the 1600L.

- In January 1982, the last of the small-engined Capris, the 1300L, was finally laid to rest – and for those who think it was never worth producing, let me remind you that that no fewer than 202,000 1.3-litre Capris had been made in thirteen years – a highly-profitable operation.

- Also during 1982 (and with the 2.8i now taking most of the media's attention, as described in the following chapter), Ford cut back ruthlessly on the number of different Capris. Out went the 1600L, the 1600GL, the 2000GL and the 2000 Ghia – leaving only the 1600LS, the 2000S, the 2.8i – and, of course, the special-edition types that had become so important to Ford's marketing activities.

A perfect way to promote the X-Pack was to line up a car alongside Britain's most successful racing Capri – Gordon Spice's Autocar-sponsored 3000S of 1978.

Two ways of showing off the X-Pack on these cars, one with extra decals on the flanks and ...

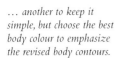

... another to keep it simple, but choose the best body colour to emphasize the revised body contours.

Special Editions ...

Seasoned (or shall I say cynical?) motor industry watchers always know that a range of cars needs a boost if special editions start to appear. As far as the Capri was concerned, this had first occurred with the Midnight models of 1975, as described in Chapter 5, but the big rush of 'Specials' came in 1980–84, when version after version of 1600 and 2000 types appeared.

Mechanically, all such cars were the same as those on which they were based, the novelty being in the dress-up package and the perceived extra value put on offer for a short time. In their own way, all such special editions have made their name with latter-day classic Capri owners, so this is a summary of what was available, and when:

GT4: this model was unveiled in February 1980, and was based on the 72bhp/1600L model. Fitted out with the S-type facia and instrument display, it also had twin coach-lines along the flanks (which feathered into almost an arrow motif close to the tail lamps) and a more emphatic bonnet decal. It was priced at £4,375.

Cameo, Tempo, and Calypso: this trio of special editions were based on the 1300L/ 1600L (Cameo), 1600L (Tempo) and 1600LS (Calypso) of the period, and introduced in July 1981.

The Cameo was a stripped-out, bargain-basement model based on the 1300L and 1600L chassis, with a side tape stripe replacing the plastic body moulding, a rubber mat instead of a boot carpet, and a lack of rear parcel

160

Opening rear quarter windows – optional on some models, standard on top-of-the-range and limited-edition types – were always popular on these cars.

The GT4 limited edition was a very successful short-run model. Here it is seen, in ideal studio conditions, with a Zakspeed Turbo Capri poster on the wall.

tray, centre console, clock or radio. Only 1,500 of both types were made, priced at £3,995 (1300 version) and £4,250 (1600 version) – both nearly £500 less than the mainstream models.

The Tempo was based on the 1600L and was also a stripped-out model, in the same way as the Cameo.

The Calypso was a much more up-market car, based on the existing 1600LS, with extra equipment including head restraints for the seats, tinted glass, rear wiper-wash and a rear carpet in the boot. Not only that, but there was unique duo-tone paint treatment – all this costing £5,120 (which was just £194 more than the standard 1600LS). Only 1,500 such models were produced, some of them with a £200 option pack that included a tilt-and-slide sun-roof, opening rear quarter windows, and a remote-control driver's door mirror.

And More, And More ...

Ford, by this time, was well into the swing of producing special editions of most of their cars (the Fiesta Supersport and the Cortina Crusader were similar dress-up jobs of the same period), so the success of these original special

Capris led them to produce another pair of cars in May 1982 – the Cabaret and Cabaret II. As before, these cars were both based on the 1600L or 2000GL:

Cabaret: this included a tilt-and-slide sun-roof, the rear spoiler normally found on S-derivatives, sports (steel) road wheels, a Ghia centre console, fabric trimmed seats, and the S/Ghia type of facia/instrument display complete with rev-counter, and tinted glass. With a choice of four two-tone solid colours, the 1600L Cabaret cost £5,106, the Cabaret 2000 £5,184.

Cabaret II: this was effectively the same car as the Cabaret, but had metallic paintwork, which cost an extra £108. Several run-out editions were produced to mark the end of Capri sales on continental Europe in early 1984.

Laser: it was not until June 1984 that another UK-market 'Special', the Laser, put in an appearance. This was based on the existing 1600 and 2000 chassis, mechanically unchanged as is the way with all such limited-edition cars, except that a five-speed manual gearbox was standard on the 2000 and optional on the 1600. Compared with the mainstream cars, a Laser had a colour-coded front grille, headlamp surrounds and door mirrors, an S-type tailgate

The Laser model was originally offered as a limited edition, but soon took over as a mainstream product in 1600 and 2000 form, and was built to the very end.

spoiler, four-spoke RS-style cast alloy wheels (with 185/70-section tyres), tinted glass, Laser-styling motifs, a leather gear-lever knob, a radio-cassette, a full S-type instrument panel and new trim.

Priced at £5,990 (1600) or £6,371 (2000) these were seen as real bargains, and were a great success. What had meant to exist only as a limited-production offer was so popular that Ford turned it in to a regular production line model almost at once, where the Laser replaced the 1600LS and the 2000S from mid 1984 – both these cars carrying on until the end of

Capri assembly in December 1986, the last cars being sold from Ford showrooms in 1987.

Fuel-Injection to Follow, and the Grand Finalé

As every Capri enthusiast surely knows, in March 1981 the range was completely rejuvenated by the arrival of the fuel-injected 2.8i model. This had such far-reaching consequences, and did so much to revive the image of the entire line-up of Capris, that it deserves a final chapter to itself.

Four new Capri IIIs grouped together; the message was that an entire range, not just one model, was available.

German-Market, German-Built Capri IIIs, 1978–81

As with British-market Capri IIIs, because overall sales had fallen (and looked like continuing to do so), the range of German-market Capri IIIs was more restricted than before.

Capri III assembly was concentrated on Cologne, with cars for the British market always outselling those for the German and European markets.

As is clear from the main text in this chapter, from 1978 UK-market Capri IIIs were built as 1300, 1600, 1600S, 2000 and 3000 models. Those built for Germany and the rest of Europe (which was now of very limited interest to the Capri marketing staffs) lined up as follows:

1300	1298cc, 4-cylinder, overhead-valve	54bhp @ 5,500rpm
1600	1593cc, 4-cylinder, overhead-valve	72bhp @ 5,500rpm
2000	1998cc V6, overhead-valve	90bhp @ 5,000rpm
2300	2293cc V6, overhead-valve	108bhp @ 5,100rpm
3000	2994cc V6, overhead-valve	138bhp @ 5,000rpm

Compared with the British-market cars, the familiar Cologne V6s – in 90bhp 2-litre and 108bhp 2.3-litre forms – continued. Maybe they were not as modern in layout as the Pinto 4-cylinder engine, but they were simple, easy to maintain, and smooth. German customers, and the dealer network, loved them – it was as simple as that.

As with the UK-market cars, there was an important engine re-shuffle in the autumn of 1979 (effectively, for the start-up of 1980 model year). To summarize:

1600	This was de-tuned to 68bhp @ 5,500rpm
2000	This V6-engined car ran through unchanged
2000	Effectively a 2000GT, this new type had a Pinto, 4-cylinder, overhead-camshaft engine, rated at 101bhp @ 5,200rpm

This range then carried on, gradually being reduced in scope after the 2.8i model, described in the following chapter, as follows:

- In 1981, the 1998cc V6-engined car was withdrawn, this leaving the Pinto-engined 2000 as the only 2-litre Capri III still on sale in Europe.
  As in the UK, with right-hand-drive cars, the 2994cc Essex 3-litre-engined car was dropped when the 2.8i model made its début. Late in the year, the last-ever 1300 Capri III was built, this model officially being withdrawn early in 1982.
- In 1983, the 1.6-litre model was withdrawn, though it carried on in right-hand-drive guise, for sale to the UK.
- In November 1984, left-hand-drive Capri assembly came to an end. From that time the Capri was therefore withdrawn from the German and related European markets.

2.3 Ghia? No. Never sold in the UK, but one of the most popular Capri III derivatives sold in Germany and the rest of Europe, where the Cologne V6 engine was a well-liked installation.

Capri III Specifications (1978–86): UK-Market Cars

Engines

1300 Kent
Layout	4-cylinder, in-line, overhead-valve
Bore × stroke	80.9 × 62.99mm
Capacity	1298cc
Compression ratio	9.2:1
Maximum power	57bhp @ 5,500rpm (60bhp @ 5,750rpm from 1979–80)
Maximum torque	67lb ft @ 3,000rpm (68lb ft @ 3.000rpm from 1979–80)
Fuel system	Ford/Motorcraft GPD carburettor

1600 Pinto
Layout	4-cylinder, in-line, single overhead-camshaft
Bore × stroke	87.65 × 66mm
Capacity	1593cc
Compression ratio	9.2:1
Maximum power	72bhp @ 5,500rpm (73bhp @ 5,300rpm from 1979–80)
Maximum torque	87lb ft @ 2,700rpm (86lb ft @ 2,700rpm from 1979–80)
Fuel system	Ford/Motorcraft GPD carburettor

1600S Pinto
Layout	4-cylinder, in-line, single overhead-camshaft
Bore × stroke	87.65 × 66mm
Capacity	1593cc
Compression ratio	9.2:1
Maximum power	88bhp @ 5,700rpm (91bhp @ 5,900rpm from 1979–80)
Maximum torque	92lb ft @ 4,000rpm
Fuel system	Weber compound dual-choke carburettor

2000GT Pinto
Layout	4-cylinder, in-line, single overhead-camshaft
Bore × stroke	90.8 × 76.95mm
Capacity	1993cc
Compression ratio	9.2:1
Maximum power	98bhp @ 5,200rpm (101bhp @ 5,200rpm from 1979/1980)
Maximum torque	112lb ft @ 3,500rpm
Fuel system	Weber compound dual-choke carburettor

3000GT Essex V6
Layout	6-cylinder, in 60-degree V, overhead-valve
Bore × stroke	93.66 × 72.44mm
Capacity	2994cc
Compression ratio	9.0:1
Maximum power	138bhp @ 5,100rpm
Maximum torque	174lb ft @ 3,000rpm
Fuel system	Weber compound dual-choke carburettor

2.8i Cologne V6
Layout	6-cylinder, in 60-degree V, overhead-valve
Bore × stroke	93 × 68.5mm
Capacity	2792cc
Compression ratio	9.2:1
Maximum power	160bhp @ 5,700rpm
Maximum torque	162lb ft @ 4,200rpm
Fuel system	Bosch K-Jetronic fuel-injection

Transmission

Gearbox	All synchromesh manual 4-speed. Optional 5-speed on 1600 and 1600S models from 1983. 5-speed standard on the 2000 from 1983, standard on 2.8i from 1983–84. Optional 3-speed automatic with 1600, 1600S, 2000 and 3000GT engines
Final drive	4.125:1 (1300), 3.89:1 (1300), 3.77:1 (1600), 3.75:1 (1600S), 3.44:1 (2000), 3.09:1 (3000GT/Ghia/S and 2.8i)

Suspension

Front	MacPherson strut, coil springs, anti-roll bar, telescopic dampers
Rear	Live axle, half-elliptic leaf springs, anti-roll bar, telescopic dampers
Steering	Rack and pinion (power-assisted on 3000 and 2.8i models)
Brakes	Disc front, drum rear, vacuum servo standard on all other types

Running Gear

Wheels	13in steel wheels, several styles, or cast alloy wheels on 1600S, 2000, 3000, and 2.8i models
Tyres	Radial-ply on all models from 165-section (1300) to 185/70 section (1600S, 2000, 3000 models). 205/60 section on 2.8i model

Dimensions

Wheelbase	100.8in (2,559mm)
Front track	53.3in (1,353mm)
Rear track	54.5in (1,384mm)
Length	172.3in (4,376mm)
Width	66.9in (1,698mm)
Height	52.1in (1,323mm)
Weight (unladen)	From 2,227lb (1,010kg) for the 1300, to 2,580lb (1,170kg) for the 3000, and 2,712lb (1,230kg) for the 2.8i

In 1981 and 1982, the Capri 2.8 Turbo was marketed as an officially-approved conversion by Ford-Germany. It was based on the Capri 2.8i, with the following differences:

Engine

Maximum power	188bhp @ 5,500rpm
Maximum torque	206lb ft @ 4,500rpm
Fuel system	Dual-choke compound Weber carburettor, and KKK turbocharger
Gearbox	All-synchromesh manual 4-speed. Optional automatic transmission not available.

Running Gear

Wheels	Cast-alloy wheels, 235/60VR-13in tyres

Dimensions

Width	70in (1,780mm)
Height	51in (1,295mm)
Weight (unladen)	2,695lb (1,225kg)

8 Capri 2.8 Injection – The Final Frontier

By the end of 1980 the Capri looked as if it was coasting towards retirement and, frankly, most of the media and many regular Ford customers were getting rather bored with it. The glory days of this sports coupé, it seemed, were now behind it, no important style changes had been made for some years, and it seemed to have lost its novelty value.

In marketing terms, the Unique Selling Proposition (USP) had dissolved. No longer sold in the USA (where a great number of sales had originally been made), it was no longer the glamorous car of the early 1970s. In Britain and in Europe, it was about to be rendered impotent in motor sport touring car racing because of proposed rule changes.

Production was sagging and the sales force was in despair. Down from 85,420 in 1979 to 41,755, it seemed as if demand would plunge even further. Then suddenly, the 2.8 Injection (2.8i) was introduced, and immediately rescued the image. And it at all started with a simple phone call from Germany to Dunton.

Although it wasn't Rod Mansfield who personally saved the Capri, it was his new department – Special Vehicle Engineering (SVE) – that provided that impetus. Having engineered several famous Escort RS models at the Advanced Vehicle Operation (AVO) in the mid-1970s, there had been no glamour for him since then, and he could see nothing exciting in the future. Until, that is, February 1980, when the phone rang: 'It was Gerhard Hartwig, chief engineer of vehicle engineering,' Rod recalls, 'asking me to found Special Vehicle Engineering. I thought for about three seconds, and said "Yes, please!"'

Special Vehicle Engineering

Rod Mansfield was an early Advanced Vehicle Operation (AVO) member, and was also responsible for setting up Ford's Special Vehicle Engineering (SVE) department in 1980.

From 1970, Mansfield worked for Bob Howe at AVO, replaced Henry Taylor in 1972, and later engineered all AVO products until that project closed in 1975. After five years in relative obscurity, he was suddenly asked to set up SVE.

SVE's brief was to develop cars that were more sporty and more specialized than those normally covered by Ford's engineering team. Like AVO before it, SVE was really a team within a team, though liaison with all other departments was maintained.

SVE's first successful projects were the Capri 2.8i and the original Fiesta XR2, these being followed by the original Escort XR3i and the Sierra XR4x4. Although SVE then worked on finalizing the still-born RS1700T, the next to go on sale (in 1984) was the first-generation fuel-injected Escort RS Turbo.

Other cars such as the Escort Cabriolet and the Sierra RS Cosworth were also important SVE projects, but serious work on the Escort RS Cosworth was a vital responsibility after 1989, and included several little-publicized 'why-don't-we...?' dabbles with rear-drive Escorts, some driven by Cosworth (Scorpio-type) 24-valve V6 engines.

Mansfield himself then enjoyed a colourful 1990s, which included spells at Aston Martin, setting up a SVE-like operation at Ford-USA, and even spending time as Managing Director of Lotus. However, SVE developed strongly without him, and worked on every fast and special Ford that the company announced thereafter.

The reason was simple. Since the Advanced Vehicle Operation (AVO) had closed down in 1975, Ford's sporting image had slipped back, and the marketing staff wanted that trend to be reversed. Even so, it was really Mike Moreton (who, let us remind ourselves, had product planned the RS3100 in 1973) who really sparked off that change. When Mike slipped back into Product Planning from AVO:

> I took what was left of AVO with me, which was virtually nothing, then wrote a Strategy Paper on 'Specialist Vehicles in Ford-of-Europe', pointing out that specialist cars could certainly be built at Saarlouis and in Cologne, but that they needed to be backed by a specialist engineering activity. I would argue that this was really the beginning of what became Special Vehicle Engineering.

That was thirty years – ago the SVE legend has grown steadily ever since then, and its list of completed projects is now long and proud. This team within a team not only developed other successful cars as remarkable as the 'whale-tail' Sierra RS Cosworth, the Escort RS Turbo and the Escort RS Cosworth, but had taken a hand in most of Ford's modern four-wheel-drive (FWD) projects, its cabriolets, and a number of strange but esoteric derivatives. Although SVE is still an important part of Ford's heritage, in a generation it changed almost beyond measure. Starting with no more than a dozen engineers, Mansfield rapidly built it up to more than fifty at its peak.

Small Beginnings

Initially, Mansfield's problems were time and money. There was never any difficulty in attracting engineers:

> Once they heard about SVE, I got a stream of applications to join ... Money, in the form of operating budgets, was always tight, as was time – because Sales and Marketing was crying out for fast, smart and sexy derivatives. Bright ideas, expansive ideas, and advanced ideas, would all have

to wait. Ford's product planners wanted to see results within a year – earlier if possible!

Even then, when cars were simpler to engineer, that was not easy, but Mansfield – the experienced negotiator, 'fixer' and runner of meetings – soon found a way. FWD, turbocharging and an even more exotic chassis would have to wait. The original SVE products, therefore, were cheap and cheerful – both the Capri 2.8i and the Fiesta XR2 went from 'good idea' status to the assembly lines in no more than a year – and in each case SVE had a flying start.

Conceived way back in AVO days in the mid-1970s but then cancelled ('This was the obvious successor to the Capri RS2600', Mike Moreton recalls), the Capri 2.8i was mainly a packaging job, while the XR2 was little more than a careful amalgam of US-specification Fiesta engineering and Fiesta Supersport styling.

But it got the show on the road, and immediately brought SVE to the motoring world's attention. Although these were, indeed, 'Specials', they didn't look that way. A 'Special' tends to look bitty, unfinished, raunchy, but somehow 'garden-shed' built, yet all the cars from SVE were as well detailed as any other new models coming from this major corporation, and that was one of their strengths.

Ford normally doesn't like to make personalities out of its engineers, but it made an exception in this case – for Rod Mansfield, the fluent talker, dinner-guest and symposium leader, was an ideal subject.

Within a year SVE was looking further into Ford's future, not initiating projects, but taking on those which mainstream engineering found too cumbersome. It was not long before SVE made a speciality of such activities – where administrative corners had to be cut, where favours had to be called in, and where deals had to be done, they were supreme.

This was where Mansfield shone. Disliked by some of his colleagues because of his high-profile reputation, he was the figurehead who built up SVE as a 'can-do' organization. There are those who said that he made a speciality of missing deadlines, but there are many more who admit that his enthusiastic team was superbly qualified.

Capri 2.8 Injection – First Thoughts

Developing the final high-performance Capri, the 2.8 Injection (2.8i), was as much about rummaging in the available Ford 'parts bin' as of developing new equipment. Not only was time very short (Ford meant what they said when they insisted on a new car being ready within a year), but the budget was low for new engineering. SVE's first priority, therefore, was to sit down, survey the state of the ageing 3-litre car, and see what could be done to improve it. In fact an unrelated prototype had been built at Ford-Germany Motorsport in 1977–78, so most of the physical 'can-it-fit?' problems were well-known.

Almost at once, it was decided that the old Essex 3-litre V6 engine should be abandoned.

By 1980, in any case, it was no longer being used in any other British Ford private car, for since 1977 the latest Granada range had always used Ford-Cologne V6 types instead. Economically, it made a lot of sense to drop the Essex, for once that was done, the manufacturing facility at Dagenham could be dismantled and all the specialized tooling could be moved out: in fact it was soon to be sent off to Ford-South Africa, where that engine would be used for several more years.

It was altogether typical of motor industry 'PR-speak' that Ford suggested that existing 3-litre S and Ghia types would carry on until early 1982 (when they would no longer be able to meet proposed European toxic emissions regulations), though this never happened in practice. We now know that the last 3-litre-engined Capri was built in April 1981, and the last showroom stocks were just moving out when the 2.8i arrived.

Almost automatically, therefore, the engine of the new car chose itself – the most powerful version of the 2792cc Cologne V6 that

The engine bay of the Capri 2.8i was well filled; all the Bosch hardware was shared with the Granada saloons of the period and therefore very familiar to Ford technicians and dealerships.

could be provided. Since this would be no more than a modified, enlarged and updated version of the 2.3-litre unit already being used in German-market Capri IIIs, SVE knew that they would not have a major packaging problem to resolve.

Wistful enthusiasts who still harked back to the RS2600 of the early 1970s looked for some form of rebirth in this car, though that car's 150bhp/2.6-litre version of the 'Cologne' engine was no longer made, as Ford no longer used Kugelfischer fuel-injection. Instead, it was decided to use a slightly up-rated version of the fuel-injected 2.8-litre derivative as used in Granada 2800i models: for the Capri it was to be rated at 160bhp at 5,700rpm.

For the Capri, this involved placing the major fuel-injection units towards the front nearside (nearside, that is, in the UK) of the engine bay, the engine being topped by a cast aluminium plenum chamber, in a particularly neat installation. Hidden away was an oil/water heat exchanger on the cooling side, and a large-bore twin-pipe exhaust system.

Compared with the old 3-litre, there was less peak torque – 162lb ft instead of 174lb ft – but as the new car was only to be made available with manual transmission, and was expected to be driven more vigorously, SVE was convinced that few customers would complain. Nor did they.

No changes were made to the transmission/drive line, which meant that the final drive ratio remained at 3.09:1, and here was the only minor problem with this car. If and where it was legally possible, on an open road, a Capri 2.8i could cruise easily at 100mph (161km/h), which equated to 4,700rpm. Did this make an extremely fast car seem slightly under-geared? Some owners (which included the author, who soon bought a new 2.8i) thought so – but at the time no one could have realized that SVE was already eyeing up the 5-speed gearbox that was being developed for the still-secret Sierra XR4i: when this was eventually fitted, with fifth gear acting as an overdrive, it made all the difference.

SVE, who were soon recognized as specialists in this sort of engineering, transformed the handling, not only by lowering the car by 0.8in (20mm) on its suspension, but by beefing up the front and rear springs, adding firmer anti-roll bars at front and rear and specifying Bilstein gas-filled struts and rear dampers. Not only that, but Wolfrace Sonic cast alloy wheels (the famous 'pepper-pot' style alloys) with 7in rims and Goodyear 205/60VR-13 tyres were fitted, along with ventilated front wheel disc brakes.

Inside the cabin, which was trimmed to 3-litre Ghia specifications, the only obvious change was that S-specification Recaro seats (with 'tennis racket' type head restraints) and a shorter gear lever (which gave the effect of a slicker, more sporty, gear change) were fitted. Power-assisted steering, of course, was standard.

Transformed? Most independent road testers thought so, and so did I. My personal opinion, it seems, lined up with that of many other long-time Capri enthusiasts – that I was no longer in love with the old 3-litre type, which neither handled well enough, nor was as quiet and refined as I now wanted. The new 2.8i, on the other hand, not only went faster than ever, but felt much more civilized while doing it – and the handling was considerably better balanced and responsive than the old 3-litre had been.

It was no wonder that *Autocar's* test report, written by John Miles, was positively glowing, for it summarized as follows, that:

> In terms of road holding, handling, refinement, looks and performance, the Capri 2.8 Injection is a vast improvement over the now rather agricultural-feeling Essex engined 'S' and Ghia, and shows how a simple down-to-earth concept (with the attendant relatively simple maintenance) can be kept more than competitive.

Ford revealed the new car in March 1981, with deliveries in Germany beginning soon afterwards, but UK-market deliveries did not begin until June. Priced at £7,995 – the last of the 3000S types had cost £6,220, the final 3-litre

When the 2.8i was introduced in 1981, it completely rejuvenated the Capri's image. This German-registered car shows off just how the handling had also been improved.

Ghia £7,334 – that price hike certainly did not deter buyers. Figures released many years later show that only 2,131 3-litre types had been sold in the whole of 1980, while no fewer than 5,747 of the 2.8i's were produced in 1981 (in which production did not begin until April–May of that year) and 4,091 would follow in 1982.

Other Capri derivatives died out at this time – the last 1.3-litre cars disappeared in 1982, the last 2-litre V6-engined cars (German market) were dropped in 1981, and all versions of the 1.6-litre and 2-litre cars except for the 1600LS and 2000S were also discontinued before the end of 1982, too.

From 1981, there were only three models in the Capri range. Much the most charismatic, though not the best-seller, was the new 2.8i (at the front of this group), which transformed the car's image.

Mean, moody and magnificent? Effective and fast too – this being the 2.8i of 1981.

Well, if you believe this, you'll believe anything. Although the police loved the Capri Injection for its performance, they could not stow as much emergency gear inside it as – say – in a Granada, or other competing saloon. Great picture though!

In the early 1980s, 'spy photographers' didn't have to go far to spot a new Ford being paraded for photography, for this was usually done on the A12 or the A127 close to the Dunton technical centre. Here was a pre-launch shot of a 2.8i and …

… a different car, caught by the same cameraman, on a different day, in a different location.

In the Meantime – Capri 2.8 Turbo

Even while SVE was finalizing the original Capri 2.8i, another version, similar but not the same, was being developed in Germany. Like the 2.8i, it would go on sale in 1981, but unlike the 2.8i it was only a short-term, limited-edition product.

Except in Germany and Switzerland, this, the turbocharged Capri, is the least known of all derivatives. It was only in production for a short time, it was only ever built in left-hand-drive form, and it was officially never sold in the UK. Nor was it well known in its native Germany, for only 200 were ever built, all of them being sold on the Continent.

Deep down, the 2.8 Turbo was intended to benefit from the great publicity garnered by the flamboyant Zakspeed 'silhouette' race cars of the late 1970s. Although the aerodynamic add-ons in the Turbo gave an impression of these two cars being related, in fact they had nothing in common. Even so, the 'halo' effect of one must surely have helped the other.

The key to this development was Zakspeed, the much-respected German tuning house based at Niederzissen, for all 200 cars were part fettled there, by modifying partly completed production Capri 2.8i body shells that had been transported from Cologne. The GRP wheel arches, in fact, were glued rather than riveted into place – which sometimes caused

Ford-Germany marketed this car, the 2.8 Turbo, purely for sale in Germany during the early 1980s, and only 200 such cars were produced. The engine featured a carburettor/turbocharged combination, and conversion was by Zakspeed. This shot was taken at the Nürburgring race circuit.

some quality problems, especially on finished cars. They were then returned to Cologne for completion.

It is important to realize, however, that these were *not* turbocharged versions of the 2.8i – for the Turbo had a carburetted engine. Except on the very first cars (which were 3000S types), the 'base' car, indeed, was a 2.8i Capri, but the power train was actually taken from a carburetted version of the 2792cc V6 engine, as was normally being fitted to the Granada at this time. Zakspeed completed the tune-up by fitting a Garrett turbocharger: much of the development work had been completed by

Consultant Engineer Michael May, who had recently been linked with work on the very latest V12 engines fitted to the Jaguar XJ-S.

Even though maximum boost was only 0.4 bar, this was enough to push peak power up from 135bhp (normally aspirated) to 188bhp (Zakspeed Turbo). This engine, in fact, was so lusty that 160bhp (Capri 2.8i peak levels) was already being developed at 4,000rpm, at which point the power curve was still thrusting confidently upwards.

No changes were made to the familiar, beefy, old four-speed gearbox (there never was a five-speed Capri Turbo), though a limited-

A head-on view of the 200-off Capri Turbo, sold only in Germany in 1981–82, shows the deep front spoiler and the 'Turbo' decal on the front of the bonnet panel.

The Germany-only 2.8 Turbo had 188bhp, and could reach up to 140mph (225km/h) – here it is seen diving into the famous 'concrete ditch' of the Karussel curve on the Nürburgring race circuit.

slip differential was always optionally available in the (Atlas-type) rear axle.

Because this was a torquey, rather than a peak-output, turbocharging tune, the Turbo had easy-to-find, stump-pulling performance, for which Ford-Germany claimed a top speed of 134mph (215km/h) and 0–62mph acceleration in 8 seconds. As far as I can see, there were no independent tests, but both these, surely, were conservative figures – for tests showed that the 160bhp 2.8i was almost as fast.

Zakspeed went all out to make the Turbo obvious, so it attached a deep front spoiler under the front bumper and an even more flamboyant plastic rear spoiler on the hatch-back. Flared glass-fibre wheel arches were also added. The visual effect was completed by the chunky 6.5in (some cars even had 7.5in Ford Motorsport-style four-spokers) alloy wheels and the 235/60-section tyres.

Except for the use of Ford RS-branded velour seating and an Escort RS1600i type of four-spoke steering wheel, that was the extent of the conversion, which, crucially, left the braking and suspension unmodified. The result was a mixture of features and merits, not as elegantly as SVE had evolved the Ford-UK 2.8i car, and although it did its job (and all 200 cars were sold in the year in which they were marketed) it never became an icon in the way that the British model most certainly did. Except for the Tickford Capri, which I describe next, this was the fastest of all factory-approved

Capris – yet there was no obvious category in which it could go motor racing, and I have not traced any successes in that field.

Tickford Capri – 1983–87

Although it was not officially a production Capri, I must not forget the charismatic Tickford Capri. Although there *were* some factory connections, the Tickford Capri had rather complex origins. First came the enthusiasm of ex-F1 driver John Miles, a Capri fanatic and accomplished engineer who was then working for *Autocar* magazine. Next came Aston Martin Tickford (AMT), who were keen to build high-performance, high-quality cars in numbers, and finally there was Ford-UK, who were originally persuaded to back its development.

That, though, was in 1981, but by the time it was ready for sale at the end of 1983, Ford's support had degraded. Instead of cash, they would only provide sales support. Advertised as being 'available through selected Ford and other dealers', this was always an expensive car. Tickford Capris started life as complete and conventional Capri 2.8is (or, later 2.8 'Specials') built at Cologne, before being transported to an ageing factory in Bedworth, near Coventry (this was the same building that later produced the Sierra RS500 Cosworths, and re-prepared most of the RS200s for sale as road cars), where they were stripped out, completely re-engineered and re-equipped.

Because of their high prices, and because there were so many optional extras that could be added at the build stage, these cars were never built from stock. Each and every one was produced in response to an order, and no two cars seemed to be exactly alike.

How to summarize? Think of the best handling of all fuel-injected Capris, make it a whole lot faster with a turbocharged engine, improve the handling and traction with modified suspension, then keep this all in check with a conversion to four-wheel disc brakes. Then, to round it all off, make it look sensational, order it with lots of value-adding extras, have it painted in an eye-catching colour (not all of them were in specially enhanced diamond white, but that seemed to be favourite), and go out to make every other Capri owner jealous.

That was the whole ethos of the Tickford Capri. John Miles and Victor Gauntlett (who controlled AMT at the time) effectively set out to create an 'eight-tenths scale Aston Martin Vantage' (Aston's 5.3-litre 170mph/273km/h flagship coupé of the period) and many people think they achieved just that. The problem was that exclusivity cost money, so in October 1983, at a time when the normal Capri 2.8 retailed at £8,653, a 'bare' Tickford was listed at £14,985, but by the time you had added a

leather interior, Wilton carpets and more to the interior, the invoice price had probably risen to £18,000 and more, which was a good reason why few customers could be found for a special Capri costing at least twice that of the unmodified car. For that price, incidentally, you could also have bought a Porsche 944, a BMW 628CSi, a Lotus Excel or a TVR 350i, and you would have a lot of change to buy a commuting car too, which may explain why Tickford Capris were always rare.

While the basis of the car was Capri 2.8i, there were major changes to the engine, the rear suspension, the brakes, the bodywork and the interior. The fact that the engine produced 205bhp, instead of 150bhp, tells us a lot.

Although the 2.8-litre Ford-Cologne V6 was to be turbocharged, the original 9.2:1 compression ratio was not reduced. Sophisticated electronics, together with a low-boost (7.5psi) Japanese IHI turbocharger, helped keep the engine in one piece, and this in any case was high-revving, rather than a low-speed 'grunter'.

Because of the way that the engine, its accessories and the engine bay sheet metal was arranged, the turbocharger had to be placed ahead of the engine, the Bosch fuel-injection gizmos were moved across the engine bay, an intercooler was fitted, and the water-cooling

The Capri Tickford might have sold well if it could have been announced earlier and had not been quite so expensive. There was no question that its style was dramatic and effective, and surviving cars soon became enduring classics.

This interior study of the Capri Tickford, showing off the leather trim and seats and the wooden facia, emphasizes that this was meant to be the most special, as well as the fastest, Capri ever built.

radiator was pushed well forward into the nose. Incidentally, if you are wondering about the location of the battery – it had been relocated, in the boot compartment.

Surprisingly, no changes were made to the existing 2.8i/Sierra XR4i-type T9 five-speed gearbox, nor to the back axle (which, by this time, had been fitted with a limited-slip differential as standard): like the standard car, a long-legged 3.09:1 final drive ratio was retained.

Although front spring and damper settings were left alone (Rod Mansfield's SVE engineers had already done a re-tuning job when the 2.8i was being developed in 1980–81), the rear suspension was considerably improved.

This was done to stop the axle's tendency to wind up, and to move sideways under hard cornering as the leaf springs distorted. Better location was achieved with what Tickford engineers called an 'A frame', this actually comprising two diagonally located radius arms that linked the axle centre piece to the front end of the spring-mountings. In geometry terms, something similar had been done under the original Lotus-Cortina saloons of 1963–64, but this was far better detailed.

The brakes, too, were re-jigged at the rear, with solid rear discs taking the place of the drums. We now know that most of this hardware was not Ford, but came from an unspecified

The engine bay of the Capri Tickford, complete with the turbocharger high up and placed well forward where it could take advantage of any cooling air, was impressive and carefully detailed.

contemporary Peugeot model. The French connection could easily be explained by the fact that by the early 1980s Peugeot owned the ex-Chrysler, ex-Rootes manufacturing business in Coventry, and was building large numbers of Peugeots and Talbots just a few miles away.

Tickford Capri Style Changes

The most obvious visual differences were to the style, and when you remember the 'eight-tenths Aston Martin' quip, that resemblance is clear. Tickford's task was not only to provide the car with fresh looks to match its fresh performance, but to make it handle better and feel more stable at high speeds. John Miles, who had already owned (and improved) several rather wayward 3-litre Capris, had insisted on that.

The result was that although the chassis platform of the Tickford Capri was no lower than the standard car, the extra-sized front and rear bumpers, which were closer to the deck, made it look like that. Under the skin, the Capri monocoque was virtually standard, except that the front edge of the steel bonnet was re-worked by hand, by craftsmen and a planishing tool, to align it with the new front spoiler.

Tickford then used glass-fibre to mould a striking body kit that included two very large integrated front and rear bumpers, which also helped to manage the airflow, sill kits along the flanks, a complete blanking panel for the front grille (remember the AM Vantage?), which also surrounded the four circular headlamps, and a large but effective spoiler mounted on the hatchback.

The original grille had never been very functional in any case, so blanking this off caused no overheating problems: most of the radiator cooling air (and air for the intercooler) for the Tickford entered through a large slot moulded into the new bumper.

We now know, incidentally, that the kit helped damp down the drag *and* the tendency to lift at high speeds: the drag coefficient was claimed to be Cd=0.37, while compared with the standard Capri, front and rear lift were reduced by 40 per cent. During the build period of 1983–87, incidentally, there were two different types of road wheel, starting with the standard 2.8i 'pepper-pot' style (that could be sprayed body colour), then later the seven-spoke variety from the 280 'Special' was fitted instead.

The interior was revised, with a new and more impressive plastic (but leather covered) instrument panel surround, and with a wooden facia insert. Early cars used walnut veneer, later cars had satin black veneer instead. The standard instruments were all retained.

Just to make it all above-board, Tickford then fitted their own VIN plate on the front cross-panel. Naturally the VIN number of the standard car was not changed.

Every panel fitted to the Capri Tickford had a function as well as artistic appeal, for this car was intended to be a 140mph (225km/h) plus machine that held the road like no other Capri had ever done.

Colour and trim? Surprisingly, not as many as you might think were white with black leather interiors, though such cars seem to have hogged the limelight over the years. Basically there were three colours – cardinal red, black and diamond white – and leather was always an expensive option (£1,885 in 1983, becoming more costly as the years passed).

Although white was the most common paint colour, one or two oddball colours were also provided by Tickford, which was always able to provide such a hand-tailoring service. (I still recall that when I arranged to pick up a Ford-owned RS200 in the late 1980s, I was offered a Ferrari rosso red re-spray before delivery – and accepted that!)

Prices started at £14,985 in 1983, but there was always a long options list to help boost the sticker value, and at least one car, delivered in 1984, went for £21,000. Tickford, incidentally, was not prepared to sell the body panels for 'kit' purposes – you had to buy a complete car to achieve this!

Because of this, Tickford stylist Simon Saunders later moved on from the company and set up his own – KAT – to make and sell body kits for Capris. At first Tickford thought these were too close to their own trade-marked layout and threatened legal action, after which those styles were modified enough to keep all parties happy.

From time to time, people have attempted to mock-up normal 2.8-litre Capris to look like Tickfords, but these usually fall down on detail. None of the body kits, not even the KAT design, have exactly the same style, and of course the special Tickford badges are extremely rare. The rear suspension and disc brake installation, too, is very rare, and difficult to replicate. Supply of special Tickford parts was always difficult, but in later years the moulds were preserved so that replacement panels or sections could be re-manufactured. If this description makes you want to go out and buy a Tickford Capri, your first problem will be to find one. Exactly 100 cars were built before 1987 and latter-day estimates are that there are less than fifty roadworthy survivors in this country.

Tickford Capri Specifications

Engine

2.8i Cologne V6

Layout	6-cylinder, in 60-degree V, overhead-valve
Bore × stroke	93 × 68.5mm
Capacity	2792cc
Compression ratio	9.2:1
Maximum power	205bhp @ 5,000rpm
Maximum torque	260lb ft @ 3,000rpm
Fuel system	Bosch K-Jetronic fuel-injection, with IHI RHB6 turbocharger. 7.5 psi boost

Transmission

Gearbox	All synchromesh manual 5-speed. Automatic transmission not available
Final drive	3.09:1

Suspension

Front	MacPherson strut, coil springs, anti-roll bar, telescopic dampers
Rear	Live axle, half-elliptic leaf springs, anti-roll bar, A-bar axle location, telescopic dampers
Steering	Rack and pinion (power-assisted)
Brakes	Disc front and rear, with vacuum servo

Running Gear

Wheels	13in cast alloy wheels
Tyres	205/60VR–13in

Dimensions

Wheelbase	100.8in (2,559mm)
Front track	53.3in (1,353mm)
Rear track	54.5in (1,384mm)
Length	172.3in (4,376mm)
Width	66.9in (1,698mm)
Height	52.1in (1,323mm)
Weight (unladen)	From 2,650lb (1,202kg), depending on extras fitted

And Only Three Models Remained...

From 1981 to the end of 1986, Capri after Capri derivative was gently allowed to die away. Once the last mechanical updates had been made in late 1979 (as already described in Chapter 7), all except the 2.8-litre engined cars carried on, basically unchanged, until the end, though several special editions were put on sale to make the final years more interesting. It is also important to realize that, although Capri assembly was in Germany until the end, that from late November 1984 only right-hand-drive cars were assembled – all of those cars being destined for British customers. This is how the range gradually contracted or was kept going with limited/special-editions:

- 1.3-litre engined cars – 1300L finally dropped in January 1982. Such Kent-engined cars had been on sale since 1969.
- 1.6-litre engined cars – Calypso, Cameo and Tempo limited editions, all based on the 1600L and 1600LS, were launched in July 1981.
- The Cabaret and Cabaret II special edition (based on the 1600LS) followed in May 1982.
- The Laser 1600 (originally a special edition car, later a mainstream product) followed in January 1984, that car having the 5-speed transmission as standard.
- The 1600LS was dropped in June 1984, but the Laser 1600 carried on to the end, in December 1986.
- 2-litre engined cars – 2000GL and 2000 Ghia models were dropped during 1982, leaving only the 2000S in series production.
- The Laser 2000 replaced the standard 2000S in January 1984, that car having a 5-speed transmission as standard. The standard 2000S was dropped in January 1984. The Laser 2000 then carried on to the end of Capri assembly, in late 1986.

Even so, throughout this time sales of these cars held up remarkably, invariably outselling the glamorous but more specialized 2.8-litre injected car. No fewer than 40,832 1.6-litre-engined cars were produced in the last five years (1982–86 inclusive), which compared with 28,880 2.0-litre-engined cars and 18,845 fuel-injected 2.8-litre cars in the same period.

It would be fair to say, though, that as far as the media was concerned (and, in fact, by all except a few dedicated Ford dealers) the 4-cylinder-engined Capris had been forgotten by the mid-1980s. Their end came quietly, at the end of 1986, for it was only the last fuel-injected type of all that would get a sales reprieve into 1987, even after series assembly had ceased.

2.8i 'Specials' and 280 Brooklands – The Final Flourish

After 1982, all the Capri product action – as far as engineering, rather than dress-up details, was concerned – was concentrated on the 2.8-litre fuel-injected cars. Road test reports, after all, had been universally favourable, sales had bounced back, and the biggest, fastest and glossiest of all Capris once again became a real icon.

Later models of the 2.8i and all Injection 'Specials' and 280s, were fitted with a five-speed gearbox (look at the markings on the gear lever), though the facia/instrument style was never significantly changed.

My experience provides a suitable anecdote for what was fairly typical. Having already owned two new 2-litre Capris since the mid-1970s, then moving to larger, faster, fuel-injected Granadas, I thought that my Capri-owning days were over. Until, that is, I had a chat with Rod Mansfield in early 1981, drove a pre-launch demonstrator car, and was convinced. I then took delivery of a brand-new 2.8i model in the summer of 1982, and enjoyed it thoroughly for the next two years – a period that included getting a 'fastest time of the day' award from the Somerset police force on the A303!

In the end Ford, and SVE, found time (and investment priorities) to make three distinct improvements to this car in the next four years – first to fit a five-speed gearbox, then to introduce the 'Special' model, and finally to introduce the run-out model, a 280 Brooklands type for 1987.

It is fair to say that without the arrival of the mass-market Sierra (that appeared in September 1982) there might never have been a five-speed Capri, for it was from that car (and the Granada, which benefited too) that the major and important 'building block' was lifted. This gearbox, internally known as T9 at Ford, was a much-modified update of an existing four-speeder, and therefore not ideally engineered, but it included the direct top gear and the overdrive fifth gear, which made the car a much better cruiser.

No change was made to the rear axle ratio – which was 3.09:1 on both four-speed and five-speed cars – but this is a comparison of internal gear box ratios :

4-speed: 3.16, 1.95, 1.41, 1.00, reverse 3.46
5-speed: 3.36, 1.81, 1.26, 1.00, 0.825, reverse
            3.37

The change was officially made to the Capri in January 1983 (the first flood of supply had gone to the Sierra assembly lines in Belgium), and at the same time, the 2.8i got a new design of upholstery fabric and (more important, perhaps) the provision of opening rear-quarter windows as standard, with tinted glass all round.

Little more than a year later, the injected car was upgraded yet again – from April 1984 in Germany as the 2.8 Super Injection, but from September 1984 the same car was sold as the 2.8i 'Special', replacing the original 2.8i model. From November 1984, of course, assembly of all left-hand-drive Capris ceased, the final two years of production being in right-hand drive, for sale only in the UK.

Although there were few technical innovations, the Special appealed to Capri enthusiasts for two main reasons – the use of extremely smart seven-spoke RS-style alloy wheels and a Salisbury-type limited-slip differential as standard. The wheel nuts could be locked into place – which was invaluable, as the wheels looked (and were) very desirable and much coveted by British low-life, while the limited-slip differential brought extra grip, traction and balance to a car that always seemed to be about to defeat its 1960s-generation chassis technology.

Externally, a 'Special' could be identified by its wheels, its body-colour grille and headlamp surrounds, and by the arrival of leather trim on various parts of the interior package (including the steering wheel rim, and the edges of the Recaro seats). The price, naturally, had risen since 1981, the 1985 model 'Special' retailing at £9,500, still good value for money, and low enough to keep demand up. Ford made it clear that they would carry on building the Capri until the end of 1985 but, as we now know, the end did not come until December 1986.

Closing down the Capri lines at that time was rather a surreal occasion, for it was weeks before Ford officially admitted that it had already happened. Not only was the last Capri to be assembled not the one with the highest VIN/chassis number (that had already been built!), but the announcement of a new run-out model was made weeks after the last cars had already been completed. Not only that, but a posed picture around the last Capri in the Cologne works showed total Capri assembly as being 1,886,647 cars, though later analysis showed that this figure should actually have been 1,922,847. So where had the missing

The 2.8i 'Special' was introduced in late 1984, fitted with these special seven-spoke alloy wheels, and a limited-slip differential was also part of the standard specification.

36,200 cars been hiding? Search me – and Ford never bothered to explain either!

Amazingly enough, in spite of Ford's reticence, every insider seemed to know of the nostalgic day, the sad day, the significant day, which fell on 19 December 1986, just before Ford-Cologne closed down for its winter break. British but, significantly, no German photographers were there in numbers to record the occasion, and a notice on the roof of the last car spelled out, poignantly, in English: 'bye-bye, Capri'.

Except that it was not quite over. Ford knew it, the media knew it, and Capri enthusiasts seemed to know it too. Late in February 1987, Ford-UK made a double announcement – that the Capri had finally and irrevocably been killed off, but that 1,039 of a very special run-out model, officially to be known as the '280', but unofficially known as the '280 Brooklands'

(every one of the cars was painted in Brooklands green) were about to go on to the market. All these cars, of course, had already been built, so if demand exceeded supply, all that would happen would be that second-hand prices would go through the roof!

What actually happened is that Britain's criminal fraternity soon discovered how easy it was to steal one of these cars – and many of them disappeared in the first few months. Although I have often wondered who would buy any one of these cars – for each of these limited-edition models could certainly be traced very quickly – the fact is that quite a number were stolen and never seen again.

The 280 Brooklands was an instant success, and I suspect that more than the number produced could certainly have found owners. By any measure, it was the most desirable fuel-injected Capri of all, and no one seemed to

The 2.8i 'Special' was a fast, very well-balanced and exhilarating car to drive at speed. Costing only £9,500 when new, it was a real performance bargain that embarrassed many of its competitors.

The 280 Brooklands model was the last Capri of all, a batch being built at the end of 1986 but sold in the UK in 1987.

Limited-edition 280 Brooklands types were available in the UK in 1987, but were not actually announced until all assembly of Capris had ended in Germany. The limited supply was immediately snapped up by enthusiasts – though many would be stolen in the years that followed.

complain about the £11,999 asked for it. Mechanically it was identical with the 'Special' on which it was based, though the seven-spoke road wheels were now 15in (instead of 13in) in diameter, still with 7in rim width, but with 195/50 section tyres.

Inside, the 280 Brooklands received the full leather treatment – all cars getting the same type of grey seats with burgundy piping, and matching gear-lever knob and steering wheel rim coverings.

So now it really *was* all over and no more Capris would ever be built in Europe. Even so, Ford seemed to have been wise, for sales figures later published by the SMM & T show that no fewer than 4,408 Capris were sold in 1987 (which proves just how large the 'car

This was the special grey interior of the final 280 Brooklands model.

Soon after Ford dropped the Capri, Brian Hart, then Cosworth, developed this V6 engine, which was a completely civilized, road-going twin-overhead-camshaft-per-bank conversion of the Cologne V6 engine. In production form it was rated at 195bhp (later 210bhp) in Ford Scorpio saloons and hatchbacks of the early 1990s. Of course it could be fitted to a Capri too, but came along just too late. But there's a thought ....

Final Capri III Prices in the UK (1986–87)		
Model	Engine size /power	Retail Price
1.6 Laser	1,593cc/73bhp	£7,152
2.0 Laser	1,993cc/101bhp	£7,607
2.8 Special	2,792cc/160bhp	£11,002
280 [Limited Edition]	2,792cc/160bhp	£11,999

At a great age, in great distinction, the Capri had come to the end of a successful career. No matter how much some might sneer about the way that third- and fourth-hand cars slipped down the market, the figures prove that Ford had always been right to take the gamble. Not even the most cynical cost accountant could wince at the sale of 1.9 million examples in eighteen years, especially as little new investment in engine, transmission or chassis engineering had ever been needed.

Not only had the Capri been a sales success in many markets – not least the United States – but it had helped to create a new market section in Europe, and to rejuvenate the palate of many a family man who wanted to put some 'sports car' back into his motoring. Truly, for many people – including this author – it was 'the car you always promised yourself'.

park' of unsold examples actually was when the end came in 1986) and – amazingly – 156 remained to be registered in 1988, and a final and nostalgic three machines in 1989. I am confident, by the way, that those last three cars were 280 Brooklands types held back by 'investors' hanging on for a profit, and finding it not actually there!

When Ford built the last Capri of all (a 280 Brooklands) this posed picture tells its own story. In later years, and after a careful recount, that production figure was raised to more than 1.9 million. A magnificent achievement.

Appendix I
Capris in the USA

In 1970–77 no fewer than 464,729 Capris were sold in the USA, this being one in three of all Capris being built in that time and half of the output of the Capri lines in Cologne. Each US-market Capri was built by Ford-Germany in Cologne, and all were sold through Lincoln-Mercury dealerships in that vast continent.

That short paragraph, I hope, may have altered your overall view of the Capri's place in Ford's worldwide market. The lesson, certainly, is that it would be far too easy for Europeans to forget just many Capris were sold outside the UK or Germany, and to ignore how important those sales must have been to the viability of the entire project.

The Capri was not always destined to be sold in the USA, for it was not until the new model was actually launched in Europe in 1969 that the first marketing studies were made. This explains, no doubt, why the Capri's European launch was in January 1969, whereas the unveiling of a model for the USA, at the New York Auto Show, came as late as April 1970. Incidentally – and this cannot possibly have been a marketing accident (Ford didn't 'do' marketing accidents in those days!) – this date was exactly six years to the day after the original Mustang had been introduced in the USA.

Let us also make something else quite clear – the Capri was never likely to be such an immediate, massive success in the USA as it had been in Europe. Quite simply, by American standards, in 1970 a Capri looked like a pretty toy rather than a real car. American Ford enthusiasts wanting what they called a *real* ponycar had always bought a home-grown Mustang, preferably one with a very large, very powerful, and a 'don't-care-if-it-only-does-15mpg' (19ltr/100km) V8 engine. In the 1960s Ford had tried to sell the 105E Anglia in the USA, without any success, and then the Cortina, which sold a little better but not in large quantities. Not even a successful Lotus-Cortina racing car programme in the USA helped that much.

Times, though, were slowly changing. In 1969 Ford-USA had already launched the 4-cylinder-engined Maverick saloon, which was something approaching Capri size but less specialized, and in 1970 they would not only announce the 'cheap-as-chips' family car range, but a new 4-cylinder overhead-camshaft engine (the Pinto) to go with it. As we now know, but did not at the time, the Pinto power unit would become a vital building block for use in several European Fords.

There was more. In the background, but gradually and unstoppably becoming more important, were the first exhaust emission limitation laws in the USA, which required the development of new engine, carburation and combustion technology, along with a whole raft of safety measures which would eventually include the fitment of what became known as '5mph bumpers' – which were shaped to withstand a 5mph (8km/h) impact without deforming enough to damage the car's sheet metal coachwork.

If they were to market these cars on the other side of the Atlantic, Ford-of-Europe's first important task was to decide which of the multifarious engines should be offered, and through which showrooms the cars should be retailed.

It did not take long for Ford to decide to sell the Capri through the Lincoln-Mercury dealer chain, mainly because they would therefore not have to show the car in the same showrooms as the soon-to-be-launched Pinto and also because it was likely to provide a marketing lift to the image of the Lincolns and Mercury models that were then on the market. A dig back into history shows that 1970s Mercury models were a middle-price-level brand, intended to bridge the marketing gap between mass-market Ford-USA cars and the much more expensive Lincolns, while the Lincoln Continental range relied on engines of 7.5-litres, and elephantine bulk, in a successful attempt to face up to Cadillac.

In the USA, it seems, the Capri was not to be a Ford, nor a Mercury and certainly not a Lincoln, but a plain Capri – a new brand. To emphasize that, where European-market types all boldly stated 'Ford' on the nose of the bonnet pressing, US-market cars would simply be 'Capri' types.

At first there was no choice of engines, for Ford took the easy way out and sold the American Capri only with a 71bhp Kent overhead-valve engine. This pragmatic decision was made not only because it put the Capri in the correct marketing slot, but because that engine was already established in the USA (it had been used in Cortinas) and the same engine would also be the 'entry-level' power unit in the soon-to-be-announced Ford-USA Pinto range. Even so, this meant that the first USA-market cars were not fast nor very sporty.

For sale in the USA, too, this Capri was the first to use the four circular headlamp nose that would soon appear on the European RS2600, and eventually on several other more up-market Capris. Because of the lighting regulations that applied to cars sold in the USA at the time, this, of course, had been considered at the original styling stage.

With such a low-powered car, Ford then took the very brave step of advertising it as 'The Sexy European' and the 'European Sporty Car', but the public seemed to take all this with good humour, especially at the bargain price, and sales took off far better than Ford had ever forecast. More than 17,000 cars were sold in 1970, which made the new car a real success and allowed Ford to bring in the larger and more powerful engines

that were deemed to make it even more attractive to North American buyers.

For 1971, a 2-litre/100bhp Pinto engine was also made available – which raised the top speed to a claimed 108mph (174km/h) – this being the engine that would soon become such a part of the Ford-of-Europe scene in cars as small as the Escort RS2000 and as large as the Granada 2-litre.

Yet more power became available in 1972, with the introduction of the 2.6-litre/107bhp Cologne V6 engine, and in the same year the original 1.6-litre Kent engine type was dropped. Ugly and rather visually intrusive '5mph' bumpers were added for 1973, and for 1974 the definitive 2.8-litre Cologne V6 engine took over from the 2.6-litre type, though only with an emissions-restricted 105bhp (US SAE rating), which delivered 105mph (169km/h).

The last of all Capri Is was delivered in 1975, bringing total sales in the USA up to 408,288, which was quite remarkable for a new brand: along with Canada, the USA was much the largest Capri market throughout the world at this time.

The Capri II hatchback model was introduced to the USA in March 1975 and was available only in two forms – the 'entry-level' car being a 2.3-litre/88bhp Lima-engined type (Lima was an enlarged and more robust derivative of the original overhead-camshaft Pinto, and was being made in the USA), the other version having the 2.8-litre Cologne V6 in 109bhp guise. Prices started at US$4,117, but European inflation and the inexorable rise of the deutschmark/dollar exchange rate was taking its toll, as this car was more costly than the equivalent USA-built Mustang II.

Although Ford tried to shrug this off, the Capri II hatchback never captured the imagination in the same way as the original car had done, and it must count as a marketing failure in the USA as only 56,441 cars were sold in three years. Because the Capri brand was about to be applied to a new Mercury Capri model from late 1978, the European car was therefore discontinued at the end of the 1977 model year.

Appendix II
Production Figures –
Year on Year

Calendar Year	Britain (Halewood)	Germany (Cologne and Saarlouis)★
1968	3,097	758
1969	79,635	134,344
1970	84,973	169,740
1971	47,148	168,726
1972	47,005	152,120
1973	49,392	183,933
1974	38,932	146,429
1975	21,225	78,826
1976	27,033★★	74,069
1977	–	
1978	–	69,112
1979	–	85,420
1980	–	41,755
1981	–	34,658
1982	–	25,832
1983	–	27,618
1984	–	19,508
1985	–	9,262
1986	–	10,710
Totals:	398,440	1,524,407

★   All Capris sold to the USA, and often known (inaccurately) as 'Mercury' Capris, were assembled in Germany.
★★ UK assembly, at Halewood, ended in October 1976.

Appendix III
Production Figures –
All Models

Model	Built	Production
1300 (Kent 4 and Cologne V4 combined)	1969–81	202,000★
1500 (Cologne V4)	1969–72	93,575
1600 (Kent V4)	1969–86	567,000★
1700 (Cologne V4)	1969–72	124,427
2000 (Essex V4, Cologne V4, Pinto combined)	1969–86	510,000★
2300 (Cologne V6)	1969–84	112,354
2600 (Cologne V6)	1970–73	105,935
RS2600 (Cologne V6)	1970–75	3,532
2800 (Cologne V6)	1973–77	115,565
2.8i (Cologne V6)	1981–86	24,592
3000 (Essex V6)	1969–81	62,852
RS3100 (Essex V6)	1973–74	248
Total:		1,922,847

★ Due to the vagaries of surviving production records from Halewood, these figures are only approximate.

Appendix IV
Capri Sales in the UK

Year	Numbers Sold	Comment
1969	33,086	
1970	38,186	
1971	33,944	
1972	42,437	
1973	38,793	
1974	37,553	Capri II introduced in February
1975	27,678	
1976	36,098	
1977	42,816	
1978	31,642	Capri III introduced in March
1979	49,147	
1980	31,187	
1981	22,289	Capri 2.8i introduced in June
1982	19,403	
1983	22,254	
1984	16,328	
1985	11,075	
1986	8,149	Capri assembly ended in December
1987	4,408	
1988	156	
1989	3	

Appendix V
Engines Used in Capri
Road Cars – 1969–86

Type/Size	Peak Power	Years Used
Kent, 4-cylinder, overhead-valve 1298cc	52bhp (later 57bhp, later 50bhp, 54bhp, or 55bhp or 60bhp)	1969–82
1298cc (GT)	64bhp (later 72bhp or 73bhp)	1969–71
1599cc	64bhp (later 68bhp, 72bhp, or 73bhp)	1969–72
1599cc (GT)	82bhp (later 86bhp)	1969–72
Pinto, 4-cylinder, overhead-camshaft 1593cc	63bhp, 72bhp or 73bhp)	1972–86
1593cc	88bhp	1972–80
1993cc (GT)	98bhp (later 101bhp)	1974–86
Lima, 4-cylinder, overhead-camshaft 2301cc	88bhp (later 91.5bhp)	1975–77
Essex (Ford-UK), V4 & V6, overhead-valve 1996cc V4	93bhp	1969–74
2994cc V6	128bhp (later 138bhp)	1969–81
3091cc V6	148bhp	1973–74
Ford-Cologne, V4, overhead-valve 1305cc	50bhp (later 55bhp)	1969–74
1498cc	60bhp (later 65bhp)	1969–72
1699cc	75bhp	1969–72

Type/Size	Peak Power	Years Used
Ford-Cologne,V6, overhead-valve 1998cc	85bhp (later 90bhp)	1969–84
2293cc	108bhp (later 114bhp)	1969–84
2293cc	125bhp	1969–70
2550cc	125bhp	1970–74
2637cc	150bhp	1970–74
2792cc	160bhp	1981–86
2792cc	188bhp	1981–82
Ford-USA, overhead-valve/V8 (for South Africa) 4949cc	281bhp	1970–74

The following engines all had specific engine tunes for USA-market cars: 1599cc, 1993cc, 2301cc (enlarged version of 1993cc), 2550cc and 2792cc.

Appendix VI
Capri Performance –
Selected Models

	Top Speed mph (km/h)	0-60mph (secs)
Capri I		
1300	84/86 (135/138)	23.0/22.0
1600GT	96/100 (154/161)	
2000GT (V4)	106 (170.5)	10.6
2600GT (V6 German)	118 (190)	10
3000GT/3000GXL	114/122 (183/196)	9.2/8.3
Perana (V8)	143 (230)	6.6
Capri II		
1300	89 (143)	19.4
1600GT	106 (170.5)	13.5
2000GT	108 (174)	11.1
2300GT (German)	112 (180)	12
3000GT/S/Ghia	122 (196)	9
Capri III		
1300	89/91 (143/146)	20/19.5
1600S	106/109 (170.5/175)	12.5/12.0
2000	111 (178.5)	10.8
3000	122 (196)	8.5
2.8i	130 (209)	7.8
2.8 Turbo (German)	137 (220)	8
Tickford Turbo	140 (225)	6
RS Models		
RS2600	126 (203)	8.6
RS3100	125 (201)	7.3

(Where two figures are quoted, this is to take account of engine changes made in mid-run)

Index

Index